COLORED
MINORITIES
in GREAT BRITAIN

COLORED
MINORITIES
in GREAT BRITAIN

compiled by Raj Madan

a comprehensive bibliography, 1970-1977

GREENWOOD PRESS
Westport, Connecticut

Library of Congress Cataloging in Publication Data

Madan, Raj.
  Colored minorities in Great Britain.

  Includes indexes.
  1. Blacks—Great Britain—Bibliography. 2. South
Asians in Great Britain—Bibliography. 3. Great
Britain—Race relations—Bibliography. I. Title.
Z2027.N4M3 [DA125.N4] 016.30145'1'0941 78-74656
ISBN 0-313-20705-4

Library of Congress Catalog Card Number: 78-74656
ISBN: 0-313-20705-5

First published in 1979

in Great Britain by Aldwych Press Limited
3 Henrietta Street, London WC2E 8LU

in the United States of America by Greenwood Press, Inc.
51 Riverside Avenue, Westport, Conn. 06880

Printed in the United States of America

10 9 8 7 6 5 4 3 2 1

CONTENTS

Preface   ix

I.   General Works   3
     A. Books
     B. Periodical Articles
     C. Statistical Sources

II. Immigration   14
     A. Books
     B. Periodical Articles

III. History and Politics   22
     A. Books
     B. Periodical Articles

IV. Racism   34
     A. Books
     B. Periodical Articles

V.   Law and Legislation   46
     A. Books
     B. Periodical Articles

VI. Inter-Ethnic Relations   57
     A. Books
     B. Periodical Articles

VII. Employment   65
     A. Books
     B. Periodical Articles

VIII. Social Conditions   79
      A. Books
      B. Periodical Articles
 IX. General Culture, Family, and Community Life   86
      1. General   86
         A. Books
         B. Periodical Articles
      2. Culture Conflict   93
         A. Books
         B. Periodical Articles
  X. Education   97
      1. General   97
         A. Books
         B. Periodical Articles
      2. Educational Problems   106
         A. Books
         B. Periodical Articles
      3. English as a Second Language   112
         A. Books
         B. Periodical Articles
      4. Multi-Racial Education   118
         A. Books
         B. Periodical Articles
      5. Teacher Training   125
         A. Books
         B. Periodical Articles
      6. Racial Discrimination in Textbooks   127
         A. Books
         B. Periodical Articles
 XI. Housing   129
      A. Books
      B. Periodical Articles
XII. Health   137
      A. Books
      B. Periodical Articles
XIII. Social Services   140
      A. Books
      B. Periodical Articles
XIV. Race Relations in the Mass Media   147
      A. Books
      B. Periodical Articles

XV.   Police and the Colored Minorities   150
      A. Books
      B. Periodical Articles

APPENDIX A.   List of Periodicals, with Addresses, That
              Primarily Deal with the Colored Minorities   155

APPENDIX B.   List of Organizations Concerned with the
              British Colored Minorities' Problems   159

Author Index   161
Title Index   175
Subject Index   185

PREFACE

The mass movement of British Commonwealth immigrants from the West Indies, India, Pakistan, Sri Lanka, Kenya, and Uganda to Great Britain in the past two decades has created immense racial, economic, and social problems which have received worldwide attention. The writings and surveys on this issue make it evident that the racial sentiments and attitudes established during colonial rule still operate today. The increasing racial tension between the so-called colored people, who make up approximately 6 percent of the total population, and the white majority has become a source of major concern for the British government and interested individuals because of its volatile nature.

The British, recently critical of the United States for its discrimination against blacks and other ethnic minorities, are now themselves faced with the same dilemma. Their dilemma, it may be said, results directly from their colonial rule.

A great deal has been written about the plight of the colored minorities in Great Britain and the attitudes of British whites toward them. Access to this information, however, is scattered in various indexes and bibliographies. The present bibliography attempts to bring together all the English-language sources published between 1970 and 1977, with the exception of newspaper articles, which are not included.

The date 1970 was chosen because an earlier work entitled *Coloured Minorities in Britain* by Ambalavaner Sivanandan, a librarian at the Institute of Race Relations in London, covers works from 1950 to 1969.[1] This bibli-

1. Ambalavaner Sivanandan. *Coloured Minorities in Britain*, 3d ed. London: The Institute of Race Relations, 1969. 110 pp.

ography may be considered a successor to Sivanandan's bibliography, which is still in print and should be used for retrospective coverage.

The use of the word "colored" in the title of this bibliography needs explanation. The term or word "colored" has a special connotation in the British context. Unlike the United States where the word is used to denote Negroes, in English society it stands for all the non-white people from Asia, Africa, and the West Indies, be they brown, black, or yellow. Therefore, Indic peoples (even though technically Caucasian) who have brown skin and people from the West Indies and Africa are all called colored.

Another frequently used term is "immigrant," which again refers to non-whites from Asia, Africa, and the West Indies. Socially the word "immigrant" is also used for the children of immigrants who were born and raised in England and are bona fide English citizens. Therefore, in the literature cited here, readers will find that the words "colored," "blacks," and "immigrants" have been used interchangeably. This usage indicates the extent to which prejudice is prevalent in Great Britain today.

ORGANIZATION OF THE ENTRIES

The organization of the materials, in this complex field of race relations, has been determined primarily by usefulness to the reader rather than by academic criteria. The subject matter is divided into fifteen broad categories which form the parts of the Bibliography. Each part is subdivided into subsections. Most parts, with the exception of Parts I, IX, and X, have two subsections: Subsection A lists books, pamphlets, government publications, theses, and dissertations, and Subsection B lists periodical articles. Part I, which covers the category General Works, has a Subsection C, which lists statistical sources; these statistical sources, although books, have been placed in a separate section in order to make the statistical information more accessible. Part IX, on General Culture, Family and Community Life, and Part X, on Education, have been subdivided into narrower categories, and these subcategories have then been divided into Subsections A and B.

Entries are listed by author or government agency within each subsection and contain complete bibliographic information, i.e., author, title, subtitle, publisher, date and place of publication, and pagination. In a few cases the name of the country has been supplied for clarification. For periodical articles the author, title, periodical title, volume number and/or issue number, page numbers, and date of the article have been supplied. The entries are numbered consecutively throughout. When available, reviews have been provided right after the work.

APPENDIXES

Appendix A lists titles and addresses of periodicals that deal primarily with race relations in Britain. Appendix B lists the names and addresses of organizations concerned with British colored minorities' problems and are a source of useful information on them.

INDEXES

The importance of consulting the subject index in using this bibliography cannot be overemphasized. For reasons of brevity and economy, works cited only once and placed in the most appropriate broad category. For example, a book dealing with housing problems, which might also throw some light on economic and social conditions, would be entered in the housing section, but it would also appear in the subject index under social and economic conditions. Therefore, to find all citations concerning the economic and social conditions of minorities, users are advised to check the subject index in addition to the sections on social conditions and employment.

For the convenience of users, author and title indexes are also included in the bibliography. The title index, which lists only titles of books, has been supplied to provide an easy access to government publications, which in most cases have complicated main entries.

It is hoped that this bibliography will be used by persons with a wide variety of interests and needs: researchers, race relations experts, students of British race relations, sociologists, humanists, and librarians.

ACKNOWLEDGMENTS

I would like to express my gratitude to my husband, who supported me in this endeavor and patiently looked after our children, and without whose help and understanding this work would not have been possible. My appreciation goes to Elizabeth Maine and Marion Wells, who proofread the manuscript, and Virginia Cameron, who at various points offered constructive criticism of the work. Most of all I am deeply indebted to Joan Carlile and Annabelle Day, who did a wonderful job in typing the manuscript.

Raj Madan

Brockport, N.Y.

COLORED
MINORITIES
in GREAT BRITAIN

I.

GENERAL WORKS

A. BOOKS

1. Anglo-French Conference on Race Relations in France and Great Britain, Brighton, England, 1968. Colloque Franco-Britannique sur les Relations Raciales en France et en Grande Bretagne. Paris: Mouton, 1972. 209 p.

   "Text in French and English."

2. Bagley, Christopher. The Dutch Plural Society: A Comparative Study in Race Relations. London: Oxford University Press, 1973. 293 p.

   Review by Frank Bovenkerk. Race 15: 2 (October 1973): 261-264.

3. Banton, Michael Parker. The Idea of Race. London: Tavistock Publications, 1977. 190 p.

4. Banton, Michael Parker and Jonathan Harwood. The Race Concept. London: Newton, Abbot, David and Charles, 1975. 159 p.

   Review by Jenny Bourne. Race and Class 17: 2 (August 1975): 202-204.

5. Banton, Michael Parker. Racial Minorities. London: Fontana, 1972. 192 p.

6. Bloom, Leonard. Social Psychology of Race Relations. London: Allen & Unwin, 1971. 198 p.

7. Bowker, Gordon and John Carrier, eds. Race and
    Ethnic Relations: Sociological Readings. New
    York: Holmes & Meier, 1976. 400 p.

8. Burnham, Colin. Race. London: Batsford, 1971. 96 p.

9. Campbell-Platt, Kiran. Ethnic Minorities in Society:
    A Reference Guide. London: Community and Race
    Relations Unit of the British Council of Churches
    and Runnymede Trust, 1976. 55 p.

10. Cohen, Abner, ed. Urban Ethnicity. London: Tavistock
    Publications (Disbributed in the U.S.A. by Harper
    & Row, Barnes & Noble Import Division), 1974.
    391 p.

    Review by Maurice Freedman. New Community 5
    (Autumn 1976): 181-188.

11. Deakin, Nicholas, ed. Immigrants in Europe. London:
    Fabian Society, 1972. 36 p.

12. Ehrlich, Paul R. and Shirley Feldman. The Race Bomb:
    Skin Color, Prejudice and Intelligence. New York:
    Quadrangle, 1977. 256 p.

13. Field, Frank and Patricia Haikin, eds. Black Britons.
    London: Oxford University Press, 1971. 132 p.

14. Great Britain. Central Office of Information.
    Reference Division. Race Relations in Britain.
    London: H.M.S.O., 1972. 29 p.

15. Great Britain. Central Office of Information.
    Reference Division. Race Relations in Britain.
    2d ed. London: H.M.S.O., 1977. 45 p.

16. Great Britain. Community Relations Commission.
    Audio-Visual Aids, Aspects of Community Relations:
    Cultural and Religious Backgrounds, Social
    Development and Welfare, Prejudice and Specialized
    Items for Selected Age and Interest Group. London:
    Community Relations Commission, 1970. 31 p.

17. Great Britain. Community Relations Commission. Film
    Catalogue. Produced jointly by Community Relations
    Commission and Race Relations Board. London:
    The Commission; The Board, 1975. 30 p.

18. Great Britain. Community Relations Commission. Race
    Relations in Britain: Selected Bibliography with
    Emphasis on Commonwealth Immigrants. 2d ed.
    London: Community Relations Commission, 1971.
    19 p.

19. Great Britain. Community Relations Commission. Race
     Relations in Britain: A Select Bibliography with
     Emphasis on Commonwealth Immigrants. 3d ed.
     London: Community Relations Commission, 1973.
     23 p.

20. Great Britain. Community Relations Commission. Race
     Relations in Britain: A Select Bibliography.
     4th ed. London: The Commission, 1974. 29 p.

21. Great Britain. Community Relations Commission. Race
     Relations in Britain: A Select Bibliography.
     5th ed. London: The Commission, 1975. 29 p.

22. Great Britain. Community Relations Commission. Race
     Relations in Britain: A Select Bibliography.
     6th ed. London: The Commission, 1976. 24 p.

23. Krausz, Ernest. Ethnic Minorities in Britain. London:
     MacGibbon & Kee, 1971. 175 p.

          Review by Michael J. Hill. Race 14: 1
          (July 1972): 90-92.

24. Krausz, Ernest. Ethnic Minorities in Britain. London:
     Paladin, 1972. 175 p.

25. Lambeth Libraries. Black Britons. A Select Biblio-
     graphy on Race. Compiled by John Buchanan.
     London: London Borough of Lambeth, 1972. 24 p.

26. Mason, Philip. Patterns of Dominance. London:
     Published for the Institute of Race Relations
     by Oxford University Press, 1970. 337 p.

27. Mason, Philip. Race Relations. London: Oxford
     University Press, 1970. 169 p.

28. Rex, John. Race Relations in Sociological Theory.
     London: Weidenfeld and Nicolson, 1970. 169 p.

29. Rose, Arnold Marshall and Caroline B. Rose. Minority
     Problems. 2d ed. New York: Harper, 1972. 483 p.

30. Santa Cruz, Hernan. Racial Discrimination. New York:
     United Nations, 1971. 324 p.

31. Santa Cruz, Hernan. Racial Discrimination. New York:
     United Nations, 1976. 284 p.

32. Seminar on Measures to be Taken on the National Level
       for the Implementation of United Nations Instru-
       ments Aimed at Combating and Eliminating Racial
       Discrimination and for the Promotion of Harmonious
       Race Relations, Yaounde, Cameroon, 1971. Seminar
       on Measures to be Taken on the National Level for
       the Implementation of United Nations Instruments
       Aimed at Combating and Eliminating Racial Dis-
       crimination and for the Promotion of Harmonious
       Race Relations: Symposium on the Evils of Racial
       Discrimination. Organized by the United Nations
       Division of Human Rights in co-operation with the
       Government of the Federal Republic of Cameroon.
       New York: United Nations, 1971. 36 p.

33. Sivanandan, Ambalavaner and Hazel Waters. Register of
       Research on Commonwealth Immigrants in Britain.
       5th ed. London: Institute of Race Relations:
       Distributed by Research Publications, 1970. 36 p.

34. Sivanandan, Ambalavaner and Cheryl Kelly. Register of
       Research on Commonwealth Immigrants in Britain.
       6th ed. London: Institute of Race Relations,
       1972. 26 p.

35. Social Science Research Council (Great Britain).
       Research Unit on Ethnic Relations. Ethnic
       Relations: The Work of the SSRC Research Unit on
       Ethnic Relations at the University of Bristol,
       1970-74. Bristol: The Unit, 1975. 23 p.

36. Stephens, Leslie. Human Rights and Race in the U.K.
       London: U.N.A. Trust, 1970. 36 p.

37. Thomson, Grant. Race Relations. Glasgow: Blackie,
       1977. 66 P.

38. Watson, P. Psychology and Race. London: Penguin,
       1973. 491 p.

B. PERIODICAL ARTICLES

39. Abbott, Simon. "Race Studies in Britain." Social
       Science Information 10 (February 1971): 91-101.

40. Alcock, A. E. "A New Look at Protection of Minorities
       and the Principle of Human Rights." Community
       Development Journal 12: 2 (April 1977): 85-95.

41. Bagley, Christopher. "Racialism and Pluralism: A
       Dimensional Analysis of Forty-eight Countries."
       Race 13: 3 (January 1972): 347-354.

42. Ball, R. "How Europe Created its Minority Problem."
     Fortune 88 (December 1973): 130-133.

43. Banton, Michael Parker. "The Adjective Black: A
     Discussion Note." New Community 5 (Spring/
     Summer 1977): 480-482.

44. Banton, Michael Parker. "The Future of Race Relations
     Research in Britain: The Establishment of a
     Multi-Disciplinary Research Unit." Race 15: 2
     (October 1973): 223-229.

45. Beloff, Max. "Racial Dimensions." Encounter 36
     (May 1971): 72-75.

46. Bonham-Carter, Mark. "Race Relations in Britain."
     United Asia 22 (March/April 1970): 79-82.

47. Bracken, H. M. "Essence, Accident and Race."
     Hermathena 116 (Winter 1973): 81-96.

48. Collard, David. "The Future of Race Relations Research
     in Britain: Economists in Race Relations Research-
     A Personal View." Race 15: 3 (January 1974):
     383-389.

49. Cooper, Mark N. "Racialism and Pluralism as Dimensions
     of Nations: A Further Investigation." Race 15: 3
     (January 1974): 370-381.

50. Dickie-Clarke, Hamish. "Some Issues in the Sociology
     of Race Relations." Race 15: 2 (October 1973):
     241-247.

51. Drake, S. "Colour Problem in Britain: A Study in
     Social Definitions." Sociological Review 3
     (December 1975): 197-217.

52. Grove, John. "Differential, Political and Economic
     Patterns of Ethnic and Race Relations: A Cross-
     National Analysis." Race 15: 3 (January 1974):
     303-328.

53. Hatch, Stephen. "Priority for Research in Race
     Relations." New Community 3 (Autumn 1974):
     397-398.

54. "How Unhappy Minorities Upset Europe's Calm." U.S.
     News and World Report 82 (31 January 1977):
     37-39.

55. Howells, William W. "The Meaning of Race." New
     Community 3 (Winter/Spring 1974): 26-30.

56. Jahoda, Marie. "The Roots of Prejudice." New Community
     4 (Summer 1975): 179-187.

57. Lambert, John and C. J. Filkin. "Race Relations
     Research: Some Issues of Approach and Application."
     Race 12: 3 (January 1971): 329-335.

58. Little, Alan and David Kohler. "Are Race Relations
     Getting Worse: Report on a New Survey of Race
     Relations in Britain." CRC Journal 5: 1
     (December/January 1976/77): 10-11.

59. Lyon, Michael H. "Ethnic Minority Problems: An Overview
     of Some Recent Research." New Community 2
     (Autumn 1973): 329-352.

60. Milner, David. "The Future of Race Relations Research
     in Britain: A Social Psychologist's View." Race
     15: 1 (July 1973): 91-99.

61. Moore, Robert. "Race Relations and the Rediscovery
     of Sociology." British Journal of Sociology 22
     (March 1971): 97-104.

62. "Publishing in a Multi-Racial Society: Editors'
     Conference." Bookseller (9 June 1973): 2724-2726.

63. "Race in Britain." Economist 251 (27 April 1974):
     23-24, 27-28.

64. "Race, Sex and Equality." New Statesman (6 April
     1973): 491-493.

65. Reynolds, V. "Human Racial Variation: Current Know-
     ledge and Future Trends." New Community 3
     (Winter/Spring 1974): 31-35.

66. Richmond, Anthony H. "Black and Asian Immigrants in
     Britain and Canada: Some Comparisons." New
     Community 4 (Winter/Spring 1975/1976): 501-516.

67. Rolph, C. H. "Minority is Always Right to Shout."
     Observer Magazine (14 December 1975): 8-10.

68. Rose, Richard. "Do the British Exist?" New Community 1
     (Summer 1972): 271-276.

69. Scase, Richard. "Images of Inequality in Sweden and
     Britain." Human Relations 28 (April 1975):
     261-277.

70. Walvin, James. "The First Black Minorities."
     Listener 92 (14 November 1974): 634-635.

71. Waters, Hazel. "Guide to the Literature on Race Rela-
        tions in Britain, 1970-75." Sage Race Relations
        Abstracts 1: 2 (March 1976): 97-105.

C. STATISTICAL SOURCES

72. Annual Abstract of Greater London Statistics. London:
        Greater London Council, 1966- Vol. 1- Annual.

73. Britain: An Official Handbook. London: H.M.S.O., 1971-
        Annual.

        Continues the same title issued by Great Bri-
        tain. Central Office of Information.

74. Colour in Britain: The Facts in Detail. London: Runny-
        mede Trust, 1974. 3 p.

75. Education Statistics, 1974-75: The Chartered Institute
        of Public Finance and Accountancy and the Society
        of County Treasurers. C.I.P.F.A., Society of Coun-
        ty Treasurers, 1974. 21 p.

76. Facts and Figures 1972: Statistics on Immigration. Lon-
        don: The British Council of Churches, Community and
        Race Relations Unit and the Institute of Race Rela-
        tions, 1972. Unpaged.

77. Farid, S. M. The Current Tempo of Fertility in England
        and Wales for the Office of Population Censuses
        and Surveys. London: H.M.S.O., 1974. 94 p.

78. Great Britain. Central Statistical Office. Annual Ab-
        stract of Statistics. London: H.M.S.O., 1840/53-
        Vol. 1- Annual.

        Supplemented in many respects by Monthly Digest
        of Statistics.

79. Great Britain. Central Statistical Office. Monthly Di-
        gest of Statistics. London: H.M.S.O., 1946- Vol.
        1- Monthly.

        In many ways it supplements the Annual Abstract
        of Statistics.

80. Great Britain. Commonwealth Immigration Advisory Coun-
        cil. Report. London: H.M.S.O., 1963- Vol. 1-

        Issued in the series of Parliamentary Papers as
        Papers by Command.

81. Great Britain. Department of Education and Science.
     Education Survey. London: The Department, 1967-
     Vol. 1- .

82. Great Britain. Department of Education and Science.
     Statistics of Education. London: The Department,
     1963- Annual.

          Supersedes a publication with the same title is-
          sued by the Ministry of Education.

83. Great Britain. Department of Employment. Department of
     Employment Gazette. London: The Department, 197 -
     Vol. 79- .

          Continues the Department of Employment and Pro-
          ductivity's Employment and Productivity Gazette.

84. Great Britain. Department of Employment. New Earnings
     Survey. London: H.M.S.O., 1970- Annual.

          Continues the publication with the same title is-
          sued by the Department under an earlier name:
          Department of Employment and Productivity.

85. Great Britain. Department of Employment and Productivi-
          ty. Statistics on Incomes, Prices, Employment and
          Production. London: H.M.S.O., No. 1- .

86. Great Britain. Department of Health and Social Security.
     On the State of the Public Health: The Annual Report
     of the Chief Medical Officer. London: H.M.S.O.,
     1968- Annual.

          Continues the same title issued by the Ministry
          of Health.

87. Great Britain. Department of Health and Social Security.
     Social Security Statistics. London: H.M.S.O.,
     1972- Vol. 1- Annual.

88. Great Britain. Department of the Environment. Direc-
          torate of Statistics. Housing and Construction
          Statistics. London: H.M.S.O., 1972- No. 1-
          Quarterly.

          Formed by the union of its Housing Statistics:
          Great Britain and the Monthly Bulletin of Con-
          struction Statistics issed by the Department's
          Statistics Construction Division.

89. Great Britain. Department of the Environment. Direc-
          torate of Statistics. Housing Statistics - Great
          Britain. London: H.M.S.O., 1972- No. 24- Quar-
          terly.

Continues the same title issued by the Ministry
of Housing and Local Government.

90. Great Britain. Department of the Environment. Direc-
torate of Statistics. Local Housing Statistics:
England and Wales. London: H.M.S.O., 1973-
No. 27- Quarterly.

Continues the same title issued by the Ministry
of Housing and Local Government. Prepared
jointly with the Welsh office.

91. Great Britain. Government Actuary. Population Projec-
tions: No. 2, 1971-2011; England and Wales,
Scotland, Northern Ireland, Great Britain, United
Kingdom. London: H.M.S.O., 1972. 115 p.

At head of title: Office of Population Censuses
and Surveys.

92. Great Britain. Home Department. Control of Immigration
Statistics. London: H.M.S.O., 1965- Annual.

Continues Immigration Statistics. Subseries of
Great Britain. Parliament. Papers by Command.
Volumes for 1975- issued by the Department under
a variant form of name: Home Office.

93. Great Britain. Home Department. Immigration Statistics.
London: H.M.S.O., Vol.- .

Issued in the series of Parliamentaty Papers as
Papers by Command. Some volumes issued by the
Department under a variant form of name: Home
Office. Continued by Control of Immigration
Statistics.

Also previously published in 2 volumes as Common
wealth Immigrants Acts - 1962 and 1968, Control
of Immigrant Statistics and Statistics of Foreigners Entering and Leaving the United Kingdom.

94. Great Britain. Home Department. Statistics of Foreigners Entering and Leaving the United Kingdom.
London: H.M.S.O., 1939- Vol. 1- Annual.

Issued in the series -- Great Britain. Parliament. Papers by Command.

95. Great Britain. Home Department. Statistics of Persons
Acquiring Citizenship of the United Kingdom and
Colonies. London: H.M.S.O., 1962- Vol. 1-
Annual.

Issued in the series of parliamentary papers as
Papers by Command.

96. Great Britain. Ministry of Housing and Local Govern-
     ment. Local Housing Statistics: England and Wales.
     London: The Ministry, 1967- No. 1- Annual.

     Issued in cooperation with the Welsh office.

97. Great Britain. Office of Population Censuses and Sur-
     veys. Census 1971, England and Wales: Advance
     Analysis. London: H.M.S.O., 1972- Vol. 1- .

98. Great Britain. Office of Population Censuses and Sur-
     veys. Census 1971, England and Wales: Preliminary
     Report, etc. London: The Office, 1971. 45 p.

99. Great Britain. Office of Population Censuses and Sur-
     veys. Census 1971, Great Britain: Country of
     Birth Tables. London: H.M.S.O., 1974. 194 p.

100. Great Britain. Office of Population Censuses and Sur-
     veys. Population Projections 1970-2010. Prepared
     by the Government Actuary. London: The Office,
     1971. 145 p.

101. Great Britain. Office of Population Censuses and Sur-
     veys. Population Trends. London: Government Sta-
     tistical Office, 1975- Vol. 1- Quarterly.

102. Great Britain. Office of Population Censuses and Sur-
     veys. The Registrar General's Annual Estimate of
     the Population of England and Wales and of Local
     Authority Areas. London: The Office, Vol. 1-
     Annual.

103. Great Britain. Office of Population Censuses and Sur-
     veys. Registrar General's Statistical Review of
     England and Wales. London: H.M.S.O., 1970- Vol.
     1- .

     Continues the same title issued by the Office
     under its earlier name: General Register Office.
     Supplements accompany some issues.

104. Great Britain. Office of Population Censuses and Sur-
     veys. Immigrant Statistics Unit. The Coloured
     Population of Great Britain. London: Runnymede
     Trust, 1976. 8 p.

105. Great Britain. Office of Population Census and Sur-
     veys. Immigrant Statistics Unit. Country of Birth
     and Colour 1971-4. London: Runnymede Trust, 1975.
     8 p.

106. Great Britain. Parliament. House of Commons. Select
      Committee on Race Relations and Immigration. Sta-
      tistics of Immigrant School Pupils: First Special
      Report from the Select Committee on Race Relations
      and Immigration, Session 1971/72. London: H.M.S.O.,
      1972. 26 p.

107. Greater London Council. Intelligence Unit. 1971 Cen-
      sus Data on London's Overseas Born Population and
      Their Children. Compiled by A. M. Field, et al.
      London: Greater London Council, 1974. 19 p.

108. Housing Survey Reports. London: Great Britain Ministry
      of Housing and Local Government, 1969- No. 1- .

109. Kohler, David Frank, ed. Ethnic Minorities in Britain:
      Statistical Data. London: Community Relations
      Commission, 1974. 19 p.

110. Kohler, David Frank, ed. Ethnic Minorities in Britain:
      Statistical Data. 2d ed. London: Community Rela-
      tions Commission, 1974. 20 p.

111. Kohler, David Frank, ed. Ethnic Minorities in Britain:
      Statistical Data. 3d ed. London: Community Rela-
      tions Commission, 1974. 18 p.

112. Kohler, David Frank, ed. Ethnic Minorities in Britain:
      Statistical Data. 4th ed. London: Community Re-
      lations Commission, 1975. 20 p.

113. Kohler, David Frank, ed. Ethnic Minorities in Britain:
      Statistical Data. 5th ed. London: Community Re-
      lations Commission, 1975. 21 p.

114. Lomas, Glenys Barbara Gillian. Census 1971: The Col-
      oured Population of Great Britain: Preliminary
      Report. London: Runnymede Trust, 1973. 118 p.

115. London Facts and Figures. London: Greater London Coun-
      cil, 1972- No. 1- .

          Subseries of the Council's publication No. 1
          compiled by the Intelligence Unit of the Greater
          London Council.

116. Morrey, C. R. 1971 Census: Demographic, Social and
      Economic Indices for Wards in Greater London.
      London: Greater London Council, 1976. 2 vols.

117. Nandy, Dipak. How to Calculate Immigration Statistics.
      London: Runnymede Trust, 1970. 13 p.

118. Runnymede Trust. Immigration and Settlement, 1963-1970.
      London: Runnymede Trust, 1971. 5 p.

II.

IMMIGRATION

A. BOOKS

119. Akram, Mohammed and Jan Elliot. Firm But Unfair: Immi-
      gration Control in the Indian Sub-Continent: A
      Preliminary Report. London: Runnymede Trust,
      1976. 11 leaves.

120. Bonham-Carter, Mark. Migration and Race: Fact and
      Fiction. Newcastle Upon Tyne: University of
      Newcastle Upon Tyne, 1970. 12 p.

121. Bottomley, Arthur and Sir George Sinclair. Control of
      Commonwealth Immigration: An Analysis and Summary
      of the Evidence Taken by the Select Committee on
      Race Relations and Immigration, 1969-70. London:
      Runnymede Trust, 1970. 48 p.

122. Campbell-Platt, Kiran. Census 1971: The Coloured Popu-
      lation of Great Britain. Preliminary Report by
      G. B. Gillian Lomas. Summarized by K. Campbell-
      Platt. London: Runnymede Trust, 1974. 23 p.

123. Economic Issues in Immigration: An Exploration of the
      Liberal Approach to Public Policy on Immigration.
      London: Institute of Economic Affairs, 1970.
      155 p.

124. Eversley, David Edward Charles. A Question of Numbers?
      London: Runnymede Trust, 1973. 32 p.

           Review in New Community 2 (Spring 1973):
           218-219.

125. Facts Paper on the United Kingdom. London: Institute
      of Race Relations. Distributed by Research Publi-
      cations, 1970. 48 p.

126. Freeman, Gary Pete. "British and French Policies on
      Immigration and Race Relations, 1945-1974."
      Doctoral dissertation, University of Wisconsin,
      1975. 470 p.

127. Great Britain. Central Office of Information. Refer-
      ence Division. Immigration Into Britain. London:
      British Information Services, 1974. 13 p.

128. Great Britain. Parliament. A Register of Dependents:
      Report of the Parliamentary Group on the Feasibil-
      ity and Usefulness of a Register of Dependents.
      Presented to Parliament by the Secretary of State
      for the Home Department. London: H.M.S.O., 1977.
      30 p.

129. Great Britain. Prime Minister. Immigration From the
      Commonwealth. London: H.M.S.O., 1970. 17 p.

130. Jones, Catherine. Immigration and Social Policy in
      Britain. London: Tavistock Publications, 1977.
      291 p.

          Review by Lee Bridges. Race and Class 19:2
          (Autumn 1977): 211-212.

131. Jones, Kathleen and A. D. Smith. The Economic Impact
      of Commonwealth Immigration. Cambridge, England:
      University Press, 1970. 177 p.

132. Katznelson, Ira. Black Men, White Cities: Race,
      Politics and Migration in the United States, 1900-
      30 and Britain 1948-68. London: Oxford University
      Press, 1973. 219 p.

          Review by Harold Pollins. New Community 3
          (Summer 1974): 294-296.

          Review by Lee Bridges. Race 15: 4 (April 1974):
          535-537.

133. Labour Party. (Great Britain) Immigration and Racial-
      ism. Researched by Liz Atkins. London: Labour
      Party, 1977. 4 p.

134. Labour Party. (Great Britain) Study Group on Immigra-
      tion. Citizenship, Immigration and Integration.
      London: Labour Party, 1972. 47 p.

135. Liberal Party. (Great Britain) Panel on Immigration,
      Race and Community Relations. Immigration and
      Race Relations: A Liberal Party Report. London:
      Liberal Publication Department, 1974. 29 p.

136. Liberal Party. (Great Britain) Panel on Immigration,
      Race and Community Relations. Immigration: Report
      of the Liberal Party Panel on Immigration, Race
      and Community Relations. London: Liberal Publica-
      tion Department, 1977. 32 p.

137. Mamdani, Mahmood. From Citizen to Refugee: Uganda
      Asians Come to Britain. London: Francis Pinter,
      1973. 127 p.

138. Moore, Robert Samuel and Tina Wallace. Slamming the
      Door: The Administration of Immigration Control.
      London: Robertson, 1975. 126 p.

      Review by Jenny Bourne. Race and Class 18: 1
      (Summer 1976): 95-96.

139. Nicolson, Colin. Strangers to England: Immigration
      to England 1100-1952. London: Wayland, 1974.
      128 p.

140. Palmer, Howard. Immigration and the Rise of Multi-
      Culturalism. London: Heinemann, 1970. 216 p.

141. Phillips, K. Diana, ed. Immigration Appeals: Selected
      Determinations of the Immigration Appeal Tribunal
      and of Immigration Appeal Adjudicators on Appeals
      Under the Immigration Act 1971, and Including
      Reports of Decisions of the House of Lords Appel-
      late Committee and the Supreme Court of Judicature
      on Reference from Decisions of the Immigration
      Appellate Authorities. London: H.M.S.O., 1977.
      117 p.

142. Philpott, Stuart B. West Indian Migration: the
      Montserrat Case. London: Athlone Press, 1973.
      210 p.

143. Stephen, David. Immigration and Race Relations.
      London: Fabian Society, 1970. 32 p.

144. Thomas, Brinley. Migration and Economic Growth: A
      Study of Great Britain and the Atlantic Economy.
      2d ed. Cambridge, England: University Press,
      1973. 498 p.

145. Tinker, Hugh. The Banyan Tree: Overseas Emigrants
      from India, Pakistan and Bangladesh. New York:
      Oxford University Press, 1977. 204 p.

146. Whitfield, Sylvia. People in Paper Chains: Final
      Report. Birmingham: Birmingham Community
      Development Project, 1977. 32 p.

B. PERIODICAL ARTICLES

147. Anwar, Muhammad. "Pakistanis and Indians in the 1971
      Census: Some Ambiguities." New Community 3
      (Autumn 1974): 394-396.

148. "Asian Immigration." Community Relations in Social
      Services 1: 3 (September 1975): 1-3.

149. Beeson, T. "Uganda Exodus." Christian Century 89
      (20 September 1972): 912.

150. Bourne, Richard. "The Last Asians." New Society
      (31 May 1973): 484-485.

151. "Breathing Space." Economist 251 (8 June 1974): 22.

152. "Britain Takes the Asians." New Commonwealth 51: 6/7
      (8 September 1972): 312.

153. "Britain's Democracy in Action." America 128
      (17 February 1973): 131.

154. "Confess Now." Economist 265 (3 December 1977): 26.

155. "Corked Up." Economist 261 (9 October 1976): 43.

156. Cosgrave, Patrick. "Immigration and Statistics."
      Spectator (10 January 1976): 5.

157. Cosgrave, Patrick. "Where Will All the Blacks Go Now?"
      Spectator (3 February 1973): 133.

158. Cosgrave, Patrick. "Who Goes Home?" Spectator
      (23 June 1973): 775.

159. Deakin, Nicholas. "Citizens and Immigrants in Britain."
      Round Table No. 242 (April 1971): 283-292.

160. Deakin, Nicholas. "Harold Macmillan and the Control
      of Commonwealth Immigration." New Community 4
      (Summer 1975): 191-194.

161. "Demos and Deafening Silence." Economist 244
      (2 September 1972): 21.

162. "Don't Blame Us." Economist 253 (23 November 1974):
      38.

163. "The Door Opens to the Whites But Closes on the Asians."
      Economist 246 (27 January 1973): 19.

164. Dykes, Hugh. "Immigration vs. Race Relations."
      Spectator (22 April 1972): 639, 664.

165. European Commission o n Human Rights. "Decision on
        Admissibility of Applications by East African
        Asians against United Kingdom, October 10, 1970."
        International Legal Materials 10 (January 1971):
        6-55.

166. "Evacuation." Economist 261 (20 November 1976): 71-72.

167. "False Fears and Real Fears." Economist 245 (25
        November 1972): 17-18.

168. Fenton, James. "Life Assurances." New Statesman
        (9 August 1974): 186.

169. "For the Record." Economist 259 (26 June 1976): 56.

170. Fox, A. D. "Attitudes to Immigration: A Comparison
        of Data From the 1970 and 1974 General Election
        Surveys." New Community 4 (Summer 1975): 167-
        178.

171. "Further Notes on the Asian Minorities of East Africa."
        New Community 1 (Autumn 1972): 417-420.

172. Gates, H. L., Jr. "Black London." Antioch Review 34
        (Spring 1976): 301-317.

173. "Getting Ready for Them." Economist 244 (26 August
        1972): 18, 21.

174. "God on His Side." Economist 244 (12 August 1972):
        13-14.

175. Gupta, A. "Ugandan Asians, Britain, India and the
        Commonwealth." African Affairs 73 (July 1974):
        312-324.

176. "Happy Families." Economist 250 (23 March 1974):
        29-30.

177. "The Hard News." Economist 246 (27 January 1973): 37.

178. "Here They Come at Last." Economist 244 (23 September
        1972): 26.

179. Hitchens, Christopher. "Absolute Beginners." New
        Statesman (23 May 1975): 684.

180. "How Happy." Economist 248 (29 September 1973): 32.

181. "How Wide a Welcome." Economist 244 (23 September
        1972): 41-42.

182. Huxley, E. "England Faces the Great Migration."
      National Review 24 (13 October 1972): 1124-1125.

183. "Immigrants to Come." Economist 259 (29 Mary 1976):
      12-13.

184. Jones, Kathleen and A. D. Smith. "The £SD of
      Immigration: The Economic Aspects of Commonwealth
      Immigration." Race Today 2: 8 (August 1970):
      251-252.

185. Kirby, Alexander. "Unwilling Passage to India." New
      Statesman (18 January 1974): 73.

186. Kohler, David Frank. "A Black Trickle." New Society
      (20 February 1975): 460.

187. Kohler, David Frank. "Commonwealth Coloured Immigrants
      and the 1971 Census." New Community 2 (Winter
      1972/1973): 80-84.

188. Kohler, David Frank. "Illegal Immigrants." New
      Society (16 August 1973): 401-402.

189. Kohler, David Frank. "Public Opinion and Illegal
      Immigrants." New Community 2 (Autumn 1973):
      427-428.

190. Kohler, David Frank. "Public Opinion and the Ugandan
      Asians." New Community 2 (Spring 1973): 194-197.

191. Kohler, David Frank. "Statistics Concerning Minority
      Ethnic Groups." New Community 3 (Summer 1974):
      311-312.

192. Lapping,,Anne. "Whom Man Is Keeping Apart." Observer
      (16 July 1972): 25.

193. Legum, Colin and Adam Raphael. "A Bottomless Pool."
      Observer (30 May 1976): 11.

194. Lomas, Glenys Barbara Gillian. "Colour in the Census."
      New Society (24 January 1974): 196.

195. "Long Struggle Back." Economist 248 (11 August 1973):
      21.

196. Lyon, Alex. "Immigration: A Matter of Principle."
      New Statesman (28 May 1976): 701-703.

197. McKenzie, Robert, et al. "'Welcome' and Keep Out':
      The Two Signs on Britain's Door." Listener 98
      (15 September 1977): 325-326.

198. Marks, Laurence. "Enoch Slips up in the Numbers
          Game." Observer (28 February 1971): 2.

199. "No Longer Anyone's Guess." Economist 264
          (17 September 1977): 20, 23.

200. Peach, G. C. K. and S. W. C. Winchester. "Birthplace,
          Ethnicity and the Under-Enumeration of West
          Indians, Indians and Pakistanis in the Censuses
          of 1966 and 1971." New Community 3 (Autumn
          1974): 386-393.

201. Plender, Richard. "The Expulsion of Asians from
          Uganda: Legal Aspects." New Community 1
          (Autumn 1972): 420-427.

202. "A Powellite Triumph and a Case of Double Indebtedness."
          Spectator (6 March 1971): 308.

203. "Pushing Off." Economist 253 (12 October 1974): 144.

204. "Race and Immigration." Venture 23 (January 1971):
          3-37.

205. "Registering with Reggie." Economist 238 (6 March
          1971): 26.

206. "Roll Back the Carpet." Economist 252 (10 August
          1974): 47.

207. "A Short Stay." Economist 245 (7 October 1972): 28.

208. Sye, Robert J. "Frost on Immigration." Focus 1: 3
          (August 1973): 23-27, 53-56.

209. "They Are Falling." Economist 265 (29 October 1977):
          19.

210. "They Got Here Anyway." Economist 245 (11 November
          1972): 29.

211. "Uganda: The Outcast's Story." Newsweek 80
          (25 September 1972): 58-62.

212. "Ugandan Asians: Getting Ready for Them." Economist
          244 (26 August 1972): 18, 21.

213. "Victims in Flight." Economist 234 (14 February
          1970): 18.

214. Wallis, Susan. "The Asian's Arrival." New Society
          (27 May 1976): 472-473.

215.   Ward, Robin H.   "The Decision to Admit: A Note on
           Governmental Attitudes to Immigration."   New
           Community 1   (Autumn 1972): 428-434.

216.   "We Don't Need Anymore: Question of Accepting Ugandan
           Asians."   Newsweek 80   (11 September 1972): 30.

217.   West, Richard.   "The Ugandans Come to Brent."   New
           Statesman   (27 October 1972): 585-586.

218.   West Indian Immigration.   Community Relations in
           Social Services 1: 4   (November 1975): 1-2.

219.   Wicker, B.   "Uganda's Asians: Half a Welcome."
           Commonweal 97   (20 October 1972): 52-53.

220.   "Will Britain Balk."   Economist 249   (6 October 1973):
           68.

221.   Winchester, S. W. C.   "Immigrant Areas in Coventry
           in 1971."   New Community 4   (Winter/Spring 1974/
           1975): 97-104.

222.   Wood, Susanne.   "Coloured Population of Great Britain."
           Political Quarterly 45: 2   (April/June 1974): 251.

III.

HISTORY AND POLITICS

A. BOOKS

223. Barclay, William, Krishna Kumar and Ruth P. Simms.
Racial Conflict Discrimination and Power: Histori-
cal and Contemporary Studies. New York: AMS
Press, 1976. 436 p.

224. Berkeley, Humphry. The Odyssey of Enoch Powell: A
Political Memoir. London: Hamish Hamilton, 1977.
160 p.

225. Bolt, Christine. Victorian Attitudes to Race. London:
Routledge & Kegan Paul, 1971. 254 p.

   Review by V. G. Kiernan. Race 13: 2 (October
   1971): 257-258.

226. Bonhomme, Samuel. Enoch Powell and the West Indian
Immigrants. London: Afro-American and West Indian
Publishers, 1971. 83 p.

227. Crewe, Ivor, ed. The Politics of Race. New York:
Wiley, 1975. 298 p.

228. Great Britain. Commission for Racial Equality. Strategy Statement: A Programme for Action. London:
The Commission, 1977. 12 p.

229. Great Britain. Community Relations Commission.
Citizenship of the United Kingdom and Colonies:
What Registration Means to You. London: The
Commission, 1972. 38 p.

230. Great Britain. Community Relations Commission. List
      of Community Relations Councils. London: Com-
      munity Relations Commission, 1973. 18 p.

231. Great Britain. Community Relations Commission. Report.
      London: H.M.S.O., 1968-69- Annual.

          Issued in the series of reports and papers of
          the House of Commons of Parliament.

232. Great Britain. Community Relations Commission. Sum-
      mary of the PEP Report on Racial Discrimination.
      London: The Commission, 1970. 8 p.

233. Great Britain. Community Relations Commission.
      Towards a Multi-Racial Society. London: The
      Commission, 1970. 34 p.

234. Great Britain. Community Relations Commission.
      Reference and Community Services. Refuge or
      Home? A Policy Statement on the Resettlement of
      Refugees. London: The Commission, 1976. 68 p.

235. Great Britain. Community Relations Commission.
      Reference Division. One Year On: A Report on the
      Resettlement of the Refugees from Uganda in Bri-
      tain. London: Community Relations Commission,
      1974. 60 p.

236. Great Britain. Home Office. The Organisation of Race
      Relations Administration: Observations on the Re-
      port of the Select Committee on Race Relations
      and Immigration. London: H.M.S.O., 1976. 21 p.

237. Great Britain. Home Office. Racial Discrimination.
      London: H.M.S.O., 1975. 31 p.

238. Great Britain. Home Office. Advisory Committee on
      Race Relations Research. Race Relations Research:
      A Report. London: H.M.S.O., 1975. 43 p.

239. Great Britain. Home Office. Uganda Resettlement Board.
      Final Report. London: H.M.S.O., 1974. 24 p.

240. Great Britain. Parliament. House of Commons. Select
      Committee on Race Relations and Immigration.
      Minutes of Proceedings, Session 1973-74. London:
      H.M.S.O., 1974. Unpaged.

241. Great Britain. Parliament. House of Commons. Select
      Committee on Race Relations and Immigration. The
      Organisation of Race Relations Administration:
      Select Committee on Race Relations and Immigration,
      Session 1974/75. London: H.M.S.O., 1975. 3 vols.

          Vol. 1. Report.   Vol. 2. Evidence.
          Vol. 3. Appendices.

242. Great Britain. Parliament. House of Commons. Select
      Committee on Race Relations and Immigration.
      Special Report. London: H.M.S.O., 1975. 8 p.

243. Great Britain. Parliament. House of Commons. Select
      Committee on Race Relations and Immigration. Sub-
      ject of Inquiry: First Special Report from the
      Select Committee on Race Relations and Immigration:
      Session 1972/73. London: H.M.S.O., 1972. Unpaged.

244. Great Britain. Parliament. House of Commons. Select
      Committee on Race Relations and Immigration. Sub-
      ject of Inquiry: First Special Report from the
      Select Committee on Race Relations and Immigration:
      Session 1975-76. London: H.M.S.O., 1976. Unpaged.

245. Great Britain. Parliament. House of Commons. Select
      Committee on Race Relations and Immigration. Sub-
      ject of Inquiry: Second Special Report from the
      Select Committee on Race Relations and Immigration.
      London: H.M.S.O., 1971. 4 p.

246. Great Britain. Parliament. House of Commons. Select
      Committee on Race Relations and Immigration. Sub-
      ject of Inquiry: Second Special Report from the
      Select Committee on Race Relations and Immigration:
      Session 1974-75. London: H.M.S.O., 1975. 3 p.

247. Great Britain. Parliament. House of Commons. Select
      Committee on Race Relations and Immigration. The
      West Indian Community: Report from the Select Com-
      mittee on Race Relations and Immigration: Session
      1976-1977. London: H.M.S.O., 1977. 2 vols.

      Vol. 1. Report with Minutes of Proceedings
      and Appendices to the Report. Vol. 2. Evi-
      dence.

248. Great Britain. Race Relations Board. Report. London:
      The Board, 1967- Annual.

      Ceased in 1973.

249. Hill, Michael J. and Ruth M. Issacharoff. Community
      Action and Race Relations: A Study of Community
      Relations Committees in Britain. London: Oxford
      University Press for the Institute of Race Rela-
      tions, 1971. 317 p.

      Review by Sheila Allen. Race 14: 1 (July 1972):
      92-93.

250. Huttenback, Robert Arthur. Racism and Empire: White
      Settlers and Coloured Immigrants in the British
      Self-Governing Colonies, 1830-1910. Ithaca and
      London: Cornell University Press, 1976. 359 p.

251. Immigration and Race Relations: A Reference Guide for
      Candidates. London: Runnymede Trust, 1970. 15 p.

252. Irvine, Keith. The Rise of the Coloured Races: A
      History of Their Cultures, Societies, and Inter-
      play with the White World. London: Allen and
      Unwin, 1972. 646 p.

253. Kidman, Brenda. A Handful of Tears. London: British
      Broadcasting Corporation, 1975. 200 p.

254. Kiernan, E. Victor Gordon. The Lords of Human Kind:
      European Attitudes Towards the Outside World in
      the Imperial Age. Rev. ed. Harmondsworth:
      Penguin, 1972. 354 p.

255. Kuepper, William George, Lynne Lackey and Nelson
      Swinerton. Ugandan Asians in Great Britain:
      Forced Migration and Social Absorption. London:
      Croom Helm, 1975. 122 p.

256. Little, Kenneth. Negroes in Britain: A Study of Racial
      Relations in English Society. Rev. ed. London:
      Routledge and Kegan Paul, 1972. 309 p.

            Review by Roderick J. MacDonald. Race 15: 2
            (October 1973): 258-259.

257. Lorimer, Douglas Alexander. "British Attitudes to the
      Negro, 1850-1870." Doctoral dissertation,
      University of British Columbia, 1972.

258. Mazov, V. End Colonial and Racial Crimes. Moscow,
      Novosti Press Agency Publishing House, 1971. 70 p.

259. Morrell, William Parker. British Overseas Expansion
      and the History of the Commonwealth: A Select
      Bibliography. 2d ed. London: Historical Associa-
      tion, 1970. 48 p.

260. Mullard, Christ. Black Britain: With an Account of
      Recent Events at the Institute of Race Relations
      by Alexander Kirby. London: Allen and Unwin,
      1973. 194 p.

            Review by J. H. Taylor. New Community 2
            (Summer 1973): 316-317.

261. Newton, Kenneth. Second City Politics. London:
      Oxford University Press, 1976. 244 p.

262. O'Brien, Justin. Brown Britons: The Crisis of the
      Ugandan Asians. London: Runnymede Trust, 1972.
      23 p.

263.   Onyeama, Dillibe. John Bull's Nigger. London: Frewin,
       1974. 159 p.

264.   Rex, John. Race, Colonialism and the City. London:
       Routledge and Kegan Paul, 1973. 310 p.

       Review by Lucy Mair. New Community 2 (Summer
       1973): 315-316.

265.   Roth, Andrew. Enoch Powell: Tory Tribune. London:
       MacDonald, 1970. 393 p.

266.   Runnymede Trust. The First Fifteen Months: A Report.
       London: The Trust, 1970. Unpaged.

267.   Runnymede Trust. Strategy and Style in Local Community
       Relations: A Report. Collated by Anthony Barker.
       Prepared for the Runnymede Trust and submitted to
       the House of Commons Select Committee on Race Re-
       lations and Immigration, May 1975. London: The
       Trust, 1975. 57 p.

268.   Russell, Alan Gladney. Colour, Race and Empire. Port
       Washington, London: Kennikat Press, 1973. 278 p.

269.   Schoen, Douglas E. Enoch Powell and the Powellites.
       London: Macmillan, 1977. 317 p.

270.   Schoen, Douglas E. Enoch Powell and the Powellites.
       New York: St. Martin's Press, 1977. 317 p.

271.   Scobie, Edward. Black Britannia: A History of Blacks
       in Britain. Chicago: Johnson, 1972. 316 p.

272.   Shyllon, Folarin Olawale. Black People in Britain:
       1555-1833. London: Oxford University Press for the
       Institute of Race Relations, 1977. 300 p.

273.   Shyllon, Folarin Olawale. Black Slaves in Britain.
       London: Oxford University Press for the Institute
       of Race Relations, 1974. 252 p.

274.   Sivanandan, Ambalavaner. Race and Resistance: The IRR
       Story. London: Race Today Publications, 1974.
       36 p.

275.   Stacey, Tom. Immigration and Enoch Powell. London:
       Author, 1970. 208 p.

276.   Tinker, Hugh. Race, Conflict and the International
       Order: From Empire to United Nations. New York:
       St. Martin's Press, 1977. 157 p.

277. Tinker, Hugh. Separate and Unequal: India and the
      Indians in the British Commonwealth, 1920-1950.
      London: C. Hurst, 1976. 460 p.

278. Tucker, Peter, ed. Citizenship of the United Kingdom
      and Colonies: What Registration Means to You?
      2d ed. London: Community Relations Commission,
      1974. 63 p.

279. Walvin, James. Black and White: The Negro and English
      Society, 1555-1945. London: Allen Lane, 1973.
      239 p.

          Review by F. O. Shyllon. Race 15: 2 (October
          1973): 255-258.

280. Walvin, James. The Black Presence: A Documentary His-
      tory of the Negro in England, 1555-1860. London:
      Orbachs and Chambers, 1971. 222 p.

          Review by Richard Blackett. Race 14: 1 (July
          1972): 86-88.

281. Weintraub, Allen L. "Race and Local Politics in Eng-
      land: A Case Study of Willesden." Doctoral dis-
      sertation, Columbia University, 1972. 432 p.

282. Wood, John. Powell and the 1970 Election. Kingswood,
      England: Elliot Right Way Books, 1970. 125 p.

283. Yearbook of Social Policy in Britain. London: Rout-
      ledge & Kegan Paul, 1971- v. 1- Annual.

B. PERIODICAL ARTICLES

284. "Advance on All Fronts." Economist 260 (10 July 1976):
      18, 22.

285. "America for Equal Rights." Economist 256 (26 July
      1975): 17-18.

286. Ankrah Dove, Linda. "Immigrant School Leavers and
      Political Life." Teaching Politics 4 (May 1975):
      95-104.

287. Anwar, Muhammad. "Asian Participation in the October
      1974 General Election." New Community 4 (Autumn
      1975): 376-383.

288. Anwar, Muhammad. "Pakistani Participation in the 1972
      Rochdale By-Elections." New Community 2 (Autumn
      1973): 418-423.

289. Anwar, Muhammad. "Pakistani Participation in the 1973
      Rochdale Local Elections." New Community 3
      (Winter/Apring 1974): 67-72.

290. Asher, Wayne. "Powellism, Racism and the Conservative
      Party Today." International Socialism No. 87
      (March/April 1976): 6-7.

291. "Asian Minorities in East Africa and Britain." New
      Community 1 (Autumn 1972): 406-416.

292. "Asians from Uganda in European Transit Camps." New
      Community 2 (Summer 1973): 276-277.

293. Bagley, Christopher. "Racial Prejudice and the Con-
      servative Personality: A British Sample." Politi-
      cal Studies 18: 1 (March 1970): 134-141.

294. Bayles, Michael D. "Reparations to Wronged Groups."
      Analysis 33 (June 1973): 182-184.

295. Beith, Alan. "A New Immigration Policy for Britain."
      Contemporary Review 225 (September 1974): 121-126.

296. "Belt Up You Big Bore: Views of E. Powell." Time 109
      (7 February 1977): 44-45.

297. Bentley, Stuart. "Intergroup Relations in Local Poli-
      tics: Pakistanis and Bangladeshis." New Community
      2 (Winter 1972/1973): 44-48.

298. "Better Late." Economist 241 (16 October 1971): 24.

299. "The Black Man in Britain: Registration and Politics."
      Listener 93 (6 February 1975): 168-169.

300. "Black Racism in Uganda - White Man's Burden for Bri-
      tain." U.S. News and World Report 73 (4 Sep-
      tember 1972): 48-49.

301. "Blunderbuss." Newsweek 84 (4 November 1974): 45-46.

302. Bolt, Christine and Philip Mason. "Cold Baths, Prudery
      and Empire: Victorian Attitudes to Race."
      New Society (4 February 1971): 201-202.

303. Bonham-Carter, Mark. "Of Macaulay and the Black-Haired
      People." Listener 96 (12 August 1976): 163-165.

304. Bourne, Richard. "Monitoring Social Policy." New
      Society (7 March 1974): 567-569.

305. Bridges, Lee. "The Ministry of Internal Security:
      British Urban Social Policy, 1968-74." Race and
      Class 16: 4 (April 1975): 375-386.

306. Bridges, Lee. "Race Relations Research: From Colo-
      nialism to Neo-Colonialism: Some Random Thoughts."
      Race 14: 3 (January 1973): 331-341.

307. Bristow, Mike. "Britain's Response to the Uganda
      Asian Crisis: Government Myths Versus Political
      and Resettlement Realities." New Community 5
      (Autumn 1976): 265-279.

308. Bristow, S. "Up the Poll in Slough." Race Today 3: 6
      (June 1971): 202-203.

309. "The British Campaign to Stop Immigration: Pressure
      Groups at the Polls." Race Today 4: 6 (June 1972):
      208-209.

310. "Calling the Tune." Economist 243 (1 April 1972):
      24-26.

311. Cameron, James, et al. "The Ship of Good Hope: How
      Jamaica Came to England." Listener 92 (8 August
      1974): 165-166.

312. "Clobber Powell?" Economist 262 (29 January 1977):
      19-20.

313. Cosgrave, Patrick. "How Many Nations." Spectator
      (2 February 1974): 126.

314. Crabbe, Pauline. "The First Fifty Years." New Com-
      munity 2 (Winter 1972/1973): 62-66.

315. Cunningham, Sir Charles. "The Uganda Resettlement
      Board and Hiving-Off: Some Possibilities for
      Future Research." Public Administration 51
      (Autumn 1973): 251-260.

316. Cunningham, Sir Charles. "The Work of the Uganda Re-
      settlement Board." Contemporary Review 222
      (May 1973): 225-230.

317. Cunningham, Sir Charles. "The Work of the Uganda Re-
      settlement Board." New Community 2 (Summer 1973):
      261-267.

318. "The Dangers of Apathy." CRC Journal 5: 1 (December/
      January 1976/1977): 7.

319. Deakin, Nicholas. "Political Rights and Minority
      Groups." New Community 1 (Summer 1972): 189-192.

320. Deakin, Nicholas and Jenny Bourne. "Powell, the Mi-
      norities and the 1970 Election." Political Quar-
      terly 41: 4 (October/December 1970): 399-415.

321. Deakin, Nicholas and Jenny Bourne. "Powell - the Mi-
          norities and the General Election 1970." Race
          Today 2: 7 (July 1970): 205-206.

322. Dhesi, A. "The Immigrant Vote: Asian Variants." Race
          Today 2: 7 (July 1970): 234-235.

323. Dummett, M. "CARD Reconsidered." Race Today 5: 2
          (February 1973): 42-44.

324. "Experts Confounded." Economist 263 (7 May 1977):
          24-26.

325. "Fast Work Could Still Save the New Race Commission."
          Economist 263 (18 June 1977): 19-20.

326. Frasure, Robert C. "Constituency, Racial Composition
          and the Attitudes of British M.P.'s." Comparative
          Politics 3 (January 1971): 201-210.

327. Great Britain. Parliament. House of Commons. Select
          Committee on Race Relations and Immigration. "The
          Organisation of Race Relations Administration."
          New Community 4 (Autumn 1975): 314-316.

328. Greaves, Mary. "A Policy for Change." Observer
          (8 October 1972): 46.

329. Hamilton-Paterson, James. "Camp on John Bull's Is-
          land." Nova (April 1973): 68-72, 75.

330. Hill, Michael. "Community Buffers." New Society
          (14 June 1973): 624.

331. Horowitz, Dan. "The British Conservatives and the
          Racial Issue in the Debate on Decolonization."
          Race 12: 2 (October 1970): 169-187.

332. Johnson, R. W. and D. Schoen. "The Powell Effect: Or
          How One Man Can Win." New Society (22 July 1976):
          168-172.

333. Johnstone, T. "An Overview of Ethnic Services in the
          Department of Education." Journal of Education
          4: 2 (Spring 1977): 15-18.

334. Katznelson, Ira. "The Politics of Racial Buffering in
          Nottingham, 1954-1968." Race 11: 4 (April 1970):
          431-446.

335. Laird, A. F. and D. Wood. "A Reply to Ira Katznelson
          on the Politics of Racial Buffering in Nottingham,
          1954-68." Race 12: 2 (October 1970): 237-238.

336. Layton-Henry, Zig. "Race and Politics in Ladywood: The
      Parties and the Campaign." New Community 6 (Winter
      1977/1978): 130-142.

337. Layton-Henry, Zig and Stan Taylor. "Race at the Polls."
      New Society (25 August 1977): 392-393.

338. Makins, Virginia. "Can David Lane's Soft Answer Turn
      Away Racial Wrath?" Times Higher Educational
      Supplement No. 3231 (6 May 1977): 9.

339. Narayan, Rudy. "The Immigrant Vote: West Indian Pri-
      orities." Race Today 2: 7 (July 1970): 235-236.

340. "A New CRC." Race and Class 17: 1 (Summer 1975): 78-79.

341. "Not Just Enoch." Economist 262 (8 January 1977): 25.

342. "Numbers Game." Economist 260 (24 July 1976): 23-24.

343. "Organisation of Race Relations Administration - Sum-
      mary of Recommendations of the Select Committee on
      Race Relations and Immigration." New Community 5
      (Autumn 1975): 314-316.

344. Pearson, David G. "The Politics of Paradox: Community
      Relation and Migrant Response in Britain." Social
      and Economic Administration 10: 3 (Autumn 1976):
      167-181.

345. Phillips, Melanie. "Race of Monoliths." New Society
      (5 May 1977): 228-229.

346. Phillips, Michael. "Landfall." Listener 92 (21 Novem-
      ber 1974): 660-661.

347. Phillips, Ron. "The Black Masses and the Political
      Economy of Manchester." The Black Liberator 2: 4
      (January 1975-August 1976): 290-300.

348. Potter, Tim. "Lessons of Lewisham." International
      Socialism No. 101 (September 1977): 18-23.

349. Power, Jonathan. "This Britain, An Unhappy Nation."
      New Society (21 February 1974): 443-444.

350. "Racing on With Enoch." Economist 258 (10 January 1976):
      22-23.

351. "Reconciling the Concilliators." Economist 256 (5 July
      1975): 45.

352. "Red Tape Around the Camps." Economist 245 (21 October
      1972): 21.

353. "Resettling Ugandan Asians." World Development 1
      (June 1973): 54.

354. Rex, John. "Sociological Research and the Politics
      of Racial Justice." Race 14: 4 (April 1973):
      481-487.

355. Richardson, C. and J. Lethbridge. "The Anti-Immigrant
      Vote in Bradford." Race Today 4: 4 (April 1972):
      120-122.

356. Rose, Hannan. "Extreme Right and Election Campaign."
      Race Today 2: 8 (August 1970): 275-276.

357. Roy, Amit. "The Asian Vote." Spectator (14 February
      1976): 10-12.

358. Schaefer, Richard T. "Party Affiliation and Prejudice
      in Britain." New Community 2 (Summer 1973):
      296-299.

359. Scott, Duncan. "West Pakistanis in Huddersfield:
      Aspects of Race Relations in Politics." New
      Community 2 (Winter 1972/1973): 38-43.

360. Scott, Gavin. "Department of Education and Science
      Rapped for Not Knowing Race Facts." Times Educa-
      tional Supplement No. 3138 (25 July 1975): 5.

361. Sills, Patrick. "Community Relations Councils: What
      Kind of Shot in the Arm?" New Community 4
      (Winter/Spring 1975/1976): 434-435.

362. Smith, Jef. "The Early History of West Indian Immigrant
      Boys." British Journal of Social Work 1 (April
      1971): 73-84.

363. Stadlen, Frances. "Public Poll Shows Signs of Progress
      in Race Relations." Times Educational Supplement
      No. 3170 (5 March 1976): 6.

364. Stapleton, John. "Time to Listen." Listener 95
      (17 June 1976): 766.

365. Stephen, David. "Sir Charles's Settlers." New
      Statesman (1 September 1972): 275-276.

366. Studler, Donley T. "British Public Opinion, Colour
      Issues and Enoch Powell: A Longitudinal Analysis."
      British Journal of Political Science 4 (July
      1974): 371-381.

367. Taylor, Stan. "The National Front: Backlash or Boot
      Boys." New Society (11 August 1977): 283-284.

368. "Thumbs Down." _Economist_ 244 (2 September 1972):
      21-22.

369. Tinker, Hugh. "Race and Neo-Victorianism." _Encounter_
      38 (April 1972): 47-55.

370. "Tinker's Reprieve." _Economist_ 243 (22 April 1972):
      66.

371. "The True Voice of Britain." _Economist_ 244
      (16 September 1972): 12-13.

372. "Under Inspection." _Economist_ 243 (24 June 1972):
      22, 25.

373. Underwood, Chris. "One Immigrant Voice." _Listener_ 96
      (29 July 1976): 103.

374. Ward, Robin H. "How Plural is Britain?" _New Community_
      1 (Summer 1972): 263-270.

375. Ward, Robin H. "What Future for the Uganda Asians?"
      New Community 2 (Autumn 1973): 372-378.

376. "What Future for Cousin's Commission?" _Economist_ 236
      (29 August 1970): 18-19.

377. Workman, G. "Thomas Carlyle and the Governor Eyre
      Controversy: An Account with Some New Material."
      Victorian Studies 18 (September 1974): 77-102.

IV.

RACISM

A. BOOKS

378. Abbott, Simon. The Prevention of Racial Discrimination in Britain. London: Oxford University Press for the United Nations Institute for Training and Research and the Institute of Race Relations, 1971. 502 p.

> Review by Sheila Allen. Race and Class 14: 1 (July 1972): 92-93.

379. Bagley, Christopher. Social Structure and Prejudice in Five English Boroughs: A Report Prepared for the IRR Survey of Race Relations in Britain. London: Institute of Race Relations. Distributed by Research Publications, 1970. 78 p.

380. Bidwell, Sidney. Red, White and Black: Race Relations in Britain. London: Gordon and Cremonesi, 1976. 213 p.

> Review by Jenny Bourne. Race and Class 18: 3 (Winter 1977): 318-320.

381. Bogan, Robert. Racial Prejudice. London: Darton, Longman and Todd, 1971. 28 p.

382. Bronnert, David. Race: The Challenge to Christians. London: CPAS Publications, 1973. 24 p.

383. CIS (Counter Information Service). Racism: Who Profits? London: CIS in Cooperation with the Institute of Race Relations, 1976. 40 p.

384. Catholic Commission for Racial Justice. Where Creed
      and Colour Matter: A Survey on Black Children
      and Catholic Schools. Abbots Langley, England,
      Catholic Commission for Racial Justice, 1975.
      47 p.

385. Deakin, Nicholas with Brian Cohen and Julia McNeal.
      Colour, Citizenship and British Society. London:
      Panther Books for the Institute of Race Relations,
      1970. 396 p.

          Review by Thomas Pettigrew and Marie Jahoda.
          Race 12: 3 (January 1971): 345-352.

386. Dummett, Ann. A Portrait of English Racism. Harmonds-
      worth: Penguin Books, 1973. 300 p.

          Review by Harold Pollins. New Community 3
          (Summer 1974): 294-296.

387. Edgington, David William. Christians and Colour in
      Britain. London: Scripture Union, 1970. 136 p.

388. Emecheta, Buchi. Second Class Citizen. London:
      Allison and Busby, 1974. 175 p.

          Review by Hermoine Harris. Race and Class
          16: 4 (April 1975): 433-435.

389. Emecheta, Buchi. The Slave Girl: A Novel. London:
      Allison and Busby, 1977. 179 p.

390. Eysenck, Hans Jurgen. The Inequality of Man. London:
      Temple Smith, 1973. 288 p.

391. Foot, Paul. Workers Against Racism. London: Inter-
      national Socialist, 1973. Unpaged.

392. The Fourth World: Victims of Group Oppression. Eight
      Reports from the Field Work of the Minority Rights
      Group. Edited by Ben Whitaker. London: Sidgwick
      and Jackson, 1972. 342 p.

393. Gilroy, Beryl. Black Teacher. London: Cassell, 1976.
      196 p.

394. Heinemann, Benjamin W. The Politics of the Powerless:
      A Study of the Campaign Against Racial Discrimina-
      tion. London: Oxford University Press for the
      Institute of Race Relations, 1972. 244 p.

          Review by Harold Pollins. New Community 3
          (Summer 1974): 294-296.

          Review by M. Glean. Race Today 5: 1
          (January 1973): 13-15.

395. Hiro, Dilip. Black British, White British. London:
        Eyre and Spottiswoode, 1971. 384 p.

              Review by Harold Pollins. New Community 1
              (Spring 1972): 235-236.

              Review by Daniel Lawrence. Race 14: 2
              (October 1972): 207-209.

396. Hiro, Dilip. Black British White British. Rev. ed.
        New York: Monthly Review Press, 1973. 346 p.

              Review by C. Sigal. New Republic 170
              (8 June 1974): 245.

397. Hooper, Rachel. Act Now: A Report on Race Relations
        in Britain, Following a Survey of August/September
        1969; With Special Reference to the Response of
        the Churches and of the Church Missionary Society.
        London: Church Missionary Society, 1970. 88 p.

398. Humphry, Derek and Gus John. Because They are Black.
        Harmondsworth: Penguin Books, 1971. 204 p.

              Review by Stuart Bentley. Race 13: 2
              (October 1971): 260-262.

399. Labour Party (Great Britain) Young Socialist.
        Racialism: A Threat to All Workers. London:
        Labour Party, 1973. 7 p.

400. McIntosh, Neil and David J. Smith. The Extent of
        Racial Discrimination. London: Political and
        Economic Planning, 1974. 55 p.

401. Miller, Ruth and Paul J. Dolan, eds. Race Awareness:
        The Nightmare and the Vision. New York, London:
        Oxford University Press, 1971. 478 p.

402. Moore, Robert Samuel. Racism and Black Resistance in
        Britain. London: Pluto Press, 1975. 115 p.

              Review by Jenny Bourne. Race and Class 17: 2
              (Autumn 1975): 202-204.

403. Nugent, N. and R. King, eds. The British Right.
        Farnborough: Saxon House, 1977. 240 p.

404. Roser, J. S. A Study of Violence on London Transport.
        London: Behavioral Science Unit, Greater London
        Council, 1976. 42 p.

405. Runnymede Trust. Race and the Dangers of 'Benign
        Neglect'. London: Runnymede Trust, 1975. 20 p.

406.   Sansbury, Kenneth. Combating Racism: The British
        Churches and the WCC Programme to Combat Racism.
        London: British Council of Churches, 1975. 78 p.

407.   Schaefer, Richard T. "The Extent and Content of Racial
        Prejudice in Great Britain." Doctoral dissertation,
        University of Chicago, 1972. 348 p.

408.   Schaefer, Richard T. The Extent and Content of Racial
        Prejudice in Great Britain. San Francisco:
        R and E Research Associates, 1976. 253 p.

409.   Smith, David John. The Facts of Racial Disadvantage:
        A National Survey. London: PEP, 1976. 307 p.

            Review by Ambalavaner Sivanandan. Race and
            Class 17: 4 (Spring 1976): 441-442.

410.   Smith, David John. Racial Disadvantage in Britain:
        The PEP Report. Harmondsworth: Penguin, 1977.
        349 p.

411.   Smith, Derek, et al. No To the Fascists. Bradford:
        Bradford Trades Council, 1976. 4 p.

412.   Stafford-Clark, David. Prejudice in the Community.
        London: Community Relations Commission, 1971.
        16 p.

413.   United Nations. General Assembly. Report of the
        Committee on the Elimination of Racial Discrimina-
        tion. New York: United Nations, 1971. 61 p.

414.   United Nations. General Assembly. United Nations
        Declaration and International Convention on the
        Elimination of All Forms of Racial Discrimination;
        International Year for Action to Combat Racism
        and Racial Discrimination. Wellington: A. R.
        Shearer, Government Printer, 1971. 19 p.

415.   United Nations. Secretary General. Elimination of
        All Forms of Racial Discrimination: International
        Year for Action to Combat Racism and Racial Dis-
        crimination: Report. New York: United Nations,
        1971. 125 p.

416.   United Nations. Secretary General. Elimination of
        All Forms of Racial Discrimination: Status of the
        International Convention on the Elimination of
        All Forms of Racial Discrimination: Report.
        New York: United Nations, 1971. 8 p.

417. United Nations Educational, Scientific and Cultural
        Organization. Race, Science and Society. Edited
        and with an introduction by Leo Kuper. Paris:
        UNESCO Press; N.Y., Columbia University Press,
        1975. 370 p.

418. Van Haute, Hans and Willy Melgert. Foreigners in Our
        Community. Amsterdam: Antwerp, 1970. 202 p.

        Review in New Community 1 (Summer 1972): 338.

419. Vincent, John James. The Race Race. London: SCM
        Press, 1970. 116 p.

420. White, Sarah, ed. The Road Made to Walk on Carnival
        Day: The Battle for the West Indian Carnival in
        Britain. London: Race Today Collective, 1977.
        23 p.

421. World Council of Churches. The Programme to Combat
        Racism of the World Council of Churches. London:
        British Council of Churches, 1974. 8 p.

422. Zubaida, Sami. Race and Racialism. London: Tavistock
        Publications, 1970. 185 p.

B. PERIODICAL ARTICLES

423. "About the Minority Question: Now Ask the British."
        U. S. News and World Report 79 (22 December
        1975): 66-67.

424. "Action Against Racism." CRC Journal 5: 1 (December/
        January 1976/1977): 6.

425. Allen, Sheila. "The Institutionalization of Racism."
        Race 15: 1 (July 1973): 99-106.

426. "Anatomy of a Riot: Racial Clashes in Liverpool."
        New Society (17 August 1972): 336-337.

427. "Angry Eruption in Notting Hill." Time 108
        (13 September 1976): 43.

428. Armitage, J. "The National Front in Huddersfield."
        Race Today 3:10 (October 1971): 335-338.

429. "Assaults on Asians." Race Today 9: 6/7 (June/July
        1977): 79.

430. "Attack on Bengals." Race Today 8: 4 (April 1976):
        79.

431. "August 1978 Proposed As Tentative Date for Anti-
      Racism Conference: World Conference to Combat
      Racism and Racial Discrimination." U.N. Chronicle
      14 (April 1977): 50.

432. Azim, Tariq. "Race and Repatriation: An Asian View-
      point." Race Today 3: 5 (May 1971): 149.

433. Beeson, T. "Britain's Blacks at the Bottom of the
      Pyramid: Concerning Statement Published by British
      Council of Churches." Christian Century 93
      (23 June 1976): 587-588.

434. Beeson, T. "Expulsion of Immigrants in Britain."
      Christian Century 90 (19 September 1973): 925.

435. Bellamy, J. "Struggle Against Racism in Britain."
      World Marxist Review 17 (March 1974): 97-105.

436. Bently, Stuart. "Race in the Census and Power in
      Society." New Community 3 (Summer 1974): 313-314.

437. "Bradford's Main-Stream Extremists." Race Today 3: 5
      (May 1971): 171-172.

438. Brock, George. "School for Hatred." Observer
      (21 August 1977): 11.

439. Brooks, Dennis and Karamjit Singh. "Does Unemployment
      Breed Racism." Race Today 4: 7 (July 1972):
      226-227.

440. Burke, Aggrey W. "The Consequences of Unplanned
      Repatriation." British Journal of Psychiatry
      123:572 (1973): 109-111.

441. "By the Colour of Their Genes." New Community 3
      (Winter/Spring 1974): 38-43.

442. Callinicos, Alex and Alastair Hatchet. "In Defence
      of Violence." International Socialism No. 101
      (September 1977): 24-28.

443. Clark, David. "The Harijans of Britain." New Society
      (26 June 1975): 765.

444. Clarke, Alva. "Candid Commentary." Community
      (January 1970): 6-7.

445. "The Coloreds Must Go: A Racist Movement Exploits
      Mounting Frustrations." Time 110 (12 December
      1977): 54-55.

446. Deming, A. and N. Proffitt. "Fire This Time."
      Newsweek 88 (13 September 1976): 68.

447. Dockrell, Bryan. "IQ: The Debate Continued." New
     Humanist 89 (January 1974): 296-297.

448. Doe, Bob. "Race Row over School Passport Checks."
     Times Educational Supplement No. 3207 (19 Novem-
     ber 1976): 8.

449. Edgar, David. "Racism, Fascism and the Politics of
     the National Front." Race and Class 19: 2
     (Autumn 1977): 111-131.

450. Edwards, J. H. "Race and IQ." New Humanist 89
     (January 1974): 298-299.

451. Egbuna, Obi Benue Joseph. "The Contradictions of
     Black Power." Race Today 3: 8/9 (August/
     September 1971): 266-268, 298-299.

452. Elkin, S. L. and W. H. Panning. "Structural Effects
     and Individual Attitudes: Racial Prejudice in
     English Cities." Public Opinion Quarterly 39
     (Summer 1975): 159-177.

453. Emecheta, Buchi. "Life in the Ditch." New Statesman
     (8 January 1971): 45-46, 77-78, 110.

454. Emecheta, Buchi. "Sitting on a Time Bomb - Brixton
     1975." Times Educational Supplement No. 3145
     (12 September 1975): 26.

455. "England in Danger." New Statesman (1 May 1970):
     601-602.

456. "England's Summer." Economist 264 (20 August 1977):
     11-12.

457. English, David, et al. "No Place for Alf." Listener
     95 (1 July 1976): 832.

458. Evans, Peter. "Learning to Laugh at the Silly Business
     of Race." New Community 1 (Spring 1972): 290-297.

459. "Facing the Front." New Statesman (12 November 1976):
     657.

460. "Fascism in Leicester." International Socialism No. 93
     (November/December 1976): 16-19.

461. Fenton, James. "Is it a Bomb or a Dinosaur?" New
     Statesman (28 May 1976): 700.

462. "Fighting Racism in the Community." Community Action
     No. 34 (November/December 1977): 18-25.

463. Flew, Antony. "Jensen: The Uproar Continues."
      Philosophy 49 (July 1974): 310-314.

464. Flew, Antony. "Reason, Racism and Obscurantism."
      New Humanist 89 (July 1973): 80-81.

465. Glean, Marion. "Whatever Happened to CARD?" Race
      Today 5: 1 (January 1973): 13-15.

466. Gretton, John. "The Race Industry." New Society
      (11 March 1971): 385-386.

467. Hanna, Max. "The National Front and Other Right Wing
      Organisations." New Community 3 (Winter/Spring
      1974): 49-55.

468. Harris, Sydney. "Spearhead of British Racialism."
      Patterns of Prejudice 7: 4 (1973): 15-19, 33.

469. Hibbert, C. "Ludds Do Your Duty Well." Horizon 16
      (Autumn 1974): 56-63.

470. Hiro, Dilip. "Untouchables; Even in Britain."
      Observer (28 November 1976): 45, 47-48.

471. Hiro, Dilip. "You Don't Have to be Afro-Asian."
      Listener 95 (20 May 1976): 636-637.

472. Holmes, Colin. "Violence and Race Relations in
      Britain, 1953-1968." Phylon 36 (June 1975):
      113-124.

473. "International Day for the Elimination of Racial Dis-
      crimination: United Nations Marks Day for Elimi-
      nation of Race Discrimination." U.N. Chronicle
      14 (April 1977): 30-33.

474. "It is Tougher on the Blacks." Economist 242
      (29 January 1972): 26.

475. "It is Worse for Immigrants." Economist 255
      (17 May 1975): 24.

476. Jensen, Arthur. "Race and Intelligence" The Case
      for Genetics." Times Educational Supplement
      No. 3095 (20 September 1974): 20-21.

477. Jones, Mervyn. "Race, Racism and Truth." New
      Statesman (30 July 1976): 136, 138-139.

478. Ketchum, Sara Ann and Christine Pierce. "Implicit
      Racism." Analysis 36 (January 1976): 91-95.

479. Kirkcaldy, John. "Black Power After Michael X."
      New Statesman (23 November 1973): 768-769.

480. Knappman, Edward W. "Color Crisis in Britain."
      Progressive 34 (June 1970): 27-31.

481. Koestler, Arthur. "Less Equal Than Others." New
      Community 3 (Winter/Spring 1974): 36-37.

482. Laishley, Jennie. "Some Perspectives on Race and
      Intelligence." New Community 2 (Spring 1973):
      187-193.

483. "Last Week It Was Soweto, This Week It is Notting Hill."
      Race Today 8: 9 (September 1976): 176-177.

484. Lawrence, Susanne. "Racial Discrimination: The Poor
      Relation." Personnel Management 7 (September
      1975): 22-26.

485. Leach, Edmund. "IQ and Race." Listener 89 (28 June
      1973): 849-851.

486. Lestor, J. "Racism Challenges Socialism." New
      Statesman (27 November 1970): 702.

487. London, Louise. "Paki-Bashing in 1970." Race Today
      5:12 (December 1973): 337-340.

488. "London's Black Carnival." Economist 260 (4 September
      1976): 12-13.

489. MacShane, Denis. "The Blacks Fight Back." New
      Statesman (21 May 1976): 670, 672.

490. Marsh, Alan. "Race, Community and Anxiety." New
      Society (22 February 1973): 406-408.

491. Marsh, Alan. "Who Hates the Blacks?" New Society
      (23 September 1976): 649-652.

492. Marshall, Roy. "Racial Discrimination: The Way Ahead."
      New Community 4 (Winter/Spring 1975/1976):
      423-428.

493. Mason, Philip. "Race, Resistance and the IRR." New
      Community 3 (Summer 1974): 285-288.

494. May, Roy and Robin Cohen. "The Interaction Between
      Race and Colonialism: A Case Study of the Liverpool
      Race Riot of 1919." Race and Class 16: 2
      (October 1974): 111-126.

495. Meacher, Michael. "Unseen Discrimination." Spectator
      (26 May 1973): 659-660.

496. Miller, Henry. "The Shockley Affair." New Community 2
      (Summer 1973): 300.

497. Milner, David. "Prejudice and the Immigrant Child."
      New Society (3 September 1971): 556-559.

498. Moore, Robert. "A Reply to George Young." Race Today
      3: 1 (January 1971): 12-13.

499. Nikolinakos, Marios. "Notes on an Economic Theory of
      Racism." Race 14: 4 (April 1973): 365-381.

500. "Not Quite Fun for Everyone at the Carnival."
      Economist 264 (3 September 1977): 15-16.

501. Nugent, Neill. "The Anti-Immigrant Groups." New
      Community 5 (Autumn 1976): 302-310.

502. "Paki Bashing." Campaign to Repeal the Immigration
      Act Bulletin No. 2 (1976): 17.

503. Palmer, Godfrey. "No Kill Nobody but a Policeman."
      Times Educational Supplement No. 2891 (16 October
      1970): 18, 63.

504. Patel, Praful R. C. "British Asians: Why They are
      Impatient?" Race Today 2: 7 (July 1970): 216-220.

505. Phillips, Mike and Lindsay MacKie. "Black Stardust:
      The Inside Outsiders." New Statesman (7 October
      1977): 469.

506. Preston, Maurice. "Wrong End of Racist Joke." Times
      Educational Supplement No. 3188 (9 July 1976): 4.

507. "Race Against Time." New Statesman (12 September
      1975): 293.

508. Race Today Collective. "Assaults on Asians." Race
      Today 8: 6 (June 1976): 123-128.

509. Race Today Collective. "Black Parents and Students
      on the Move." Race Today 8:10 (October 1976):
      195-198, 200-208.

510. Race Today Collective. "Linking the Struggle." Race
      Today 8: 5 (May 1976): 100-101.

511. Race Today Collective. "Southall: New Passions and
      New Forces." Race Today 8: 6 (June 1976):
      131-132.

512. Race Today Collective. "The Unemployed Youth and
      Students are the Target: Time to Organise." Race
      Today 8: 7/8 (July/August 1976): 149-150, 153.

513. Reynolds, Paul, et al. "The Morning After." Listener
      96 (9 September 1976): 293.

514.   Richardson, Ken and Vic Houghton. "Race and IQ: A
       Reply." New Humanist 89 (September 1973):
       159-160.

515.   Rose, John. "The Southall Youth Movement." Inter-
       national Socialism No. 91 (September 1976): 5-6.

516.   Rose, Steven. "Time to Bury This Dead Theory."
       Times Educational Supplement No. 3096. (27 Sept-
       ember 1974): 14.

517.   Rossiter, Ann. "Racism: What About Asian Women?"
       Spare Rib 49 (August 1976): 17-18.

518.   Schaefer, Richard T. "Regional Differences in Pre-
       judice." Regional Studies 9 (March 1975): 1-14.

519.   Scobie, Edward. "Britain's Blacks: Integrationists
       and Militants Struggle Against Racism of Whites."
       Ebony 28: 1 (November 1972): 109-120.

520.   Silk, Andrew. "Black Britons: The Permanent Immi-
       grants." Nation 223: 22 (25 December 1976):
       684-687.

521.   Silver, Robert. "No Backs to the Front." New
       Statesman (14 January 1977): 51.

522.   Sivanandan, Ambalavaner. "The Institute Story: The
       Unacceptable Face." Race Today 6: 3 (March
       1974): 73-75.

523.   Sivanandan, Ambalavaner. "Race, Class and Power:
       An Outline for Study." Race and Class 14: 4
       (April 1973): 383-391.

524.   Sivanandan, Ambalavaner. "Race, Class and the State:
       The Black Experience in Britain." Race and Class
       17: 4 (Spring 1976): 347-368.

525.   Sparks, Colin. "Fascism in Britain." International
       Socialism No. 71 (September 1974): 13-29.

526.   Sparks, Colin. "Fighting the Beast-Fascism: The
       Lessons of Cable Street." International
       Socialism No. 94 (January 1977): 11-14.

527.   Spittles, Brian. "Black is English." New Society
       (10 October 1974): 93.

528.   Taylor, Laurie. "The Perfect Victims." New Society
       (24 June 1976): 697-698.

529.   Taylor, Laurie. "Vigilantes - Why Not!" New Society
       (4 November 1976): 259-260.

530. "Time to Attack the Racists." New Stateman
      (11 June 1976): 759.

531. Tizard, Barbara. "In Defence of Nurture." New
      Society (10 January 1974): 73.

532. Tunteng, P-Kiven. "Ideology, Racism, and Black
      Political Culture." British Journal of Sociology
      27 (June 1976): 237-250.

533. Vestey, Michael. "The New Fires of Smithfield."
      New Statesman (1 September 1972): 276.

534. Walker, Peter. "Race and the Inner City: An Open
      Letter to the Prime Minister." New Statesman
      (18 June 1976): 804-805.

535. Watson, George. "Race and the Socialists: On the
      Progressive Principle of Revolutionary Extermina-
      tion." Encounter 47 (November 1976): 15-23.

536. Watson, Peter. "Check on Blacks' Moves." New Society
      (7 January 1971): 20.

537. Watson, Peter. "The New Outgroup: Ugandan Asians in
      Devon." New Society (23 November 1972): 444.

538. Waugh, Auberon. "Bathroom Whispers." Spectator
      (29 October 1977): 6.

539. "Why the National Front Went Marching." Economist 264
      (20 August 1977): 17-18.

540. Wicker, B. "Racial Talk-in." Commonweal 102 (18 July
      1975): 262-263.

541. Winter, J. M. "The Webbs and the Non-White World: A
      Case of Socialist Racialism." Journal of Contempo-
      rary History 9 (January 1974): 181-192.

542. Wright, Derek. "The Changed Morality of Race Dis-
      crimination." New Society (27 May 1971):
      905-906.

V.

LAW AND LEGISLATION

A. BOOKS

543. Akram, Mohammed. Where Do You Keep Your String Beds? A Study of the Entry Clearance Procedures in Pakistan. With a Commentary by Sarah Leigh. London: Runnymede Trust, 1974. 35 leaves.

544. Bindman, Geoffrey and Roger Warren Evans. The Immigration Bill, 1971. London: Runnymede Trust, 1971. 16 p.

545. Bindman, Geoffrey. A Summary of Immigration Act. London: Runnymede Trust, 1972. 5 p.

546. Burney, Elizabeth. After Four Years: A Practical Guide to the Race Relations Act After Four Years - What It Says and What It Means. London: Runnymede Trust, 1972. 11 p.

547. Claiborne, Louis. Race and Law in Britain and the United States. London: Minority Rights Group, 1974. 22 p.

548. Commonwealth Immigrants Acts 1962 and 1968: Instructions to Immigration Officers. London: H.M.S.O., 1970. 13 p.

549. Digest of Views on Review of Race Relations Legislation. London: Community Relations Commission, 1975. 25 p.

550. Dummett, Ann. Citizenship and Nationality. With a Foreword by J. E. S. Fawcett. London: Runnymede Trust, 1976. 88 p.

551. Evans, Jane Marix. Immigration Law. London: Sweet
     and Maxwell, 1976. 152 p.

552. Great Britain. Community Relations Commission. Race
     Relations Law, Legislation Against Discrimination:
     A Paper for Discussion: Review of Race Relations
     Act (1968) and the White Paper on Equality for
     Women. London: The Commission, 1975. 10 p.

553. Great Britain. Community Relations Commission. Review
     of the Race Relations Act. London: C.R.C., 1975.
     9 p.

554. Great Britain. Community Relations Commission. Supple-
     ment on the Immigration Bill 1971: Statement by
     Mark Bonham-Carter -- 24 February 1971. London:
     The Commission, 1971. Unpaged.

555. Great Britain. Home Office. Aliens: Control After
     Entry: Immigration Rules. London: H.M.S.O., 1970.
     9 p.

556. Great Britain. Home Office. Aliens: Instructions to
     Immigration Officers. London: H.M.S.O., 1970.
     18 p.

557. Great Britain. Home Office. British Nationality Law:
     Discussion of Possible Changes. London: H.M.S.O.,
     1977. 26 p.

558. Great Britain. Home Office. Commonwealth Citizens:
     Control After Entry. Immigration Rules, etc.
     London: H.M.S.O., 1970. 10 p.

559. Great Britain. Home Office. Commonwealth Immigrants
     Acts 1962 and 1968, Control of Immigration Sta-
     tistics. London: H.M.S.O., 1970. 14 p.

560. Great Britain. Home Office. Commonwealth Immigrants
     Acts 1962 and 1968, Control of Immigration Sta-
     tistics. London: H.M.S.O., 1973. 17 p.

561. Great Britain. Home Office. Commonwealth Immigrants
     Acts 1962 and 1968: Instructions to Immigration
     Officers. London: H.M.S.O., 1970. 13 p.

562. Great Britain. Home Office. Immigration Bill: Draft
     Immigration Rules: Control After Entry. London:
     H.M.S.O., 1970. 14 p.

563. Great Britain. Home Office. Immigration Bill: Draft
     Immigration Rules: Control on Entry, etc. London:
     H.M.S.O., 1971. 19 p.

564. Great Britain. Home Office. Immigration Bill: Revised
      Draft Immigration Rules: Control After Entry.
      London: H.M.S.O., 1971. 8 p.

565. Great Britain. Home Office. Racial Discrimination: A
      Guide to the Race Relations Act 1976. Prepared
      by the Home Office and the Central Office of
      Information. London: Home Office, 1977. 53 p.

566. Great Britain. Home Office. Statement of Change in
      Immigration Rules for Control After Entry. London:
      H.M.S.O., 1974. 2 p.

567. Great Britain. Home Office. Statement of Change in
      Immigration Rules for Control on Entry. London:
      H.M.S.O., 1974. 2 p.

568. Great Britain. Home Office. Statement of Changes in
      Immigration Rules for Control After Entry. London:
      H.M.S.O., 1977. 3 p.

569. Great Britain. Home Office. Statement of Changes in
      Immigration Rules for Control on Entry. London:
      H.M.S.O., 1977. 2 p.

570. Great Britain. Home Office. Statement of Immigration
      Rules for Control After Entry. London: H.M.S.O.,
      1973. 17 p.

571. Great Britain. Home Office. Statement of Immigration
      Rules for Control on Entry. London: H.M.S.O.,
      1972. 20 p.

572. Great Britain. Home Office. Statement of Immigration
      Rules for Control on Entry. London: H.M.S.O.,
      1973. 20 p.

573. Great Britain. Laws, Statutes, etc. Immigration Act
      1971: Elizabeth II, 1971. London: H.M.S.O., 1971.
      65 p.

574. Great Britain. Laws, Statutes, etc. Pakistan Act
      1974: Elizabeth II, 1974. Chapter 34. London:
      H.M.S.O., 1974. 2 p.

575. Great Britain. Laws, Statutes, etc. Race Relations
      Act 1976. Elizabeth II, 1976. Chapter 74. London:
      H.M.S.O., 1976. 67 p.

576. Great Britain. Parliament. House of Commons. Select
      Committee on Race Relations and Immigration.
      Control of Commonwealth Immigration: Appendices
      to the Minutes of Evidence. London: H.M.S.O.,
      1971. 85 p.

577. Great Britain. Parliament. House of Commons. Select
      Committee on Race Relations and Immigration.
      Control of Commonwealth Immigration: Evidence and
      Appendices. London: H.M.S.O., 1970. 2 vols.

578. Great Britain. Parliament. House of Commons. Select
      Committee on Race Relations and Immigration.
      Control of Commonwealth Immigration: Minutes of
      Evidence. London: H.M.S.O., 1971. 2 vols.

579. Great Britain. Parliament. House of Commons. Select
      Committee on the Anti-Discrimination (No. 2) Bill.
      Special Report: Session 1972-3. London: H.M.S.O.,
      1973. 17 p.

580. Great Britain. Parliament. House of Commons. Standing
      Committee B on Immigration Bill. Immigration Bill
      1971. London: H.M.S.O., 1971. Unpaged.

581. Great Britain. Parliament. House of Lords. Immigra-
      tion Bill. London: H.M.S.O., 1971. 70 p.

582. Great Britain. Parliament. House of Lords. Immigra-
      tion Bill (As Amended in Committee). London:
      H.M.S.O., 1971. 64 p.

583. Hartley, Tim. Under One Law: A Criticism of the Immi-
      gration Bill. London: Bow Group, 1971. 23 p.

584. Humphry, Derek and Michael Ward. Passports and Poli-
      tics. Harmondsworth: Penguin, 1974. 187 p.

585. Illegal Immigration and the Law: A Runnymede Trust
      Briefing Paper. London: Runnymede Trust, 1973.
      5 p.

586. Lester, Anthony and Geoffrey Bindman. Race and Law.
      Harlow: Longman, 1972. 491 p.

          Review by James Comyn. New Community 1 (Summer
          1972): 236-237.

587. Lester, Anthony and Geoffrey Bindman. Race and Law in
      Great Britain. Cambridge: Harvard University
      Press, 1972. 491 p.

588. MacDonald, Ian Alexander. The New Immigration Law.
      London: Butterworth, 1972. 285 p.

          Contains the text of the Immigration Act 1971.

589. MacDonald, Ian Alexander. Race Relations: The New Law.
      London: Butterworth, 1977. 246 p.

          Contains the text of the Race Relations Act
          1976.

590. National Council for Civil Liberties, London. Racial
          Discrimination: NCCL's Comments on the White Paper.
          Written by Nic Madge. London: N.C.C.L., 1975.
          17 p.

591. Plender, Richard Owen. Race Relations and the Law in
          Britain. J.S.D. dissertation, University of Illi-
          nois, 1972. 328 p.

592. Runnymede Trust. Questions and Answers on Race Rela-
          tions and Immigration. London: Runnymede Trust,
          1973. 26 p.

593. Runnymede Trust. Racial Discrimination: A Guide to the
          Government's White Paper. London: The Trust, 1975.
          32 p.

594. Sherman, Barrie. The Immigration Bill and the Indus-
          trial Relations Bill - A Combined Threat to Trade
          Unions: A Discussion Paper. London: National
          Council for Civil Liberties, 1971. 9 leaves.

595. Walker, Douglas James and Michael J. Redman. Racial
          Discrimination: A Simple Guide to the Provisions
          of the Race Relations Act 1976. London: Shaw,
          1977. 251 p.

          Includes Text of the Act.

B. PERIODICAL ARTICLES

596. Adam, Corinna. "Game of Human Shuttlecock." New
          Statesman (27 February 1970): 280-281.

597. Adam, Corinna. "Peter Main v. the Law." New Statesman
          (11 August 1972): 179-180.

598. Adeney, Martin. "Progress Report on the Immigration
          Bill 1971." New Community 1 (October 1971):
          77-79.

599. "Anti-Discrimination Law Now in Force." Ulster Commen-
          tary No. 327 (October 1973): 16.

600. "Asking for Guidance." Economist 250 (16 March 1974):
          59.

601. Bindman, Geoffrey. "Law and Racial Discrimination:
          The New Procedures." New Community 4 (Autumn
          1975): 284-290.

602. Bindman, Geoffrey. "Race Relations: How to Use the New
          Act - 1." LAG Bulletin (September 1977): 213-215.

603. Bonham-Carter, Mark. "Race, Sex and the Law." New
          Community 4 (Winter/Spring 1974/1975): 1-4.

604. Bonham-Carter, Mark. "The White Paper on Racial Dis-
          crimination." New Community 4 (Autumn 1975):
          281-283.

605. "Civis Britannicus Non/Sum: New Immigration Bill."
          Time 97 (8 March 1971): 28-29.

606. Claiborne, Louis F. "Law and Race in Britain." Annals
          of American Academy of Political and Social Sci-
          ence 407 (May 1973): 167-168.

607. Claiborne, Louis F. "Putting Teeth into Our Race Laws."
          Observer (20 July 1975): 9.

608. Claiborne, Louis F. "Race Relations and the Role of
          Law." Spectator (13 November 1971): 685-686.

609. "Closing the Door." Time 101 (26 February 1973): 27-28.

610. "Coggan's Conscience." Economist 260 (17 July 1976):
          21.

611. "Compassion But No Concession." Economist 247 (30 Janu-
          ary 1973): 24-26.

612. Constable, John. "Illegal Immigration Policy and Law."
          Race 15: 3 (January 1974): 361-369.

613. Constable, John. "Immigration Appeals." New Society
          (18 April 1974): 135-136.

614. Dickey, Anthony. "The House of Lords and the Race Re-
          lations Acts." New Community 2 (Autumn 1973):
          400-403.

615. Dickey, Anthony. "The Offence of Incitement to Ha-
          tred." Patterns of Prejudice 4: 1 (1970): 10-14.

616. Dickey, Anthony. "The Race Formula of the Race Rela-
          tions Acts." Juridical Review 19 (December 1974):
          282-297.

617. Evans, Jane Marix. "Immigration Act 1971." Modern Law
          Review 35 (September 1972): 508-524.

618. Garner, J. F. "Racial Restrictive Covenants in England
          and the United States." Modern Law Review 35
          (September 1972): 478-488.

619. "Good, But Not Quite Nice." Economist 239 (29 May 1971):
          28.

620. Grant, L. and G. Peirce. "Immigration: The Screw
         Tightens." Race Today 5: 3 (March 1973): 93-95.

621. Griffith, John. "Judges, Race and the Law." New States-
         man (22 November 1974): 734-735.

622. Griffith, John. "Whose Bill of Rights?" New Statesman
         (14 November 1975): 607.

623. "Half a Policy." Economist 258 (14 February 1976): 18.

624. Harrington, I. "Justice for Immigrants." New States-
         man (28 August 1970): 230.

625. Higgins, Rosalyn. "The Right in International Law of
         an Individual to Enter, Stay in and Leave a Coun-
         try." International Affairs 49: 3 (1973): 341-357.

626. Hogg, Quintin. "Race Relations and Parliament." Race
         12: 1 (July 1970): 1-13.

627. "The Immigration Act 1971." New Community 1 (January
         1972): 149-151.

628. "The Immigration Bill." Labour Research 60 (April
         1971): 60-62.

629. "Immigration Policy: Keeping Dependents Out." Race
         Today 7: 9 (September 1975): 202-207.

630. "It is Bad Enough to be Black, But Who'd be a Non-
         Patrial?" Economist 238 (27 February 1971): 25.

631. Jones, Mervyn. "Labour and the Minorities." New
         Statesman (6 August 1971): 169-170, 172.

632. "Just One Word." Economist 247 (16 June 1973): 27.

633. Kirby, Alexander. "Stop-Watch Deportation." New
         Statesman (1 February 1973): 144.

634. Kohler, David Frank. "A Ballot on Race Laws." New
         Society (19 December 1974): 762-763.

635. Kohler, David Frank. "Migrants, Work and the Law: A
         Ballot on Race Laws." New Community 4 (Winter/
         Spring 1974/1975): 62-64.

636. "Legal Status of Pakistani Immigrants in Britain."
         New Community 1 (Spring 1972): 216.

637. Legum, Colin. "What Carr Should Do?" Observer (1 July
         1973): 8.

638. Lester, Anthony. "Citizenship and the Immigrants."
         Observer (3 June 1973): 12.

639. Lester, Anthony. "Why the Next Labour Government Must
      Reform Our Immigration Laws? Wanted a Non-Racial
      Immigration Control System for Britain." Third
      World 3 (November 1973): 10-11.

640. Liu, W. H. "The Evolution of Commonwealth Citizenship
      and U.K. Statutory Control Over Commonwealth Immi-
      grants." New Community 5 (Spring/Summer 1977):
      426-447.

641. Lyttle, John. "Anti-Discrimination Law in New Zealand
      and Britain." New Community 1 (Autumn 1972):
      451-452.

642. "Mr. Maudling's Chance." Economist 236 (22 August
      1970): 19-20.

643. Munro, Colin. "The Law and Race Relations." New So-
      ciety (19 September 1974): 737-738.

644. Nandy, Dipak. "The Kith and Kin Bill." New Statesman
      (5 March 1971): 293-294.

645. "A New Law to Deal With Incitement to Hatred." Patterns
      of Prejudice 9: 5 (1975): 19-21.

646. "New Race Relations: You Can Wear Your Turbans, But
      Obey the Law." Campaign To Repeal the Immigration
      Act Bulletin 2 (1976): 13.

647. Norton, Philip. "Intra-Party Dissent in the House of
      Commons: A Case Study - The Immigration Rules,
      1972." Parliamentary Affairs 29 (Autumn 1976):
      404-420.

648. Omar, Barbara. "Towards a Repatriation Bill?" Race
      Today 4: 3 (March 1972): 93-94.

649. "On the Back of Sex." Economist 256 (13 September 1975):
      32-34.

650. "One up for Enoch." Economist 239 (10 April 1971): 26.

651. "Open and Shut." Economist 241 (25 December 1971): 20.

652. "Outlook: Stormy" Economist 238 (30 January 1971): 23.

653. "Parliamentary Gary Gilmore: Brynmor John on Powell."
      CRC Journal 5: 2 (February 1977): 16.

654. "Patrials, Progress." Economist 239 (19 June 1971): 30.

655. Pearl, David. "Dependency in Immigration Law." New
      Community 3 (Autumn 1974): 359-370.

656. Pearl, David. "Foreign Marriages and Divorces: Recent
       English Legislation" New Community 4 (Winter/
       Spring 1974/1975): 119-121.

657. Pearl, David. "Immigrant Marriages: Some Legal Prob-
       lems." New Community 2 (Winter 1972/1973): 67-
       73.

658. Pearl, David. "Legal Decisions Affecting Immigrants
       (No. 1)." New Community 4 (Summer 1975): 250-253.

659. Pearl, David. "Legal Decisions Affecting Immigrants
       (No. 2)." New Community 4 (Autumn 1975): 384-387.

660. Pearl, David. "Legal Decisions Affecting Immigrants
       (No. 3)." New Community 4 (Winter/Spring 1975/
       1976): 445-451.

661. Pearl, David. "Legal Decisions Affecting Immigrants
       and Discrimination." New Community 6 (Winter
       1977/1978): 143-149.

662. Pearl, David. "Legal Decisions Affecting Immigrants
       and Sex Discrimination - No. 5." New Community
       5 (Autumn 1976): 259-264.

663. Pearl, David. "Legal Decisions Affecting Immigrants
       and Sex Discrimination - No. 6." New Community
       5 (Spring/Summer 1977): 452-457.

664. Pearl, David. "Legal Decisions Affecting Immigrants
       and Sex Equality - No. 4." New Community 5
       (Summer 1976): 142-146.

665. Pearl, David. "Muslim Marriages in English Law."
       Cambridge Law Journal 30 (April 1972): 120-143.

666. Pearn, M. A. "Race Relations Legislation and the Role
       of Occupational Psychologist." British Psychologi-
       cal Society Bulletin (29 September 1976): 300-302.

667. Plender, Richard. "Fostering and the Race Relations
       Acts." New Community 3 (Autumn 1974): 371-378.

668. Plender, Richard. "The New Immigration Rules." New
       Community 2 (Spring 1973): 168-176.

669. Plender, Richard. "Relatives' Rights and Absolute Dis-
       cretions." New Community 2 (Spring 1973): 177-184.

670. Pritt, D. N. "Immigration Act 1971." Contemporary Re-
       view 220 (April 1972): 179-183.

671. "Race Relations Act, 1976." Department of Employment
       Gazette. 85: 5 (May 1977): 455-456.

672. "Race Relations Act, 1976." Justice of the Peace 141:26 (25 June 1977): 376.

673. "Race Relations Act, 1976." Race and Class 18: 4 (Spring 1977): 405-410.

674. "Race Relations Bill 1976: Summary of Bill." Education and Community Relations (July/August 1976): 1-4.

675. "Race Relations Board." New Community 1 (Spring 1972): 219-220.

676. "Race Relations: The Legal Measures." Labour Research 65 (July 1976): 154-156.

677. Rose, Hannan. "Does Britain Have an Immigration Problem?" New Community 2 (Winter 1972/1973): 53-61.

678. Rose, Hannan. "The Immigration Act 1971: A Case Study in the Work of Parliament." Parliamentary Affairs 26 (Winter 1972/1973): 69-91.

679. Rose, Hannan. "The New Race Relations Proposals: A Real Step Forward." New Community 4 (Winter/Spring 1975/1976): 429-433.

680. Rose, Hannan. "The Politics of Immigration After the 1971 Act." Political Quarterly 44: 2 (April-June 1973): 183-196.

681. Rose, Hannan. "Towards a Rational Immigration Policy." New Community 2 (Spring 1973): 159-167.

682. Rose, Paul. "Patrials Only." Contemporary Review 218 (May 1971): 225-229.

683. Samuels, Alec. "The United Kingdom Immigration Act, 1971." University of Western Australia Law Review 11 (June 1973): 54-67.

684. Sanders, Peter. "The Race Relations Act 1968: Two Investigations." New Community 5 (Spring/Summer 1977): 448-451.

685. Schofield, D. and Omkar Nath Channan. "Oaths of Hindu, Sikh and Muslim Witnesses." New Community 3 (Autumn 1974): 409-411.

686. Shyllon, Folarin Olawale. "Immigration and the Criminal Courts." Modern Law Review 34 (March 1971): 135-148.

687. "Society at Work: A Guide to the Race Act." New Society (3 February 1977): 230-232.

688. "Sorry Defence." Economist 238 (13 March 1971): 22.

689. Stephen, David. "Immigration Policy: A Social Policy."
      New Community 4 (Summer 1975): 188-190.

690. "The Tory Immigration Act." Labour Research 62 (October
      1973): 214-215.

691. Tucker, Peter. "Towards a New Citizenship Law." New
      Community 4 (Winter/Spring 1975/1976): 443-444.

692. "Two-Tone Citizenship." Economist 263 (30 April 1977):
      20.

693. "Watching for the Small Print." Economist 236 (11 July
      1970): 18.

694. Watkins, Alan. "Lessons of the Defeat: Immigration
      Bill." New Statesman (1 December 1972): 798.

695. Watkins, Alan. "Mr. Maudling's Missed Chance." New
      Statesman (19 February 1971): 227.

696. "What is the Immigration Act?" Campaign to Repeal the
      Immigration Act, Bulletin 2 (1976): 1, 5, 8, 10,
      12.

697. Whitfield, Sylvia. "Pakistanis or Citizens." New
      Society (3 July 1975): 17-18.

698. Zellick, Graham. "The Power of the Courts to Recommend
      Deportation." Criminal Law Review (October 1973):
      612-620.

VI.

INTER-ETHNIC RELATIONS

A. BOOKS

699. Allen, Sheila. New Minorities, Old Conflicts: Asian and West Indian Migrants in Britain. New York: Random House, 1971. 223 p.

Review by Michael J. Hill. Race 14: 1 (July 1972): 90-92.

700. Baker, Peter. Attitudes to the Coloured People in Glasgow. Glasgow: University of Strathclyde, 1970. 19 p.

701. Banner, Stephen, et al. How Black? Nine Winning Essays From the Entries for a Competition Held Annually and Open to Children in Secondary Schools -- in 1969, 1970, and 1971. Illustrations by Richard Rees. Wolverhampton: Wolverhampton Council for Community Relations, 1972. 36 p.

702. Baxter, Paul Trevor William and Basil Sansom, eds. Race and Social Difference: Selected Readings. Harmondsworth: Penguin, 1972. 495 p.

703. Great Britain. Community Relations Commission. Racial Equality: You Believe in it, Support it. London: The Commission, 1976. 4 p.

704. Great Britain. Community Relations Commission. Reference Division. Some of My Best Friends: A Report on Race Relations Attitudes. London: C.R.C., 1976. 45 p.

705.   Institute of Practitioners in Advertising. Promotion
       of Racial Harmony Planning Demonstration Held on
       11th December, 1969 at the New Theatre. London:
       The Institute, 1970. 45 p.

706.   Jackson, Barbara. Family Experiences of Inter-Racial
       Adoption. London: Association of British Adop-
       tion and Fostering Agencies, 1976. 32 p.

707.   Jenkins, Simon. Here to Live - A Study of Race Rela-
       tions in an English Town. London: Runnymede
       Trust, 1971. 44 p.

708.   Kareh, Diana. Adoption and the Coloured Child. Lon-
       don: Epworth Press, 1970. 130 p.

709.   Kentish, Barbara. Chaos or Community. London:
       Catholic Truth Society, 1977. 13 p.

710.   Kuper, Leo. The Pity of it All: Polarisation of Racial
       and Ethnic Relations. London: Duckworth, 1977.
       302 p.

711.   Lawrence, Daniel. Black Migrants, White Natives: A
       Study of Race Relations in Nottingham. Cambridge,
       England: University Press, 1974. 251 p.

           Review by Robin Ward. New Community 3 (Autumn
           1974): 442-443.

           Review by Jenny Bourne. Race and Class 16: 3
           (January 1975): 332-333.

712.   Morrison, Lionel. As They See It: A Race Relations
       Study of Three Areas from a Black Viewpoint.
       London: Community Relations Commission, 1976.
       127 p.

713.   Raynor, Lois. Adoption of Non-White Children: The
       Experience of a British Adoption Project. London:
       Allen and Unwin, 1970. 210 p.

           Review by J. Triseliotis. Race 13: 2 (October
           1971): 263.

714.   Roswith, Gerloff, et al. Partnership in Black and
       White. Westminster: Methodist Home Mission, 1977.
       37 p.

715.   Taylor, J. H. "The Education, Employment and Integra-
       tion of Indian and Pakistani Youth in New Castle
       Upon Tyne: An Empirical Study." Doctoral disser-
       tation, University of New Castle Upon Tyne, 1972.

716.   Thomas, Roger Edmund. "The Assimilation of Jamaican
       Transport Workers in England." Doctoral disser-
       tation, Yale University, 1973. 652 p.

717.   Wade, Donald William. Yorkshire Survey: A Report on
       Community Relations in Yorkshire. Leeds: York-
       shire Committee for Community Relations, 1971.
       92 p.

B. PERIODICAL ARTICLES

718.   "Action Wanted." Economist 240 (10 July 1971): 26.

719.   Adam, Corinna. "Mayhew's London Survives." New
       Statesman (17 October 1975): 464.

720.   Adam, Corinna. "Victory for Hain." New Statesman
       (25 August 1972): 245-246.

721.   Athisayam, Gillian. "Brown is to be Lived With: The
       Lessons Two Children Learned." Observer (1 Octo-
       ber 1972): 31.

722.   Bagley, Christopher. "Immigrant Minorities: Integra-
       tion and Assimilation." International Migration
       Review 5 (1971): 18-35.

723.   Bagley, Christopher. "Inter-Racial Marriages in Bri-
       tain - Some Statistics." New Community 1 (Summer
       1972): 318-326.

724.   Bennion, Francis. "Laugh at Thy Neighbour: Love Thy
       Neighbour." New Society (31 July 1975): 256-257.

725.   "Bennion 1, Hain 3." Economist 244 (26 August 1972):
       21-22.

726.   Bentley, Stuart. "Identity and Community Cooperation:
       A Note on Terminology." Race 14: 1 (July 1972):
       69-76.

727.   Beswick, W. A. "The Relationship of the Ethnic Back-
       ground of Secondary Schoolboys to Their Partici-
       pation in and Attitudes Towards Physical Activity."
       Research Papers in Physical Education 3: 2 (De-
       cember 1976): 19-21.

728.   Bingham, Stella. "Give Us a Child That Nobody Wants."
       Nova (May 1971): 62-65.

729.   "Black and White Don't Like Grey." Economist 261
       (23 October 1976): 63.

730. Bonham-Carter, Mark. "Race and Romance." New Society
      (18 November 1971): 995-996.

731. Brittan, Elaine Mary. "All Friends Together." Times
      Educational Supplement No. 3189 (16 July 1977):
      16.

732. Brooks, Dennis. "Black and White on the Buses." New
      Society (20 February 1975): 455-457.

733. Brough, D. I. "Prejudice Affecting Relationships Be-
      tween Ethnic Groups in the United Kingdom."
      Royal Society of Arts Journal 119 (May 1971):
      394-404.

734. Brown, G. A. "An Exploratory Study of Interaction
      Amongst British and Immigrant Children." The
      British Journal of Social and Clinical Psychology
      12 (June 1973): 159-162.

735. Butterworth, Eric. "Dilemmas of Community Relations -
      1." New Community 1 (Spring 1972): 205-208.

736. Cohen, Elizabeth G. "Interracial Interaction Dis-
      ability." Human Relations 25 (February 1972):
      9-24.

737. "Cricket: Black Lords." Economist 248 (1 September
      1973): 24.

738. "Cricket: I'm All White, Jack." Economist 234 (21 Feb-
      ruary 1970): 25.

739. Curtis, Sarah. "When Black is White." New Society
      (18 December 1975): 647-648.

740. Dimbleby, Jonathan. "Black and White in Liverpool,
      8." New Statesman (25 August 1972): 250-252.

741. Dove, Linda. "Racial Awareness Among Adolescents in
      London Comprehensive Schools." New Community 3
      (Summer 1974): 255-261.

742. Durojaiye, M. O. A. "Patterns of Friendship Choices
      in an Ethnically Mixed Junior School." Race 12: 2
      (October 1970): 189-200.

743. "First Impressions, Lasting Impressions: The Immigrant
      View." Listener 95 (11 March 1976): 300-301.

744. Harland, Peter. "Lions at Play." New Community 4
      (Summer 1975): 246-249.

745. Harrison, Paul. "Black and White." New Society
      (21 June 1973): 672-673.

746. Hartmann, Paul and Charles Husband. "A British Scale
     for Measuring White Attitudes to Coloured People."
     Race 14: 2 (October 1972): 195-204.

747. Headley, Jane. "Five Year Old - and Racially Preju-
     diced." Times Educational Supplement No. 3174
     (2 April 1976): 14.

748. Hill, David. "Attitudes of West Indian and English
     Adolescents in Britain." Race 11: 3 (January
     1970): 312-321.

749. Hollings, Michael. "Thoughts from Southall: A Pastoral
     Approach to Race Relations." Month 9 (September
     1976): 308-312.

750. Hope, Francis. "Uses of Diversity." New Statesman
     (5 October 1973): 473.

751. "How to Win Without Really Trying." Economist 261
     (4 December 1976): 74.

752. Hubbard, Alan. "At Stake: A Black Man's Title and a
     White Policy." Observer (25 November 1973): 27.

753. "Inter-Racial Adoption: One Family's Experience."
     Adoption and Fostering 85: 3 (1976): 55-62.

754. Jeffcoate, Robert. "Children's Racial Ideas and
     Feelings." English in Education 11: 1 (Spring
     1977): 32-46.

755. Jeffcoate, Robert. "Curing a Social Disease." Times
     Educational Supplement No. 3157 (5 December 1975):
     23.

756. Jelinek, Milena M. and Elaine M. Brittan. "Multiracial
     Education - 1: Inter-Ethnic Friendship Patterns."
     Educational Research 18 (November 1975): 44-53.

757. Krausz, Ernest. "Acculturation and Pluralism: A Clari-
     fication of Concepts." New Community 1 (Summer
     1972): 250-255.

758. Laishley, Jennie. "Can Comics Join the Multi-Racial
     Society?" Times Educational Supplement No. 3000
     (24 November 1972): 4.

759. Laishley, Jenny. "Skin Colour Awareness and Preference
     in London Nursery School Children." Race 13: 1
     (July 1971): 47-64.

760. Lawrence, Susanne. "Working Towards Racial Integra-
     tion." Personnel Management 4 (July 1972): 21-24.

761. Levine, Ned and Tripta Nayar. "Modes of Adaptation by
     Asian Immigrants in Slough." New Community 4
     (Autumn 1975): 356-365.

762. Little, Alan and Josephine Toynbee. "The Asians: A
     Threat or an Asset?" New Society (26 October
     1972): 205-207.

763. Lyon, Michael. "Race and Ethnicity in Pluralistic
     Societies: A Comparison of Minorities in the U.K.
     and U.S.A." New Community 1 (Summer 1972): 256-
     262.

764. Marsh, Alan. "Tolerance and Pluralism in Britain:
     Perspectives in Social Psychology." New Community
     1 (Summer 1972): 282-289.

765. Martin-Jenkins, Christopher. "Colourful Cricket."
     Listener 96 (2 September 1976): 268.

766. Marvell, J. "Moral Socialisation in a Multi-Racial
     Community." Journal of Moral Education 3 (June
     1974): 249-257.

767. Morrison, Lionel. "Cooling the Scene." New Society
     (5 September 1974): 615.

768. Nagenda, John. "Adoption Against the Odds." Observer
     (13 February 1972): 17.

769. "One-Love." Economist 261 (2 October 1976): 52.

770. Patterson, Sheila. "Cricket and Other Codes: Or a
     Tribute to C.L.R. James." New Community 2
     (Autumn 1973): 389-391.

771. Pryce, Kenneth. "Problems in Minority Fostering."
     New Community 3 (Autumn 1974): 379-385.

772. Reid, Vince. "Thoughts on England v. the West Indies,
     Edgbaston, 1973." New Community 2 (Autumn 1973):
     395-396.

773. Richardson, Stephen A. and Patricia Emerson. "Race
     and Physical Handicap in Children's Preference for
     Other Children." Human Relations 23 (February
     1970): 31-36.

774. Robertson, T. S. and T. Kawwa. "Ethnic Relations in a
     Girls' Comprehensive School." Educational Re-
     search 13 (July 1971): 214-217.

775. "Rugger, Mugger." Economist 247 (14 April 1973): 38.

776. Sargeant, A. J. "Participation of West Indian Boys in English Schools Sports Teams." Educational Research 14 (June 1972): 225-230.

777. Schaefer, Richard T. "Contacts Between Immigrants and Englishmen: Road to Tolerance or Intolerance." New Community 2 (Autumn 1973): 358-371.

778. Seabrook, Jeremy. "A Change of Atmosphere: Race in One-Town, Blackburn." New Society (2 September 1976): 486-491.

779. "Seen But Not Heard." Economist 257 (18 October 1975): 32-33.

780. Shiner, Roger A. "Individuals, Groups and Inverse Discrimination." Analysis 33 (June 1973): 185-187.

781. Smith, Peter B. and Michael J. Wilson. "The Use of Group Training Methods in Multi-Racial Settings." New Community 4 (Summer 1975): 218-231.

782. Stanton, Michael. "Pupil's Views of National Groups." Journal of Moral Education 1 (February 1972): 147-151.

783. Studler, Donley T. "Social Context and Attitudes Toward Coloured Immigrants." British Journal of Sociology 28 (June 1977): 168-184.

784. "Teaching Racial Tolerance." New Humanist 88 (September 1972): 208-209.

785. "A Thin White Line." Economist 261 (25 December 1976): 38-39.

786. Thomas, Clem and Geoffrey Nicholson. "The Lions Tour For and Against." Observer (5 May 1974): 26.

787. Thompson, John. "A Bradford Project in Community Involvement." Museums Journal 71 (March 1972): 161-163.

788. "The Torch That Flickered." Economist 244 (26 August 1972): 30-31.

789. Turner, Charles and Muzeyyen Sevinc. "Interaction Amongst British and Immigrant Children: A Methodological Note." British Journal of Social and Clinical Psychology 13 (June 1974): 215-217.

790. "Unruffled." Economist 260 (24 July 1976): 49.

791. Verma, Gajendra K. and Christopher Bagley. "Changing
        Racial Attitudes in Adolescents: An Experimental
        English Study." International Journal of Psy-
        chology 8 (1973): 55-58.

792. Verma, Gajendra K. "Some Effects of Teaching Race
        Relations on Friendship Patterns of Adolescents."
        New Era 56: 4 (May 1975): 95-98.

793. "Watch Out for Next Time." Economist 260 (7 August
        1976): 42-43.

794. Watson, Peter. "Colouring Children's Attitudes."
        New Society (12 August 1971): 290.

795. Wilson, Amrit. "It's Not Like Asian Ladies to Answer
        Back." Spare Rib 52 (November 1976): 10-13.

VII.

EMPLOYMENT

A. BOOKS

796. Allen, Sheila and Joanna Bornat. Unions and Immigrant Workers: How They See Each Other. Edited and summarized for Runnymede Industrial Unit by Robert Whymant. London: Runnymede Trust, 1970. 5 p.

797. Allen, Sheila, Stuart Bentley and Joanna Bornat. Work, Race and Immigration. Bradford: University of Bradford, 1977. 415 p.

798. Beetham, David. Transport and Turbans: A Comparative Study in Local Politics. London: Oxford University Press for the Institute of Race Relations, 1970. 86 p.

   Review by M. H. Lyon. Race 13: 1 (July 1971): 105-106.

799. Bell, Geoff, et al. The Battle of Grunwick: View from the Left. London: Socialist Challenge Pamphlet, 1977. 21 p.

800. Bosanquet, Nicholas. Race and Employment in Britain: A Report. London: Runnymede Trust, 1973. 16 p.

   Review in New Community 2 (Summer 1973): 317-318.

801. Brannen, P., ed. Entering the World of Work: Some Sociological Perspectives. London: H.M.S.O., 1975. 128 p.

802.   Brooks, Dennis. Race and Labour in London Transport.
        London: Oxford University Press for the Institute
        of Race Relations and the Acton Society Trust,
        1975. 389 p.

            Review by Harold Pollins. New Community 4
            (Summer 1975): 266-267.

            Review by Robin Jenkins. Race and Class 17: 2
            (Autumn 1975): 217-218.

803.   Brown, John. The Unmelting Pot: An English Town and
        its Immigrants. London: Macmillan, 1970. 240 p.

            Review by H. D. Rose. Race 14: 1 (July 1972):
            88-90.

804.   CIS (Counter Information Service). Inside Out.
        London: CIS in Cooperation with the Transnational
        Institute, 1974. 43 p.

            Review by Louis Kushnik. Race and Class 16: 3
            (January 1975): 334-335.

805.   Campbell-Platt, Kiran. Workers in Britain from
        Selected Foreign Countries. London: Runnymede
        Trust, 1975. 17 leaves.

806.   Carby, Keith and Manab Thakur. No Problems Here:
        Management and the Multi-Racial Work Force,
        Including a Guide to the Race Relations Act 1976.
        London: Institute of Personnel Management, 1977.
        156 p.

807.   Cole, Porter. Uganda Asian and Employment. London:
        Runnymede Trust, 1974. 34 p.

808.   Confederation of British Industry. Race Relations
        in Employment: Advice to Employers. London:
        C.B.I., 1970. 14 p.

809.   The Employment of Non-English Speaking Workers: What
        Industry Must Do. By Stuart Slatter in Collabo-
        ration with A. T. M. Wilson and the Reference
        Division of the Community Relations Commission.
        London: Community Relations Commission in
        Cooperation with the London Graduate School of
        Business, 1974. 32 p.

            Review by David Thomas. New Community 4
            (Summer 1975): 271-272.

810. Great Britain. Community Relations Commission.
      CRC Evidence to the Royal Commission on the
      Distribution of Income and Wealth. London:
      The Commission, 1976. 17 p.

811. Great Britain. Community Relations Commission.
      Reference Division. Unemployment and Homeless-
      ness: A Report by Reference Division, Community
      Relations Commission for the Home Office.
      London: H.M.S.O., 1974. 73 p.

812. Great Britain. Department of Employment. Take 7.
      The Report on a Survey Undertaken by the Depart-
      ment of Employment into Immigrant Labour Relations
      at Seven English Firms. London: The Department,
      1972. 118 p.

813. Great Britain. Office of Manpower Economics. Equal
      Pay: First Report by the Office of Manpower
      Economics. London: H.M.S.O., 1972. 106 p.

814. Great Britain. Office of Population Censuses and
      Surveys. Census 1971, Great Britain: Economic
      Activity. Issued by Office of Population Censuses
      and Surveys, London and General Register Office,
      Edinburgh. London: H M.S.O., 1975. 3 pts.

815. Great Britain. Parliament. House of Commons. Select
      Committee on Race Relations and Immigration.
      Employment: Report of the Select Committee on
      Race Relations and Immigration, Session 1974.
      London: H.M.S.O., 1974. 2 Vols.

          Vol. 1 Report. Vol. 2 Evidence and Appendices.

816. Grunwick. London: Socialist Worker Pamphlet, 1977.
      16 p.

817. Harrison, Robert M. Union Policy and Workplace
      Practice: A Black Worker Alleges Discrimination.
      A Case Study from a Midlands Building Site.
      London: Runnymede Trust, 1970. 8 p.

818. Hepple, Bob. Race, Jobs and the Law in Britain.
      2d ed. Harmondsworth: Penguin, 1970. 343 p.

819. Incomes Data Services. The New Race Law and Employ-
      ment. London: I.D.S., 1976. 93 p.

820. Janner, Greville Ewan. The Employer's Guide to the
      Law on Employment Protection and Sex and Race
      Discrimination. London: Business Books, 1976.
      756 p.

821.   Jones, Kathleen. Commonwealth Immigration: The
       Economic Effects. A Summary of K. Jones and
       A. D. Smith's 'The Economic Impact of Common-
       wealth Immigration'. Introduced by Nicholas
       Bosanquet. London: Runnymede Trust, 1970. 15 p.

822.   Jupp, Thomas Cyprian and Evelyn Davies. The Background
       and Employment of Asian Immigrants: A Manual for
       Preparing Short Courses, Talks and Discussion.
       London: Runnymede Trust, 1975. 177 p.

           Review by Jenny Bourne. Race and Class 17: 1
           (July 1975): 94-95.

823.   Kohler, David Frank. The Employment of Black People
       in a London Borough. London: Community Relations
       Commission, 1974. 18 p.

824.   Lee, G. L. and K. J. Wrench. Accidents Are Colour
       Blind: Industrial Accidents and the Immigrant
       Worker: A Pilot Study. London: Community Rela-
       tions Commission for the Birmingham Community
       Relations Council, 1977. 24 p.

825.   London Council of Social Services. The Inner City:
       A Preliminary Investigation of the Dynamics of
       Current Labour and Housing Markets with Special
       Reference to Minority Groups in Inner London,
       July 1974. Study Directed by Graham Lomas,
       Assisted by Lewis Donnelly: Research Officers
       Helene Middleweek and Sylvia Gilpin. London:
       Council of Social Services, 1975. 38 p.

826.   Meth, Monty. Brothers to All Men: A Report on Trade
       Union Actions and Attitudes on Race Relations.
       London: Runnymede Trust Industrial Unit, 1972.
       84 p.

827.   Monck, Elizabeth and Gillian Lomas. The Employment
       and Socio-Economic Conditions of the Coloured
       Population. London: Centre for Environmental
       Studies, 1975. 33 p.

828.   Mungham, Geoff and Geoff Pearson, eds. Working Class
       Youth Culture. London, Boston: Routledge and
       Kegan Paul, 1976. 167 p.

829.   Paterson, Peter and Michael Armstrong. An Employer's
       Guide to Equal Pay. London: Kogan Page, 1972.
       143 p.

830.   Pulle, Stanislaus. Employment Policies in the Hosiery
       Industry: With Particular Reference to the Posi-
       tion of Immigrant Workers. London: Runnymede
       Trust Industrial Unit, 1972. 30 p.

831.   Race and Jobs: 71 Questions Answered on Immigration,
       Race Relations and the Race Relations Act.
       London: Runnymede Trust Industrial Unit, 1971.
       24 p.

832.   Racialism and the Working Class: Articles from
       'Workers' Fight'. London: Workers' Fight,
       1975. 20 p.

833.   Rees, Tom. Policy or Drift? How Three London Firms
       Handle Racial Integration in the Workforce.
       London: Runnymede Trust Industrial Unit, 1971.
       10 p.

834.   Richmond, Anthony H. Colour Prejudice in Britain:
       A Study of West Indian Workers in Liverpool,
       1941-1951. Westport, Connecticut: Negro
       University Press, 1971. 184 p.

835.   Rimmer, Malcolm. Race and Industrial Conflict: A
       Study in a Group of Midlands Foundries. London:
       Heinemann Educational Books, 1972. 74 p.

       Review by Harold Pollins. New Community 1
       (Autumn 1972): 457.

836.   Rogaly, Joe. Grunwick. Harmondsworth: Penguin, 1977.
       199 p.

837.   Runnymede Trust Industrial Unit. A Race Relations
       Audit: An Independent Survey of Industrial Race
       Relations in a Major Company. London: The
       Trust, 1971. 44 p.

838.   Smith, David John. Racial Disadvantage in Employment.
       London: PEP, 1974. 109 p.

839.   Stephen, David, Elizabeth Scott and Dipak Nandy. Race
       and Jobs: 71 Questions Answered on Immigration,
       Race Relations and the Race Relations Act.
       2d ed. London: Runnymede Trust, 1971. 24 p.

840.   Stewart, Margaret. A Stitch in Time: An Employers'
       Guide to Equal Opportunity in a Multi-Racial
       Work Force. London: Runnymede Trust, 1973.
       27 p.

841.   Thakur, Manab. Industry As Seen by Immigrant Workers:
       A Summary of Research Findings from a Textile
       Mill. Edited for Runnymede Industrial Unit by
       Robert Whymant. London: Runnymede Trust, 1970.
       8 p.

842.   The Trade Union Movement and Discrimination: A
       Collection of Essays Based on Papers Given at
       a Conference Convened by Ruskin College, Oxford
       in December 1970. London: Runnymede Trust
       Industrial Unit, 1971. 12 p.

843.   Wainwright, David. Race and Employment: Managing
       a Multi-Racial Labour Force. London: Institute
       of Personnel Management, 1970. 88 p.

844.   Wandsworth Council for Community Relations. No Bloody
       Suntans. London: Wandsworth Council for Community
       Relations, 1976. 8 p.

845.   Ward, George. Fort Grunwick. London: Temple Smith,
       1977. 123 p.

B. PERIODICAL ARTICLES

846.   Adam, Corinna. "Indentured Labour." New Statesman
       (26 January 1973): 115.

847.   "After Loughborough." Economist 243 (23 December
       1972): 20.

848.   Allen, Sheila. "Race and the Economy: Some Aspects
       of the Position of Non-Indigenous Labour."
       Race 13: 2 (October 1971): 165-178.

849.   "Asian Workers Strike British Firm." U. S. News
       and World Report 74 (1 January 1973): 61.

850.   Avent, Catherine. "Discrimination is an Expensive
       Luxury." Education and Training 17 (November/
       December 1975): 260, 262.

851.   Ballard, Roger and Bronwen M. Holden. "The Employment
       of Coloured Graduated in Britain." New
       Community 4 (Autumn 1975): 325-336.

852.   Ballard, Roger and Bronwen M. Holden. "Racial
       Discrimination: No Room at the Top: Black
       Graduates." New Society (17 April 1975):
       133-135.

853.   Bandopadhyay, Nirmalya. "Working with Trade Unions."
       Ethnic Minorities and Employment No. 3 (Decem-
       ber 1976): 9.

854.   Beeson, T. "Discrimination in British Industry."
       Christian Century 88 (6 October 1971): 1156.

855. Bentley, Stuart. "Industrial Conflict, Strikes and
      Black Workers. Problems of Research Methodology."
      New Community 5 (Summer 1976): 127-138.

856. Bindman, Geoffrey. "Race Relations: How to Use the
      New Act - 2." LAG Bulletin (October 1977);
      236-239.

857. Bishop, Terry. "Immigrant Labour in Britain's
      Hospitals." Personnel Management 5 (August
      1973): 25-27.

858. "Black and Jobless." Economist 243 (3 June 1972):
      25-26.

859. "Black Employment in the Black Country." Race Today
      7: 6 (June 1975): 133-137.

860. "Blind Folly." Economist 254 (1 March 1975): 23.

861. Bosanquet, Nicholas and P. B. Doeringer. "Is There
      a Dual Labour Market in Great Britain?"
      Economic Journal 83 (June 1973): 421-435.

862. Brooks, Dennis and Karamjit Singh. "Race Relations
      Industrial Relations and Pluralism." New
      Community 1 (Summer 1972): 277-281.

863. Brooks, Dennis. "Railways, Railwaymen and Race."
      New Community 4 (Winter/Spring 1974/1975): 37-45.

864. Browne, Gilbert. "Trade Unions." Ethnic Minorities
      and Employment No. 2 (April 1976): 18-19.

865. Burke, Anthony. "Developing Relationships: Knowing
      the Differences." Training Officer 11:11
      (October/November 1975): 262-264.

866. Cambridge, A. X. "Loughborough: Black Workers and
      Trade Unions." The Black Liberator 2: 3
      (1973/1974): 70-79.

867. "Caribbean Women and the Black Community." Race
      Today 7: 5 (May 1975): 108-113.

868. Collins, Paul. "Low Paid Workers." Ethnic Minorities
      and Employment No. 4 (March 1977): 9

869. Collymore, Yvonne. "More Training for 100,000 Young
      Jobless, Say TSA." Ethnic Minorities and
      Employment No. 4 (March 1977): 14-15.

870. Connelly, Tom. "Dismissals and the Industrial Rela-
      tions Act 1971." New Community 1 (Spring
      1972): 75-76.

871   Connelly, Tom. "Race and Industrial Relations."
       Community (July 1970): 6-7.

872.   Coupland, D. E. "Aptitude Tests and Discrimination."
       International Labour Review 102 (September 1970):
       241-253.

873.   Cousins, Frank. "Discrimination or Integration?
       Frank Cousins Replies to CBI and TUC Views."
       Community (April 1970): 6-7.

874.   Cousins, Frank. "Race Relations in Employment in
       the United Kingdom." International Labour
       Review 102 (July 1970): 1-13.

875.   Daly, O. "Recruitment and Training of Ethnic Minori-
       ties in Industry." Ethnic Minorities and
       Employment No. 4 (March 1977): 16-17.

876.   Deaton, David. "The Racial Mix of London Transport
       Recruits." New Community 5 (Autumn 1976):
       316-319.

877.   Dhondy, Mala. "The Strike at Imperial Typewriters."
       Race Today 6: 6/9 (June/September 1974): 203-
       205, 223-225, 249-251.

878.   Fenton, James and C. Hitchens. "Britain's Cut-Price
       Seamen." New Statesman (30 March 1973):
       454-455.

879.   Figueroa, Peter M. E. "Employment Prospects of West
       Indian School-Leavers in London, England."
       Social and Economic Studies 25 (1976): 216-233.

880.   Findlay, Roslyn. "Young, Black and Out of Work."
       Ethnic Minorities and Employment No. 1 (December
       1976): 12-13.

881.   Foner, Nancy. "Women, Work and Migration: Jamaicans
       in London." New Community 5 (Summer 1976):
       85-98.

882.   Foner, Nancy. "Women, Work and Migration: Jamaicans
       in London." Urban Anthropology 4 (Fall 1975):
       229-249.

883.   Forester, Tom. "The Home Workers." New Society
       (4 September 1975): 509.

884.   Fowler, Bridget, Barbara Littlewood and Ruth Madigan.
       "Immigrant School Leavers and the Search for
       Work." Sociology 11: 1 (January 1977): 65-85.

885. Fowler, Bridget, et al. "Sorry the Job Has Been
     Taken." New Society (28 April 1977): 162-164.

886. Goldthorpe, John H. "Political Consensus, Social
     Inequality and Pay Policy." New Society
     (10 January 1974): 55-58.

887. Gorz, Andre. "Immigrant Labour." New Left Review
     No. 61 (May/June 1970): 28-31.

888. Gould, Stuart H. and Pierre L. Van den Berghe.
     "Particularism in Sociology Departments' Hiring
     Practices." Race 15: 1 (July 1973): 106-111.

889. Great Britain. Department of Employment. "Unemploy-
     ment Among Workers from Racial Minority Groups."
     Department of Employment Gazettee 83 (1975):
     868-871.

890. "Grunwick Gates: The Entry to Unionisation." Race
     Today 9: 4 (June/July 1977): 76-78.

891. Gunther, K. "Special Complaint Procedure Concerning
     Discrimination in Employment." International
     Labour Review 104 (November 1971): 351-365.

892. "Harder for the Young Coloured to Get Jobs." Times
     Educational Supplement No. 3149 (10 October
     1975): 11.

893. Hardie, Alan. "Employment and Community Relations
     in Thamesdown." Ethnic Minorities and Employ-
     ment No. 2 (April 1976): 5-8.

894. Hardy, Allan F. "Language, Truth and the Immigrant
     Worker." Training Officer 11:11 (October/
     November 1975): 260-261.

895. Holland, M. "Double Standards at Sea." New Statesman
     (26 March 1976): 396-397.

896. "Inequality More Costly." Economist 249 (13 October
     1973): 63-64.

897. "Job for Teacher in Race Row." Times Educational
     Supplement No. 3196 (3 September 1976): 4.

898. Jowell, R. and Patricia Clarke Prescotte. "Racial
     Discrimination and White Collar Workers in
     Britain." Race 11: 4 (April 1970): 397-417.

899. Jupp, Thomas Cyrian. "Promotion and the Immigrant."
     Personnel Management 6 (April 1974): 34-37.

900. Kapo, Remi. "Dagenham's Way With Colour: Race Rela-
      tions in the Motor Car Industry." New Statesman
      (29 October 1976): 592.

901. Kendall, Michael N. "Overseas Nurses." New Society
      (13 August 1972): 239-240.

902. "Kenilworth Strike Defeated." Race Today 6: 12
      (December 1974): 320.

903. Kerr, Alice. "Race Relations." Socialist Standard
      73:873 (May 1977): 86-87.

904. Khan, Asif. "Job Fears for Young Blacks in Midlands."
      Times Educational Supplement No. 3191 (30 July
      1976): 7.

905. Kirkham, Pat. "Asian Women on Strike." Women's Voice
      4 (1973): 11-12.

906. Knox, Valerie. "Industrial Integration in Lancashire."
      Community (January 1971): 11-15.

907. Leach, Bridget. "Postal Screening for a Minority
      Group: Young West Indians in Leeds." Urban
      Studies 12 (October 1975): 285-294.

908. Lines, S. "Training for Road Transport." Ethnic
      Minorities and Employment No. 2 (April 1976):
      20-22.

909. Lomas, Glenys Barbara Gillian. "Race and Employment."
      New Society (15 May 1975): 413.

910. "Look Who is Talking." Economist 249 (27 October
      1973): 100,103.

911. McGrath, Morag. "The Economic Position of Immigrants
      in Batley." New Community 5 (Autumn 1976):
      239-249.

912. "Migrants, Work and the Law: Trade Unions and Immi-
      grant Workers." New Community 4 (Winter/Spring
      1974/1975): 19-36.

913. Miles, R. and A. Phizacklea. "The TUC, Black Workers
      and New Commonwealth Immigration, 1945-1973."
      Working Papers on Ethnic Relations No. 6 (1977):
      1-44.

914. Moore, Robert. "Immigrant Workers in Europe: Spectre
      of New Slavery." Patterns of Prejudice 7: 4
      (1973): 1-5.

915. Morrison, Lionel. "A Black Journalist's Experience of British Journalism." New Community 4 (Autumn 1975): 317-322.

916. Morrison, Lionel. "Training for Black Youth." New Society (13 June 1974): 638-639.

917. "The NHS: Breakup of a Marriage of Convenience." Ethnic Minorities and Employment No. 4 (March 1977): 18.

918. Newell, David. "An Employment Project in Loughborough: The Future Role of Community Relations Councils." New Community 4 (Winter/Spring 1975/1976): 436-442.

919. North, David and William Weissert. "The New Immigrants: Study Shows Recent Arrivals have High Skills and Strong Work Ethic." Manpower 5 (December 1973): 25-31.

920. "Not Before Time." Economist 245 (2 December 1972): 28.

921. "Not By Jobs Alone." Economist 265 (17 December 1977): 26.

922. O'Muircheartaigh, Colm and Tom Rees. "Immigrants at Work: Migrant/Immigrant Labour in Great Britain, France and Germany." New Community 4 (Winter/Spring 1975/1976): 493-500.

923. "Positive Policy on Race Relations as Aid to Integration at Work." Department of Employment Gazette 80 (November 1972): 974-975.

924. Power, Jonathan. "The New Proletariat." Encounter 43 (September 1974): 8-22.

925. "Race, Class and the State (2)." Race and Class 19: 1 (Summer 1977): 69-75.

926. "Race in Promotion." Education 143:14 (5 April 1974): 382.

927. "Race Relations After Loughborough.: Economist 245 (23 December 1972): 20.

928. Race Today Collective. "The Grunwick Strike.: Race Today 9: 3 (April/May 1977): 52-54.

929. Race Today Collective. "We Are in the Majority at Fords." Race Today 8:11 (November 1976): 223-226.

930. "Racial Discrimination at Work." Labour Research 64
      (January 1975): 10-11.

931. "Racism in Employment: TUC Takes on Challenge." Ethnic
      Minorities and Employment No. 3 (December 1976):
      3.

932. Roberts, Celia. "Industrial English Language Training
      for Overseas Workers." New Community 4 (Autumn
      1975): 337-441.

933. Rossiter, Ann. "Risking Gossip and Disgrace: Asian
      Women on Strike." Spare Rib 54 (January 1977):
      18.

934. Rowland, V. I., "Race, Class and Occupational Choice."
      New Community 4 (Winter/Spring 1974/1975): 46-54.

935. "Rules for Europe." Economist 245 (28 October 1972):
      23.

936. Scott, Gavin. "Young Blacks Angry at Poor Prospects."
      Times Educational Supplement No. 3081 (14 June
      1974): 6.

937. Sengupta, Susan. "Asian Employment Stereotypes and
      Generalisations." Ethnic Minorities and Employ-
      ment No. 2 (April 1976): 16-18.

938. "Separate But Equal." Economist 252 (3 August 1974):
      21.

939. Shamsher, Joginder S. "The Overtime People." South
      Asian Review 5 (July 1972): 313-325.

940. Sibley, Tom. "Minorities in Industry: Trade Unions
      and Black Workers." Ethnic Minorities and
      Employment No. 3 (December 1976): 10.

941. Simmonds, Kenneth and Richard Connell. "Breaking the
      Board-Room Barrier: The Importance of Being
      British." The Journal of Management Studies
      (1974): 85-95.

942. Simpson, William. "Race Relations in the Foundary."
      Community (January 1971): 17-18.

943. Smith, David John. "Job Discrimination and the
      Function of Law." New Community 4 (Winter/
      Spring 1974/1975): 55-61.

944. Smith, David John. "The Nature of White Workers
      Resistance." New Society (June 1974): 696-699.

945. Solanki, Ramniklal. "Ethnic Minorities and the Media:
      A View of the Asian Press in Britain." New
      Community 4 (Winter/Spring 1975/1976): 471-472.

946. Sparks, D. F. "Relationship of Local Employment
      Agencies and CRCs." Ethnic Minorities and
      Employment No. 4 (March 1977): 10.

947. Stephen, Andrew. "Deadlock at the Mill." New
      Statesman (2 February 1973): 156.

948. Stephen, Andrew. "Racialism on the Shop Floor."
      New Statesman (5 January 1973): 10.

949. Stevenson, D. and P. Wallis. "Second Generation West
      Indians: A Study in Alienation." Race Today 2: 8
      (August 1970): 278-280.

950. Stewart, Margaret. "Discrimination or Integration?
      Views of CBI and TUC." Community (January
      1970): 7, 10-12.

951. "TUC - Acting in Workers Interests." Campaign to
      Repeal the Immigration Act Bulletin 2 (1976):
      13-14.

952. Taylor, John Henry. "High Unemployment and Coloured
      School Leavers: The Tyneside Pattern." New
      Community 2 (Winter 1972/1973): 85-89.

953. Taylor, Robert. "Asians and a Union." New Society
      (30 May 1974): 510-511.

954. Thakur, Manab and Roger Williams. "Immigrants at
      Work - Hopeful Travellers: A Study of Asian
      Graduates in Britain." New Community 4 (Winter/
      Spring 1975/1976): 476-492.

955. "Trade Unions and Immigrant Workers." New Community 4
      (Winter/Spring 1974/1975): 19-36.

956. "Two Worlds in Conflict." Race Today 6:10 (October
      1974): 273-275.

957. "Unions on Trial." Economist 254 (15 February
      1975): 18, 29.

958. Watson, Peter. "Race in Industry: Safety Last."
      New Society (4 February 1971): 196.

959. West, Richard. "Sex, Race and Grunwick." Spectator
      (23 July 1977): 10-11.

960. Wilby, Peter. "The Vagaries of Vouchers." New
      Statesman (7 November 1975): 566-568.

961.   Wild, Raymond and C. Ridgeway.   "The Job Expectations
       of Immigrant Workers."   _Race_ 11: 3   (January
       1970): 323-333.

962.   Wilson, David.   "Trouble at 'T' Mill."   _Observer_
       (3 December 1972): 17.

963.   "Working Party Proposes That Discrimination in Industry
       Should be Unlawful and Recommends Fair Employ-
       ment Agency."   _Ulster Commentary_ No. 326   (Septem-
       ber 1973): 15.

964.   "Young Blacks Must Wait."   _Times Educational Supple-
       ment_ No. 3205   (5 November 1976): 3.

VIII.

SOCIAL CONDITIONS

A. BOOKS

965. Bentley, Stuart. "The Structure of Leadership among Pakistanis and West Indians in Britain." M.Sc thesis, University of Bradford, 1971.

966. Bermant, Chaim. Point of Arrival: A Study of London's East End. London: Eyre Methuen, 1975. 292 p.

967. Black People in Britain. The Way Forward (Conference) London, 1975. Black People in Britain: The Way Forward: A Report. Written up and Edited by Rajeev Dhavan. London: The Post Conference Constituent Committee, 1976. 227 p.

968. Bluefoot Traveller: An Anthology of West Indian Poets in Britain. Edited with an Introduction by James Berry. London: Limestone Publications, 1976. 52 p.

969. Brendon, David. Not Proven: Some Questions About Homelessness and Young Immigrants. London: Runnymede Trust, 1973. 24 p.

970. Cameron, Gordon Campbell and Lowdon Wingo, eds. Cities, Regions and Public Policy. Edinburgh: Published for the University of Glasgow and Resources for the Future, Inc.; Washington, D. C.: by Oliver and Boyd, 1973. 337 p.

971. Castles, Stephen and Godula Kosack. Immigrant Workers and the Class Structure in Western Europe. London: Oxford University Press for the Institute of Race Relations, 1973. 514 p.

972. Clarke, Susan E. and Jeffrey L. Obler, eds. Urban
      Ethnic Conflict: A Comparative Perspective. Cha-
      pel Hill: The Institute for Research in Social
      Science, University of North Carolina at Chapel
      Hill, 1976. 257 p.

973. Davies, Paul and K. Newton. The Social and Political
      Patterns of Immigrant Areas. Birmingham, England:
      Faculty of Commerce and Social Science, University
      of Birmingham, 1971. 26 p.

974. Dewitt, John. "Indian Workers Associations in Bri-
      tain." Ph.D. dissertation, University of Chicago,
      1972.

975. Egbuna, Obi Benue Joseph. Destroy This Temple: The
      Voice of Black Power in Britain. London: Mac-
      Gibbon and Kee, 1971. 157 p.

976. Egbuna, Obi Benue Joseph. Destroy This Temple: The
      Voice of Black Power in Britain. New York:
      Morrow, 1971. 157 p.

977. Evans, Peter. The Attitudes of Young Immigrants.
      London: Runnymede Trust, 1971. 39 p.

          Review in New Community 1 (Spring 1972):
          238.

978. Gillie, Oliver. Who Do You Think You Are? Man or
      Superman: The Genetic Controversy. London: Hart-
      Davis MacGibbon, 1976. 255 p.

979. Great Britain. Community Relations Commission. The
      Multi-Racial Community: A Guide for Local Coun-
      selors. London: The Commission, 1977. 34 p.

980. Great Britain. Community Relations Commission. Urban
      Deprivation, Racial Inequality and Social Policy:
      A Report. London: H.M.S.O., 1977. 100 p.

981. Hamnett, Chris. Multiple Deprivation and the Inner
      City. Prepared by Chris Hamnett for the Open
      University Course Team. Milton Keynes: Open Uni-
      versity Press, 1976. 106 p.

982. Hill, David. "The Attitudes of Ethnic Minorities in
      Britain among Adolescents." Doctoral disserta-
      tion, University of Birmingham, 1973.

983. Hines, Vince. Britain, the Black Man and the Future.
      London: Zulu Publications, 1972. 47 p.

984. International Asian Guide and Directory (Including
      Who's Who). Ilford: Asian Observer, 1975-76.
      122 p.

985. John, Augustine. Race in the Inner City: A Report from
      Handsworth, Birmingham. With Comments from Robert
      Holman, John Lambert, and Dipak Nandy. London:
      Runnymede Trust, 1970. 53 leaves.

986. Khan, Naseem. The Arts Britain Ignores: The Arts of
      Ethnic Minorities in Great Britain. Prepared
      for the Arts Council of Great Britain, Calouste
      Gulbenkian Foundation and Community Relations
      Commission. London: The Commission, 1976. 175 p.

987. Kuper, Leo. Race, Class and Power. London: Duckworth,
      1974. 345 p.

988. Lester, Anthony. Citizens Without Status. London:
      Runnymede Trust, 1972. 16 p.

989. London: Urban Patterns, Problems and Policies. A
      Study sponsored by the Centre for Environmental
      Studies. Edited by David Donnison and David
      Eversley. London: Heinemann Educational, 1973.
      452 p.

990. Mason, Philip. Prospero's Magic: Some Thoughts on
      Class and Race. Westport, Connecticut: Greenwood
      Press, 1975. 151 p.

      Reprint of the edition published by Oxford
      University Press, London, New York, 1962.

991. The Migration and Distribution of Socio-Economic Groups
      in Greater London: Evidence from the 1961, 1966,
      1971 Censuses. Edited by K. Dugmore for the
      Greater London Council, Director-General's De-
      partment, Intelligence Unit. London: Greater Lon-
      don Council, 1975. 123 p.

992. Milner, David. Children and Race. Harmondsworth:
      Penguin, 1975. 281 p.

993. Moore, G. "Immigrants and Crime." M.A. thesis,
      Keele University, 1970.

994. Parekh, Bhikhu. Colour, Culture and Consciousness:
      Immigrant Intellectuals in Britain. London:
      Allen and Unwin, 1974. 249 p.

      Review by Ken Jordan. Race and Class 16: 2
      (October 1974): 219-223.

995. Pollak, Margaret. Today's Three Year Olds in London.
      London: Heinemann Medical for Spastics Interna-
      tional Medical Publications, 1972. 162 p.

996. Rutter, Michael and Nicola Madge. Cycles of Disad-
      vantage: A Review of Research. London: Heine-
      mann, 1976. 413 p.

997. Stewart, Philippa. Immigrants. London: Batsford,
      1976. 96 p.

998. Wandsworth Council for Community Relations. Uganda
      Resettlement Unit. Uganda Asians in Wandsworth:
      A Report. Produced by WCCR's Uganda Resettle-
      ment Unit for Sir Charles Cunningham, Chairman
      of the Uganda Resettlement Board. London: Wands-
      worth Council for Community Relations, 1973.
      30 p.

999. Woods, Robert Ivor. The Stochastic Analysis of Immi-
      grant Distribution. Oxford: School of Geogra-
      phy, University of Oxford, 1975. 35 p.

                    B. PERIODICAL ARTICLES

1000. Bagley, Christopher. "A Comparative Study of Social
       Environment and Intelligence in West Indian and
       English Children in London." Social and Eco-
       nomic Studies 20 (1971): 420-430.

1001. Bagley, Christopher. "Deviant Behaviour in English
       and West Indian School Children." Research in
       Education 8 (November 1972): 47-55.

1002. Bagley, Christopher. "Race Relations and Theories of
       Status Consistency." Race 11: 3 (January 1970):
       267-288.

1003. Bandali, Sultan G. "As Others See Us." Social Ser-
       vice Quarterly 47 (January/March 1974): 103-104.

1004. Batta, T. D., J. W. McCulloch and N. J. Smith. "A
       Study of Juvenile Delinquency Amongst Asians and
       Half-Asians: A Comparative Study in a Northern
       Town Based on Official Statistics." British
       Journal of Criminology 15 (January 1975): 32-42.

1005. Bhatti, F. M. "Language Difficulties and Social Iso-
       lation (The Case of South Asian Women in Bri-
       tain)." New Community 5 (Summer 1976): 115-117.

1006. Chase, Louis A. "Some of my Grouses." New Community
       3 (Winter/Spring 1974): 111-113.

1007. Cottle, T. J. "Cost of Hope." America 136 (12 Febru-
       ary 1977): 125-127.

1008. Cross, Crispin P. "Youth Clubs and Coloured Youths."
       New Community 5 (Spring/Summer 1977): 489-494.

1009. Cross, Malcolm. "Pluralism, Equality and Social Jus-
       tice." New Community 1 (Summer 1972): 243-249.

1010. Harrington, I. "Clubland Comes to the Boil." New
       Statesman (25 June 1971): 877.

1011. Harrison, Paul. "Prejudice and Preston." New So-
       ciety (24 October 1974): 212-213.

1012. Hill, Clifford. "Immigrant Sect Development in Bri-
       tain: A Case of Status Deprivation." Social
       Compass 18: 2 (1971): 231-236.

1013. Jefferson, Tony and John Clarke. "Down These Mean
       Streets: The Meaning of Mugging." Howard Jour-
       nal 14 (1974): 37-53.

1014. Jones, P. N. "Colored Minorities in Birmingham,
       England." Association of American Geographers
       Annals 66 (March 1976): 89-103.

1015. Kanitkar, H. A. "An Indian Elite in Britain."
       New Community 1 (Autumn 1972): 378-382.

1016. Krausz, Ernest. "Factors of Social Mobility in
       British Minority Groups." British Journal of
       Sociology (23 September 1972): 275-286.

1017. Lapping, Sir A. "London's Little Harlems: I Am the
       Mullah of Bray." Economist 262 (1 January 1977):
       32-34.

1018. Lee, Trevor R. "Immigrants in London: Trends in Dis-
       tribution and Concentration 1961-71." New Com-
       munity 2 (Spring 1973): 145-158.

1019. McCulloch, J. W. "A Comparative Study of Adult Crime
       Amongst Asians and Their Host Population."
       Probation Journal 21 (March 1974): 16-21.

1020. McGlashan, Colin. "Making of a Mugger." New States-
       man (13 October 1972): 496-497.

1021. McGlashan, Colin. "Mugging - Who Are the Victims?"
       Race Today 4:11 (November 1972): 377-379.

1022. MacInnes, Colin. "Mangrove Trial." New Society
       (23 December 1971): 1261.

1023. "Not Black and White." Economist 259 (17 April 1976):
       23-24.

1024. Parry, Jann. "The New Britons, 1." Observer (28
       November 1971): 17-22, 24-25.

1025. Parry, Jann. "The New Britons, 2: A Passage from
       India." Observer (5 December 1971): 14-18, 21-
       22.

1026. Parry, Jann. "The New Britons, 3. Even in Soho: A
       Bamboo Curtain." Observer (12 December 1971):
       38-41, 43-44.

1027. "A Patchwork Britain." New Society (26 September
       1974): 804-806.

1028. Peach, G. C. K. "Immigrants in the Inner City."
       Geographical Journal 141: 3 (November 1975):
       372-379.

1029. Perry, Norman. "What Price the Good Life." New
       Society (28 February 1974): 512-513.

1030. Prest, Mike. "Black Youth and the White Left." The
       Leveller (November 1977): 15.

1031. Preston, Barbara. "Statistics of Inequality." So-
       ciological Review 22 (February 1974): 103-118.

1032. Raban, Jonathan. "Brahmins and Pariahs." Listener
       89 (22 February 1973): 235-237.

1033. Raban, Jonathan. "The New Castes." Listener 89
       (15 February 1973): 207-209.

1034. Reubens, Edwin P. "Our Urban Ghettoes in British
       Perspectives." Urban Affairs Quarterly 6 (March
       1971): 319-340.

1035. Ritchey, P. Neal. "The Effect of Minority Group Sta-
       tus on Fertility: A Re-Examination of Concepts."
       Population Studies 29 (July 1975): 249-257.

1036. Runciman, W. G. "How Divided is Britain?" New So-
       ciety (23 May 1974): 435-438.

1037. Searle, Chris. "No Tavern Time for Blacks." Race
       Today 6:11 (November 1974): 293-294.

1038.   Sivanandan, Ambalavaner.   "The Liberation of the Black
             Intellectuals."   Race and Class 18: 4   (Spring
             1977): 329-343.

1039.   Stadlen, Frances.   "Urban Aid - Little Light in the
             Darkness."   Times Educational Supplement No.
             3167   (13 February 1976): 8.

1040.   "Suffer in Silence."   Times Educational Supplement
             No. 3170   (5 March 1976): 2.

1041.   Trussler, Denis.   "Immigrant Housewives Learn to Buy
             the Dinner."   Teacher 15:18   (1 May 1970): 13.

1042.   Weightman, Gavin.   "Poor Man's Harley Street."   New
             Society   (20 October 1977): 118-119.

1043.   Weir, Stuart, et al.   "Uganda Asians: One Year Later."
             New Community 2   (Autumn 1973): 379-388.

1044.   Werner, Eric.   "Psychological and Ethnic Correlates
             of Interpersonal Maturity Among Delinquents."
             British Journal of Criminology 15   (January
             1975): 51-68.

1045.   West, Katherine.   "Stratification and Ethnicity in
             Plural New States."   Race 13: 4   (April 1972):
             487-495.

1046.   White, David.   "Models of Politeness."   New Society
             (4 July 1974): 5-6.

1047.   Wilson, Sir Geoffrey.   "Race Relations: Clubs Concern
             Us All."   Contemporary Review 226   (March 1975):
             113-118.

IX.

GENERAL CULTURE, FAMILY, AND COMMUNITY LIFE

1. GENERAL

A. Books

1048.   Blakeley, Madeleine. <u>Nahda's Family</u>. London: A. and
        C. Black, 1977. 25 p.

1049.   Bridger, Peter. <u>A Hindu Family in Britain</u>. Oxford:
        Religious Education Press, 1975. 107 p.

1050.   Butterworth, Eric and Donald Kinnibrugh. <u>The Social
        Background of Immigrant Children from India,
        Pakistan and Cyprus</u>. London: Published for the
        Schools Council by Books for School, Ltd., 1970.
        90 p.

1051.   Cole, William Owen. <u>A Sikh Family in Britain</u>. Ox-
        ford: Religious Education Press, 1973. 101 p.

1052.   Community Work Group. <u>Current Issues in Community
        Work: A Study</u>. London: Routledge and Kegan
        Paul, 1973. 180 p.

1053.   Crishna, Seetha. <u>Girls of Asian Origin in Britain</u>.
        London: YWCA of Great Britain, 1975. 45 p.

1054.   Great Britain. Community Relations Commission. Ref-
        erence Division. <u>Muslim Burials: A Policy Paper</u>.
        London: The Commission, 1975. 12 p.

1055.   Hill, Clifford. <u>Black Churches: West Indian and Afri-
        can Sects in Britain</u>. London: British Council
        of Churches, Community and Race Relations Unit,
        1971. 23 p.

1056.   Holroyde, Peggy, Mohammed Iqbal and Dharam Kumar Vohra.
        East Comes West: A Background to Some Asian
        Faiths. London: Community Relations Commission,
        1971. 88 p.

            Review by Philip Mason. Race 12: 3 (October
            1971): 365-366.

1057.   James, Alan Geoffrey. Sikh Children in Britain.
        London: Oxford University Press for the Insti-
        tute of Race Relations, 1974. 117 p.

            Review by Roger Ballard. New Community 3
            (Summer 1974): 298-299.

1058.   Jeffrey, Patricia. Migrants and Refugees: Muslim and
        Christian Pakistani Families in Bristol.
        Cambridge, England: University Press, 1976.
        221 p.

            Review by Mohammed Asghar. Race and Class
            18: 3 (Winter 1977): 307-309.

1059.   Morrish, Ivor. The Background of Immigrant Children.
        London: Allen and Unwin, 1971. 256 p.

            Review by Sheila Patterson. New Community 1
            (Spring 1972): 237-238.

1060.   Sharma, Ursula. Rampal and His Family. London:
        Collins, 1971. 222 p.

1061.   Sookhdeo, Patrick. Asians in Britain: A Christian
        Understanding. London: Pastoral Aid Society,
        1972. 62 p.

1062.   Tilbe, Douglas. The Ugandan Asian Crisis. London:
        Community and Race Relations Unit of the British
        Council of Churches, 1972. 19 p.

1063.   Trudgian, Raymond. Community Relations. Edited by
        Robin Shepherd and Margaret Lydamore. London:
        S.C.M. Press for the Christian Education Move-
        ment, 1973. 32 p.

1064.   Wells, John Christopher. Jamaican Pronunciation in
        London. Oxford: Blackwell for Philological
        Society, 1973. 150 p.

1065.   West Indians in Great Britain, 1974/75. 2d ed.
        London: West Indian Digest, 1974. 110 p.

B. Periodical Articles

1066.   Akram, Mohammed. "Pakistani Migrants in Britain: A
        Note." New Community 4 (Winter/Spring 1974/1975):
        116-118.

1067.   Aziz, Khalid. "Daughters of Tradition." Listener
        96 (7 October 1976): 426-428.

1068.   Ballard, Roger. "Family Organisation Among the Sikhs
        in Britain." New Community 2 (Winter 1972/1973):
        12-24.

1069.   Banton, Michael. "The Migrants Choice." New Commun-
        ity 1 (Autumn 1972): 349-353.

1070.   Barot, Rohit. "A Swaminarayan Sect As a Community."
        New Community 2 (Winter 1972/1973): 34-37.

1071.   Beaumont, Tim. "Sikhs, Sabbaths and Commonsense."
        Observer Magazine (23 March 1975): 7-8.

1072.   "Bradford is Not Bengal." Economist 239 (3 April
        1971): 24-25.

1073.   Brah, A. M. Fuller, D. Louden and R. Miles. "Experi-
        menter Effects and Ethnic Cueing Phenomenon."
        Working Papers on Ethnic Relations No. 3 (1977):
        1-31.

1074.   Bristow, Mike, Bert N. Adams and Cecil Pereira.
        "Ugandan Asians in Britain, Canada and India:
        Some Characteristics and Resources." New Com-
        munity 4 (Summer 1975): 155-166.

1075.   Cashmore, Ernest. "The Rastaman Cometh." New Society
        (25 August 1977): 382-384.

1076.   Chansarkar, B. A. "A Note on the Maratha Community
        in Britain." New Community 2 (Summer 1973):
        302-305.

1077.   Churchill, R. C. "The Coloured Counties." New
        Humanist 93 (October/November 1977): 93-94.

1078.   Cohen, Gerda. "Mirpur in Yorkshire." New Statesman
        (2 July 19 .): 13-14.

1079.   Collins, Joyce. "The Social Background of Children
        from Immigrant Groups." Education for Teaching
        No. 90 (Spring 1973): 15-23.

1080. Cottle, T. J. "Jamie Horace Pinkerton." America
       136 (23 April 1977): 370-377.

1081. Dahya, Badr. "Pakistanis in Britain: Transients or
       Settlers." Race 14: 3 (January 1973): 241-277.

1082. Dahya, Badr. "Pakistanis in England." New Community
       2 (Winter 1972/1973): 25-33.

1083. Dalton, M. and J. M. Seaman. "The Distribution of
       New Commonwealth Immigrants in the London Bor-
       ough of Ealing, 1961-66." Institute of British
       Geographers Transactions (March 1973): 21-39.

1084. Dhanjal, Beryl. "Sikh Women in Southall (Some Im-
       pressions)." New Community 5 (Summer 1976):
       109-114.

1085. Doe, Bob. "Pakistan to Back Muslim Venture." Times
       Educational Supplement No. 3114 (31 January 1975):
       5.

1086. Douglas, J. W. B., et al. "Behavioral Styles of 4½
       Year Old Boys When Responding to Test Demands."
       Educational Research 14 (June 1972): 208-212.

1087. "Fewer Black Births - Census." Times Educational Sup-
       plement No. 3165 (30 January 1976): 7.

1088. Foner, Nancy. "Male and Female Jamaican Migrants in
       London." Anthropological Quarterly 49 (January
       1976): 28-35.

1089. Foner, Nancy. "The Meaning of Education to Jamaicans
       at Home and in London." New Community 4 (Summer
       1975): 195-202.

1090. "Fresh Start." Time 100 (30 October 1972): 43-44.

1091. Giles, H. and R. Y. Bourhis. "Voice and Racial Cate-
       gorization in Britain." Communication Mono-
       graphs 43 (June 1976): 108-114.

1092. Hallam, Roger. "The Ismailis in Britain." New Com-
       munity 1 (Autumn 1972): 383-388.

1093. Harrison, Paul. "The Patience of Southall." New
       Society (4 April 1974): 7-11.

1094. Hedayatullah, M. "Muslim Migrants and Islam." New
       Community 5 (Spring/Summer 1977): 392-396.

1095. Hill, Barry. "Daughters of the Temple." Times Educa-
       tional Supplement No. 2989 (1 September 1972):
       16, 45.

1096. Hill, David. "Adolescent Attitudes Among Minority
        Ethnic Groups." Educational Review 27 (November
        1974): 45-51.

1097. Hill, David. "Personality Factors Amongst Adoles-
        cents in Minority Ethnic Groups." Educational
        Studies 1: 1 (March 1975): 43-54.

1098. Hope, Francis. "Sez Leicester." New Statesman
        (8 December 1972): 863-864.

1099. "The Immigrant League." Economist 258 (31 January
        1976): 20.

1100. Iqbal, Mohammad. "Muslims in a Christian Culture."
        Times Educational Supplement No. 3060 (18 January
        1974): 2.

1101. Jeffrey, Patricia. "Pakistani Families in Bristol."
        New Community 1 (Autumn 1972): 364-369.

1102. Jones, Huw and Maureen Davenport. "The Pakistani
        Community in Dundee: A Study of Its Growth and
        Demographic Structure." Scottish Geographical
        Magazine 88 (September 1972): 75-85.

1103. Kallarackal, A. M. and Martin Herbert. "The Happiness
        of Indian Immigrant Children." New Society
        (26 February 1976): 422-424.

1104. Karmi, H. S. "The Family As a Developing Social Group
        in Islam." Asian Affairs 62 (February 1975):
        61-68.

1105. Khan, Verity Saifullah. "Pakistani Women in Britain."
        New Community 5 (Summer 1976): 99-108.

1106. Khan, Verity Saifullah. "Pakistanis in Britain: Per-
        ceptions of a Population." New Community 5
        (Autumn 1976): 222-229.

1107. Kramer, J. "The Uganda Asians." New Yorker 50
        (8 April 1974): 47-93.

1108. Kuepper, William George, G. Lynne Lackey and E. Nelson
        Swinerton. "Ugandan Asian Refugees: Resettlement
        Centre to Community." Community Development
        Journal 11 (October 1976): 199-208.

1109. Leach, Bridget. "The Social Geographer and Black
        People: Can Geography Contribute to Race Rela-
        tions?" Race 15: 2 (October 1973): 230-241.

1110. Lengermann, Patricia Madoo. "The Debate on the Struc-
      ture and Content of West Indian Values: Some Rele-
      vant Data from Trinidad and Tobago." British
      Journal of Sociology 23: 3 (September 1972): 298-
      311.

1111. Little, Alan. "Language Barriers." New Society
      (13 December 1973): 661.

1112. Lucas, Eileen. "Language in the Infants Playground."
      Multiracial School 1: 3 (Summer 1972): 18-22.

1113. Lucas, Eileen. "Language in the Infants Playground."
      Multiracial School 2: 1 (Autumn 1972): 20-23.

1114. Lyon, Michael H. "Ethnicity in Britain: The Gujarati
      Tradition." New Community 2 (Winter 1972/1973):
      1-11.

1115. MacDonald, Marcia. "The Mysterious East Comes to
      London." Contemporary Review 223 (December 1973):
      309-310.

1116. MacInnes, Colin. "Calypso Lament." New Society
      (6 April 1972): 4.

1117. "Making the Best of It." Economist 244 (19 August
      1972): 13-14.

1118. Marjoribanks, Kevin. "Ethnicity and Learning Pat-
      terns: A Replication and an Explanation."
      Sociology 6 (September 1972): 417-431.

1119. Medlicott, Paul. "Brixton Scene." New Society
      (12 April 1973): 64-66.

1120. Morris, Sam. "Moody: The Forgotten Visionary." New
      Community 1 (Spring 1972): 193-196.

1121. Muir, Christine and Esther Goody. "Student Parents:
      West African Families in London." Race 13: 3
      (January 1972): 329-336.

1122. "Muslims Warning on Role of Girls." Times Educational
      Supplement No. 3134 (20 June 1975): 9.

1123. Newall, Venetia. "Black Britain: The Jamaicans and
      Their Folklore." Folklore 86 (Spring 1975):
      25-41.

1124. Patterson, Sheila. "Latter-Day Linnaeus." New Com-
      munity 3 (Winter/Spring 1974): 56-58.

1125. Pearson, David G. "Ethnicity and Ethnic Groups: West
      Indian Communal Associations in Britain - Some
      Observations." New Community 5 (Spring/Summer
      1977): 371-380.

1126. Pettigrew, J. "Some Notes on the Social System of the
      Sikh Jats." New Community 1 (Autumn 1972): 354-
      363.

1127. Pollard, Paul. "Jamaicans and Trinidadians in North
      London." New Community 1 (Autumn 1972): 370-
      377.

1128. Poulter, S. "Talaq Divorces." New Law Journal
      (6 January 1977): 7-10.

1129. Prickett, John. "Plea for Minority Religious Educa-
      tion." Times Educational Supplement No. 3140
      (8 August 1975): 7.

1130. Raspberry, William. "Why Britain's Blacks Have No
      Leaders." Observer (19 September 1976): 11.

1131. "Reaping the Bad Harvest of Muslim Fatalism." Educa-
      tion 149:25 (24 June 1977): 424.

1132. Rowan, Iain. "What is in a Name?" New Humanist 89
      (December 1973): 267.

1133. Roy, Amit. "Summer in Southall." Spectator (19 June
      1976): 11-12.

1134. Rutter, Michael, Bridget Yule, Janis Morton, and Chris-
      topher Bagley. "Children of West Indian Immi-
      grants - III: Home Circumstances and Family Pat-
      terns." Journal of Psychology and Psychiatry and
      Allied Disciplines 16 (April 1975): 105-123.

1135. Rutter, Michael, William Yule and Michael Berger.
      "The Children of West Indian Migrants." New
      Society (14 March 1974): 630-633.

1136. Shamsher, Joginder S. and Ralph Russell. "Punjabi
      Journalism in Britain: A Background." New Com-
      munity 5 (Autumn 1976): 211-221.

1137. Simpson, R. E. D. "Birthrates: A Five Year Compara-
      tive Study." Race Today 2: 8 (August 1970):
      256-265.

1138. Simpson, R. E. D. "Family Planning Among Different
      Ethnic Groups." Race Today 2: 5 (May 1970): 131-
      133.

1139.   Smith, Richard. "Praise the Lord: West Indians at
        Church." New Society (27 May 1976): 461-463.

1140.   Spittles, Brian. "Bhushra's Life." New Society
        30 May 1974): 498.

1141.   Tambs-Lyche, Harald. "A Comparison of Gujarati Com-
        munities in London and the Midlands." New Com-
        munity 4 (Autumn 1975): 349-355.

1142.   Taylor, John Henry. "A Tradition of Respect." New
        Society (5 October 1972): 26-28.

1143.   "Turbans, Spears and Toilets." Race Today 6:11/12
        (November/December 1974): 292, 319.

1144.   "Uganda Asians: How Happy?" Economist 248 (29 Sep-
        tember 1973): 32.

1145.   Wallis, Susan. "Pakistanis in Britain." New Com-
        munity 4 (Winter/Spring 1974/1975): 105-115.

1146.   White, David. "Migrant Money: Immigrants Remittances
        to Relatives." New Society (13 April 1972): 52.

1147.   Whitehouse, R. "The Cultural Background of West In-
        dian Children in Relations to Their Educational
        Aspirations." Journal of Applied Educational
        Studies 2: 1 (Summer 1973): 10-18.

2. CULTURE CONFLICT

A. Books

1148.   Akram, Mohammed. Far Upon the Mountain: The Experi-
        ence of a Young Pakistani in Britain. London:
        Community and Race Relations Unit of the British
        Council of Churches, 1972. 24 p.

1149.   Coard, Phyllis and Bernard Coard. Getting to Know
        Ourselves. London: Bogle L'Ouverture Publishers,
        1972. 21 p.

1150.   Conference on Cultural Conflict and the Asian Family.
        University of Leicester, 1975. Cultural Conflict
        and the Asian Family: Report of a Conference Or-
        ganised by the National Association of Indian
        Youth. Edited by Pramila Parekh and Bhikhu
        Parekh. Southall: Scope Communication, 1976.
        13 p.

1151.   Ghuman, Paul Avtar Singh. The Cultural Contents of
        Thinking: A Comparative Study of Punjabi and
        English Boys. Windsor: NFER, 1975. 136 p.

1152.   Kannan, C. T. Inter-Racial Marriages in London. Lon-
        don: Author, 1972. 193 p.

            Review in New Community 3 (Summer 1974):
            297-298.

1153.   Richardson, Ken, David Spears and Martin Richards.
        Race, Culture and Intelligence. Harmondsworth:
        Penguin, 1972. 205 p.

1154.   Searle, Chris. The Forsaken Lover: White Words and
        Black People. London: Routledge and Kegan Paul,
        1972. 108 p.

1155.   Searle, Chris. The Forsaken Lover: White Words and
        Black People. Harmondsworth: Penguin, 1973.
        128 p.

1156.   Thompson, Susan S. "The Development of Ethnic Con-
        cepts in Children." M.Sc. thesis, University of
        Strathclyde, 1970.

1157.   Watson, James Lee, ed. Between Two Cultures: Migrants
        and Minorities in Britain. Oxford: Basil Black-
        well, 1977. 388 p.

1158.   Wedge, Peter and Hilary Prosser. Born to Fail. Lon-
        don: Arrow Books for the National Children's
        Bureau, 1973. 64 p.

B. Periodical Articles

1159.   Allen, Sheila. "Plural Society and Conflict" New
        Community 1 (Autumn 1972): 389-392.

1160.   Anwar, Muhammad. "Young Asians: Between Two Cultures."
        New Society (16 December 1976): 563-565.

1161.   Bagley, Christopher. "Behavioural Deviance in Ethnic
        Minority Children: A Review of Published Studies."
        New Community 5 (Autumn 1976): 230-238.

1162.   Booth, John. "Indian Girls." Libertarian Education
        No. 23 (Winter 1977): 4-7.

1163.   Dennett, Margaret. "Colour Blind." Teacher 25: 1
        (5 July 1974): 8-9.

1164. Dennett, Margaret. "Survey of Immigrants in the
       Capital's Schools." Teacher 25: 3 (19 July
       1974): 6-7, 11.

1165. Dennett, Margaret. "We Are All the Same - But a
       New Culture Grows, Anti-Home, Non-White."
       Teacher 25:2 (12 July 1974): 15.

1166. Dummett, Ann. "A Walking Dead Man." Multiracial
       School 1: 3 (Summer 1972): 13-17.

1167. Finnegan, Brian and Michael Kelly. "This Ain't
       Trinidad: Two Views of Race Relations in England
       (1) Unhappy Families (2) Culture Conscious."
       Times Educational Supplement No. 2945 (29 Oct-
       ober 1971): 4.

1168. Hall, Stuart. "Black Britons: Some Problems of
       Adjustment." Community (April 1970): 3-5.

1169. Hall, Stuart. "Black Britons - Some Teenage Problems."
       Community (July 1970): 12-14.

1170. Jacobs, David M. "Dual Loyalties: Immigrant Britons."
       Spectator (6 September 1975): 309.

1171. Jahoda, G., S. Thomas and S. Bhatt. "Ethnic Identity
       and Preferences Among Asian Immigrant Children
       in Glasgow: A Replicated Study." European
       Journal of Social Psychology 2 (1972): 19-32.

1172. Louden, D. M. "Conflict and Change Among West Indian
       Parents and Their Adolescents in Britain."
       Educational Research 20 (November 1977): 44-53.

1173. McGlashan, Colin. "England's Teenage Apartheid."
       Observer (20 August 1972): 7-8.

1174. Marsh, Alan. "Awareness of Racial Differences in
       West African and British Children." Race 11: 3
       (January 1970): 289-302.

1175. Mazrui, Ali A. "Educational Techniques and Problems
       of Identity in Plural Societies." International
       Social Science Journal 24 (1972): 149-165.

1176. Milner, David. "Identity-Conflict in Immigrant
       Children." Therapeutic Education (Spring 1972):
       19-24.

1177. Milner, David. "Racial Identification and Preference
       in 'Black' British Children." European Journal
       of Social Psychology 3 (1973): 281-295.

1178. Murari, Timeri. "Portrait of an Asian Identity."
        Twentieth Century 179:1048 (1972): 22-23.

1179. Pirani, M. "Aspirations and Expectations of English
        and Immigrant Youth." New Community 3 (Winter/
        Spring 1974): 73-78.

1180. Raspberry, William. "Black Middle-Class Kids Who
        Find it Hard to Feel British." Observer
        (26 September 1976): 4.

1181. Raspberry, William. "Young, Bitter and Black."
        Observer (5 Septebmer 1976): 19.

1182. Simsova, S. "The Marginal Man." Journal of Librar-
        ianship 6: 1 (January 1974): 46-53.

1183. Tajfel, Henri, et al. "The Devaluation by Children
        of Their Own National and Ethnic Group: Two
        Case Studies." British Journal of Social and
        Clinical Psychology 11 (September 1972): 235-
        243.

1184. Thompson, Marcus. "The Second Generation: Punjabi
        or English." New Community 3 (Summer 1974):
        242-248.

1185. Watson, G. Llewellyn: "The Sociological Relevance
        of the Concept of Half-Caste in British Society."
        Phylon 36 (September 1975): 309-320.

X.

EDUCATION

1. GENERAL

A. Books

1186. Bhatnager, Joti. Immigrants at School. London:
       Cornmarket Press, 1970. 278 p.

1187. Boyle, Edward Charles Gurney, Baron Boyle. Race
       Relations and Education. Liverpool: Liverpool
       University Press, 1970. 22 p.

1188. Driver, G. "Ethnicity, Cultural Competence and
       School Achievement: A Case Study of West Indian
       Pupils Attending a British Secondary Modern
       School." Doctoral dissertation, University of
       Illinois, 1976.

1189. Education and the Urban Crisis. Edited by Frank
       Field. London: Routledge and Kegan Paul, 1977.
       149 p.

1190. Education for Adult Immigrants. Edited by A. K. Stock
       and D. Howell. Leicester: National Institute
       of Adult Education, 1976. 142 p.

1191. Edwards, Viv K. West Indian Language: Attitudes and
       the School. Slough: National Association for
       Multi-Racial Education, 1976. 13 p.

1192. Eysenck, H. J. Race, Intelligence and Education.
       London: Maurice Temple Smith in Association
       with New Society, 1971. 160 p.

       Review by Paul Atkinson. Race 13: 3
       (January 1972): 363-367.

1193.   Great Britain.   Central Office of Information.
        Reference Division.   Education in Britain.
        Rev. ed.   London: H.M.S.O., 1971.   93 p.

1194.   Great Britain.   Community Relations Commission.
        Reference and Technical Services Division.
        A Second Chance: Further Education in Multi-
        Racial Areas.   Edited by Susan Gardiner and
        Vivien Stern.   London: The Commission, 1976.
        134 p.

1195.   Great Britain.   Department of Education and Science.
        Museums in Education.   London: H.M.S.O., 1971.
        55 p.

1196.   Great Britain.   Department of Education and Science.
        Potential and Progress in a Second Culture:
        Survey of the Assessment of Pupils from Overseas.
        London: H.M.S.O., 1971.   44 p.

1197.   Great Britain.   Schools Council.   Race Relations and
        the Curriculum: A Short Analysis and Summary of
        Work Initiated by the Schools Council.   London:
        Schools Council, 1972.   21 p.

1198.   Haynes, Judith Mary.   Educational Assessment of
        Immigrant Pupils.   Slough: National Foundation
        for Educational Research, 1971.   121 p.

1199.   Leicester Teachers.   Making Audio-Visual Materials.
        London: Association for the Education of Pupils
        from Overseas, 1972.   24 p.

1200.   London.   Inner London Education Authority.   Education
        Committee.   Further and Higher Education Sub-
        Committee.   An Education Service for the Whole
        Community: Report Presented Jointly by the
        Further and Higher Education Sub-Committee and
        the Schools Sub-Committee (of the Inner London
        Education Authority), Education Committee.
        London: I.L.E.A., 1973.   64 p.

1201.   Mabey, Christine.   Social and Ethnic Mix in Schools
        and the Relationship with Attainment of Children
        Ages 8 and 11.   London: Centre for Environmental
        Studies, 1974.   44 p.

1202. 'Payne, Joan.   E. P. A. Surveys and Statistics.   London:
        H.M.S.O., 1974.   134 p.

1203. Raynor, John and Jane Harden, eds. Readings in Urban
       Education. Edited for the Urban Education Course
       Team at the Open University. London: Routledge
       and Kegan Paul for the Open University Press,
       1973. 2 Vols.

             Vol. 1. Cities, Communities and the Young.
             Vol. 2. Equality and City Schools.

1204. Siddiqui, Hamid Rabbani. Religious Education for
       Muslim Children in Great Britain: Guidelines
       and Syllabus. London: Union of Muslim Organisa-
       tions of United Kingdom and Ireland, 1976.
       25 p.

1205. Stoker, Diana. Immigrant Children in Infant Schools.
       Rev. London: Methuen, 1970. 63 p.

1206. Taylor, John Henry. The Half-Way Generation: A
       Study of Asian Youth in New Castle Upon Tyne.
       Windsor: N.F.E.R., 1976. 267 p.

1207. Verma, Gajendra K. and Christopher Bagley, eds. Race
       and Education Across Cultures. London: Heinemann,
       1975. 375 p.

             Review by Alan Ryan. New Community 4
             (Winter/Spring 1975/1976): 562.

B. Periodical Articles

1208. "About Turn." Economist 265 (22 October 1977): 19-20.

1209. Adams, F. J. "An Example of Compensatory Education."
       Education News 14: 2 (April 1973): 13-16.

1210. Anderson, C. Arnold. "Equality of Opportunity in a
       Pluralistic Society: A Theoretical Framework."
       International Review of Education 21 (1975):
       287-300.

1211. Armor, David J. "Has Busing Succeeded?" New Society
       (18 January 1973): 120-122.

1212. Ashby, B., A. Morrison and H. Butcher. "The Abilities
       and Attainments of Immigrant Children." Research
       in Education 4 (November 1970): 73-80.

1213. "Asian Boys Come Top of Form." Times Educational
       Supplement No. 3178 (30 April 1976): 4.

1214. "Aware of Prejudice." Times Educational Supplement
       No. 3080 (7 June 1974): 3.

1215. "Back to Court." Economist 245 (7 October 1972): 57.

1216.   Barnes, Gill Gorrell. "Seen But Not Heard: Gateway
        to the Future." Social Work Today 5:22 (6 Feb-
        ruary 1975): 689-692.

1217.   Bentley, Stuart. "Politics, Ethnicity and Education:
        Some Contemporary Issues." New Community 5
        (Autumn 1976): 189-195.

1218.   "Blacks Shy Away from 'O' Levels." Times Educational
        Supplement No. 3157 (5 December 1975): 13.

1219.   Blair, Carol. "Immigrant Education and Social Class."
        Race Today 3: 8 (August 1971): 259-260.

1220.   "Blocking the Bus." Economist 244 (23 September
        1972): 49-50.

1221.   "Boyle Plea for Minorities." Times Educational Supple-
        ment No. 3127 (2 May 1975): 3.

1222.   "Busing Check." Economist 243 (10 June 1972): 60-61.

1223.   "Busing In and Out." Economist 243 (24 June 1972):
        52.

1224.   "Busing in Ealing Ruled Illegal." Race Today 8: 1
        (January 1976): 5.

1225.   Byrne, E. M. "Inequality in Education: Discrimina-
        tional Resource Allocation in Schools." Educa-
        tional Review 27 (June 1975): 179-191.

1226.   Colling, Clive. "Art Education and Immigrant
        Children." Studio International 185 (June 1973):
        253-254.

1227.   "Community Relations: An Education Digest." Education
        144: 6 (9 August 1974): 1.

1228.   Cottle, T. J. "Seeing Fate With One's Own Eyes:
        School Leave Taking in Brixton." National
        Elementary Principal 55 (May 1976): 78-80.

1229.   Davey, Alfred G. "Teachers, Race and Intelligence."
        Race 15: 2 (October 1973): 195-211.

1230.   Dhondy, Farrukh. "The Black Explosion in Schools."
        Race Today 6: 2 (February 1974): 44-47.

1231.   Dove, Linda. "The Hopes of Immigrant School Children."
        New Society (10 April 1975): 63-65.

1232.   Driver, Geoffrey. "Cultural Competence, Social Power
        and School Achievement: West Indian Secondary
        School Pupils in the West Midlands." New Commu-
        nity 5 (Spring/Summer 1977): 353-359.

1233.   "EEC Boost for Immigrants." Times Educational
        Supplement No. 3189 (16 July 1976): 3.

1234.   "Education's Apartheid: Minority Groups in Great
        Britain." New Humanist 90 (October 1974): 202.

1235.   Gibbs, Norma. "Vital Statistics." Times Educational
        Supplement No. 3256 (4 November 1977): 24.

1236.   Gilroy, Beryl. "Then and Now: A Headmistress
        Reports." Community (April 1970): 9, 12.

1237.   "Government White Paper on Racial Discrimination."
        Education and Community Relations (November/
        December 1975): 1-3.

1238.   Gretton, John and Mary Jackson. "Bussing. The Wrong
        Route for Britain." Times Educational Supple-
        ment No. 3146 (19 September 1975): 14-15.

1239.   Gretton, John and Gavin Scott. "Education May Lose
        Out in Restyled Race Relations Body." Times
        Educational Supplement No. 3144 (5 September
        1975): 5.

1240.   Grubb, Martyn. "Ealing: Goodbye to Busing." Race
        Today 4: 6 (June 1972): 206-207.

1241.   Gullick, Mary. "The Educational Background of
        Vincentian Immigrants to Britain." New Commu-
        nity 5 (Spring/Summer 1977): 405-410.

1242.   Gupta, Y. P. "Educational Aspirations of Asian
        Immigrant and English School Leaver." British
        Journal of Sociology 28 (June 1977): 185-198.

1243.   Halls, W. D. "Cultural Ideals and Elitist Education
        in England." Comparative Education Review 15
        (October 1971): 317-329.

1244.   Haynes, Judith. "The Educational Assessment of
        Immigrant Pupils." Secondary Education 2
        (Autumn 1971): 5-8.

1245.   "Heads Accused of Abusing Plan to Boost Race Staff."
        Times Educational Supplement No. 3165 (30 Jan-
        uary 1976): 3.

1246.   "Heads' Eyes Opened to Worsening Racial Tension."
        Times Educational Supplement No. 3187 (2 July
        1976): 7.

1247.   Hobbs, Maurice. "Education and Race in Britain."
        Spectrum 5 (January 1973): 54-56.

1248. Hodgkinson, C. A. "Special Education Provision for
       Immigrant Children." New Era 51 (September/
       October 1970): 262-264.

1249. Holroyde, Geoffrey. "Teamwork Fits the Bill for a
       Community Enterprise." Education 146 :10
       (5 September 1975): 239-241.

1250. Hopkins, Adam. "In Place of Turmoil." Times Educa-
       tional Supplement No. 3258 (18 November 1977):
       18.

1251. "Inequality and Education." Labour Research 62
       (October 1973): 212-213.

1252. "Integrated Studies for First Year Secondary Pupils."
       Education and Community Relations (March 1973):
       4.

1253. Iqbal, Mohammed. "Education and Islam in Britain -
       A Muslim View." New Community 5 (Autumn 1976):
       397-404.

1254. Jackson, Mark. "TUC Move to Oust Front from the
       Schools." Times Educational Supplement No. 3259
       (25 November 1977): 1.

1255. Jackson, Ray. "Jacob's Ladder: The Vocational Guid-
       ance of West Indian Children." Education and
       Training 12 (December 1970): 462-466.

1256. Jensen, Arthur Robert. "Do Schools Cheat Minority
       Children?" Educational Research 14 (November
       1971): 3-28.

1257. Johnson, S. F. "The Immigrant Child in the British
       School Situation." Educational Development
       Centre Review No. 16 (Spring 1975): 12-20.

1258. Johnson, S. F. "The Immigrant Child in the British
       School Situation." Educational Development Centre
       Review No. 17 (Autumn 1975): 20-22.

1259. Kirp, David. "Come Off Race Relations Fence." Times
       Educational Supplement No. 3239 (1 July 1977):
       2.

1260. Little, Alan. "Performance of Children from Ethnic
       Minority Backgrounds in Primary Schools."
       Oxford Review of Education 1 (1975): 117-135.

1261. Lodge, Bert. "D.E.S. Opens Race Act Loopholes."
       Times Educational Supplement No. 3246 (19 August
       1977): 3.

1262. McDowell, D. "Some Organisational Issues in the
      Education of Minorities." London Educational
      Review 2: 1 (Spring 1973): 37-42.

1263. McFie, J. and J. A. Thompson. "Intellectual Abilities
      of Immigrant Children." British Journal of
      Educational Psychology 40 (November 1970):
      348-351.

1264. McGlashan, Colin. "The Black and White of Education."
      New Statesman (7 May 1971): 625.

1265. Medlicott, Paul. "The Hidden 11 Plus." New Society
      (4 July 1974): 11-13.

1266. Medlicott, Paul. "Streaming and the Comprehensive
      Schools." New Society (14 November 1974):
      414-417.

1267. "Metro Schools." Economist 242 (22 January 1972): 42.

1268. "Mixed Schooling." Ulster Commentary No. 334 (May
      1974): 3.

1269. "More is Not Enough." Economist 241 (4 December
      1971): 16-17.

1270. "Must Appreciate, They Need Basic Education."
      Education 146:23 (5 December 1975): 587.

1271. National Foundation for Educational Research in
      England and Wales. "Immigrant Pupils - What
      Happens in Schools." Forward Trends 16
      (December 1972): 108-110.

1272. "No Race to Mix." Economist 250 (30 March 1974): 48.

1273. Ottevanger, Tim. "What the Race Relations Bill
      Promises." Education 148:11 (10 September
      1976): 230-231.

1274. "Parents in Arms." Economist 252 (21 September
      1974): 57-58.

1275. "Politics Aboard." Economist 260 (3 July 1976):
      32-33.

1276. "Punjabis Learn to Think Like English." Times
      Educational Supplement No. 3152 (31 October
      1975): 11.

1277. "Race Group Approves Schools Probe." Times Educa-
      tional Supplement No. 3256 (4 November 1977): 9.

1278. "Response to Race Reports Found Lacking." Education
      144: 9 (30 August 1974): 212.

1279. Road, Alan. "A Black Boy in Search of Schooling."
       Observer Magazine (16 December 1973): 20.

1280. Rogers, Margaret. "The Education of Children of
       Immigrants in Britain." Journal of Negro
       Education 41 (Summer 1972): 255-265.

1281. "Schools in Limbo." Economist 247 (26 May 1973):
       55-56.

1282. Scott, Gavin. "Race Complaints First Must go to
       Education Secretary." Times Educational Supple-
       ment No. 3146 (19 September 1975): 6.

1283. "Second Stage Immigrant Learners: Are Schools Meeting
       the Challenge?" Education and Community Rela-
       tions (March 1972): 1-3.

1284. "Separate But Equal." Economist 242 (25 March
       1972): 50, 53.

1285. Stadlen, Frances. "Black Professor Warns of Racial
       Dangers in U. K. Schools." Times Educational
       Supplement No. 3191 (30 July 1976): 6.

1286. Stadlen, Frances. "Council Challenge Race Board's
       Ruling." Times Educational Supplement No. 3156
       (28 November 1975): 5.

1287. Stadlen, Frances. "D.E.S. Rethinks on Racial Data."
       Times Educational Supplement No. 3240 (8 July
       1977): 5.

1288. "Stalled Bus." Economist 243 (27 May 1972): 62.

1289. Stern, Vivien. "Developments in D.E.S. Policy."
       New Community 3 (Winter/Spring 1974): 131-134.

1290. Stern, Vivien. "Further Education and Community
       Relations." Liberal Education 26 (Winter
       1973/1974): 24-26.

1291. Stern, Vivien. "Minority Report." Education 149: 5
       (4 February 1977): 87.

1292. Stern, Vivien. "The Role of the Community Relations
       Commission in the Education of Minorities."
       London Educational Review 2: 1 (Spring 1973):
       49-53.

1293. "Still the Cradle." Economist 253 (26 October 1974):
       58, 61.

1294. Syer, Michael. "Lethal Statistics." Times Educa-
       tional Supplement No. 3259 (25 November 1977):
       31.

1295. Taylor, John Henry. "New Castle Upon Tyne's Asian
       Pupils Do Better Than Whites." British Journal
       of Sociology 24 (December 1973): 443-447.

1296. "Teachers' Racism Shown in N.F.E.R. Probe." Educa-
       tion 148 : 4 (23 July 1976): 75-76.

1297. "Tipping in Canarsie." Economist 245 (18 November
       1972): 57-58.

1298. Tomilson, Sally. "Race and Education in Britain,
       1960-77: An Overview of the Literature." Sage
       Race Relations Abstracts 2: 4 (November 1977):
       3-33.

1299. Townsend, Herbert Elwood Routledge. "The Contribution
       of Current Research and Development Projects."
       London Educational Review 2: 1 (Spring 1973):
       20-24.

1300. Venning, Philip. "F. E. Offers Second Chance to
       Young Blacks." Times Educational Supplement
       No. 3170 (5 March 1976): 6.

1301. Vetta, Atam. "Ethnic Difference in I.Q.: Does it
       Exist?" British Journal of Sociology 25
       (September 1974): 398-402.

1302. Wakefield, Bernard and Dennis Bainbridge. "Immigrants
       in Schools." New Society (5 December 1974):
       622.

1303. Walker, David. "The Value of a Cool Academic Look
       at Race Relations." Times Higher Education
       Supplement 211 (7 November 1975): 6.

1304. "What the Report Recommends." Times Educational
       Supplement No. 3081 (14 June 1974): 6.

1305. "Who is Educating Who? The Black Education Movement
       and the Struggle for Power." Race Today 7: 8
       (August 1975): 180-186.

1306. "Who Will Take Notice?" Times Educational Supplement
       No. 3081 (14 June 1974): 6.

1307. "Who's Afraid of Ghetto Schools: Busing in Ealing."
       Race Today 7: 1 (January 1975): 8-10.

1308. Wilke, Ingeborg. "Select Bibliography on Education
       of Children of Migrant Workers." International
       Review of Education 21 (1975): 383-400.

1309. Willke, I. "Schooling of Immigrant Children in
       West Germany, Sweden, England: The Educationally
       Disadvantaged." International Reivew of Educa-
       tion 21 (1975): 357-382.

1310. Worrell, Keith. "All Black Schools: An Answer to
       Underperformance." Race Today 4: 1 (January
       1972): 7-9.

1311. "Young Asians Keen to Stay on and Get on." Times
       Educational Supplement No. 3245 (12 August
       1977): 6.

1312. Yule, William, Michael Berger, Michael Rutter and
       Bridget Yule. "Children of West Indian Immi-
       grants - II: Intellectual Performance and Reading
       Attainment." Journal of Child Psychology and
       Psychiatry and Allied Disciplines 16 (January
       1975): 1-17.

2. EDUCATIONAL PROBLEMS

A. Books

1313. Association of Teachers of English to Pupils From
       Overseas. Birmingham Branch. Work Group on
       West Indian Pupils. Report of the Work Group
       on West Indian Pupils. H. Alex Crump Convenor
       and Editor. Birmingham: The Association, 1970.
       76 p.

1314. Boulter, Hugh. The Work of A.T.E.P.O. Chaddesden:
       Association for the Education of Pupils from
       Overseas, 1972. 16 p.

1315. Byrne, David, Bill Williamson and Barbara Fletcher.
       The Poverty of Education: A Study in the Politics
       of Opportunity. Totowa, N.J.: Rowman and Little-
       field, 1975. 204 p.

1316. Coard, Bernard. How the West Indian Child is Made
       Educationally Subnormal in the British School
       System: The Scandal of the Black Child in Schools
       in Britain. London: New Beacon Books, 1971.
       51 p.

1317. Great Britain. Community Relations Commission.
       A Time for Growing: A Handbook for Organisers
       of Summer Projects. Edited by Eric Hawkins.
       London: The Commission, 1971. 72 p.

1318.   Great Britain. Community Relations Commission.
        Reference Division. Educational Needs of
        Children from Minority Groups. London: C.R.C.,
        1974. 24 p.

1319.   Great Britain. Department of Education and Science.
        The Continuing Needs of Immigrants. London:
        H.M.S.O., 1972. 33 p.

1320.   Great Britain. Department of Education and Science.
        Education of Immigrants. London: H.M.S.O.,
        1971. 129 p.

1321.   Great Britain. Department of Education and Science.
        Educational Disadvantage and the Educational
        Needs of Immigrants: Observations on the Report
        on Education of the Select Committee on Race
        Relations and Immigration. Presented to Parlia-
        ment by the Secretary of State for Education
        and Science. London: H.M.S.O., 1974. 16 p.

1322.   Great Britain. Home Office. The Problems of Coloured
        School Leavers: Observations on the Report of
        the Select Committee on Race Relations and
        Immigration. Presented to Parliament by the
        Secretary of State for the Home Department;
        the First Secretary of State and Secretary of
        State for Employment and Productivity and the
        Secretary of State for Education and Science,
        etc. London: H.M.S.O., 1970. 16 p.

1323.   Great Britain. Parliament. House of Commons.
        Select Committee on Race Relations and Immigra-
        tion. Education/Select Committee on Race
        Relations and Immigration, Session 1972-73.
        London: H.M.S.O., 1973. 3 Vols.

        Vol. 1 Report. Vol. 2. Evidence.
        Vol. 3. Evidence and Appendices.

1324.   Great Britain. Schools Council. Cross'd With Adver-
        sity: The Education of Socially Disadvantaged
        Children in Secondary Schools. London: Evans
        Brothers, Methuen Educational, 1970. 157 p.

1325.   Halsey, A. H. E.P.A. Problems and Policies. London:
        H.M.S.O., 1972. 209 p.

1326.   Jordanhill College of Education. The Immigrant School
        Learner: A Study of Pakistani Pupils in Glasgow.
        Written by L. Dickinson, et al for the Jordanhill
        College of Education. London: National Founda-
        tion for Educational Research, 1975. 200 p.

1327. Peaker, Gilbert Fawcett. The Plowden Children Four
       Years Later. Slough: National Foundation for
       Educational Research, 1971. 50 p.

1328. Townsend, Herbert Elwood Routledge. Immigrant Pupils
       in England: The LEA Response. London: National
       Foundation for Educational Research, 1971.
       138 p.

1329. Willes, Mary. A Survey of Books About the Education
       of Immigrants. Bedford: Association for the
       Education of Pupils from Overseas, 1971. 23 p.

B. Periodical Articles

1330. Abraham, A. S. "Time to Help the Underdog." Times
       Educational Supplement No. 3096 (27 September
       1974): 23.

1331. Angus, Anne. "Vital Priorities: ILEA Document,
       Children with Special Difficulties." New
       Society (25 July 1974): 233-234.

1332. Bagley, Christopher. "Immigrant Children: A Review
       of Problems and Policy in Education." Journal
       of Social Policy 2 (October 1973): 303-315.

1333. Bergman, Carol and Bernard Coard. "Making Children
       Subnormal: Interview." Integrated Education 9
       (September 1971): 49-52.

1334. Christopher, Lancelot. "Nottingham: West Indian
       Education in Crisis." Race Today 4: 6 (June
       1972): 205-206.

1335. "Confrontation But No Gains from Plowden." Education
       145: 9 (28 February 1975): 222.

1336. Cottle, T. J. "Time Against Race." National Elemen-
       tary Principal 56 (November 1976): 65-68.

1337. Cox, Margaret. "New Tests for Immigrants." Forward
       Trends 15 (July 1971): 79.

1338. "D.E.S. Ducking Problems of Young Blacks." Times
       Educational Supplement No. 3091 (23 August
       1974): 6.

1339. Davis, Anthony. "Rising to Meet the Immigrant
       Challenge." Education 141:13 (30 March 1973):
       395-396.

1340. "Educationally Sub-Normal and Unemployed: Gloomy
       Picture of Young Immigrants." Times Educational
       Supplement No. 3133 (13 June 1975): 9.

1341. Feinmann, Jane. "Race Commission Plan a National
       Strategy to Help Black Pupils in Need." Times
       Educational Supplement No. 3187 (2 July 1976):
       7.

1342. Fethney, Valerie. "ESN Children: What the Teachers
       Say." Race Today 4:12 (December 1972): 400-
       401.

1343. Fethney, Valerie. "Our ESN Children." Race Today
       5: 4 (April 1973): 109-115.

1344. Francis, H. "Social Background, Speech and Learning
       to Read." British Journal of Educational
       Psychology 44 (November 1974): 290-299.

1345. Gray, John. "Positive Discrimination in Education:
       A Review of the British Experience." Policy
       and Politics 4: 2 (December 1975): 85-110.

1346. Gundara, Jagdish. "Tomorrow May Be Too Late." Times
       Educational Supplement No. 3230 (29 April 1977):
       21.

1347. Halsey, A. H., et al. "Reading Standards in Educa-
       tional Priority Areas." Remedial Education 8
       (1973): 16-23.

1348. Hill, Barry. "Too Many Coloured Children Still
       Dubbed ESN." Times Educational Supplement
       No. 2971 (28 April 1972): 6.

1349. Houghton, Vic. "The White Jamaican Hypothesis."
       Race 11: 3 (January 1970): 342-346.

1350. Hudson, Bob. "Must Minorities Conform." Municipal
       and Public Services Journal 82 (10 May 1974):
       566-568.

1351. Husen, Torsten. "Problems of Securing Equal Access
       to Higher Education: The Dilemma Between Equality
       and Excellence." Higher Education 5 (November
       1976): 407-422.

1352. "Ignorance is No Help." Economist 248 (29 September
       1973): 31.

1353. "Immigrants Falling Back Into New Lower Classes."
       Times Educational Supplement No. 3116 (14
       January 1975): 9.

1354.   James, Kenneth. "Overseas Students' Listening
        Problems: An Inquiry." Spoken English 8
        (September 1975): 97-106.

1355.   Lancelot, Christopher. "West Indian Education in
        Crisis." Race Today 4: 6 (June 1972):
        205-206.

1356.   Mack, Joanna. "West Indians and School." New Society
        (8 December 1977): 510-512.

1357.   Medlicott, Paul. "Special Teaching for Special
        Children." New Society (21 March 1974): 698-
        701.

1358.   Moseley, Caroline. "Getting Through to the Children."
        Multiracial School 2: 1 (Autumn 1972): 15-19.

1359.   Moseley, Caroline. "The Problems of Communication
        in the Classroom." London Educational Review
        2: 1 (Spring 1973): 43-48.

1360.   Mowat, John. "Conversation-Work with Primary School
        Children." Multiracial School 2: 2 (Spring
        1973): 7-10.

1361.   Mundy, J. H. "D.E S. Overseas Courses to Jamaica:
        1971 and 1972." New Community 2 (Summer 1973):
        237-240.

1362.   "Not Black and White." Economist 239 (12 June 1971):
        31.

1363.   Omar, Barbara. "ESN Children - Labelled for Life."
        Race Today 3: 1 (January 1971): 2.

1364.   Pearce, K. S. "West Indian Boys in Community Home
        Schools." Community Schools Gazette 68
        (September 1974): 317-339.

1365.   Pearce, K. S. "West Indian Boys in Community Home
        Schools." Community Schools Gazette 68
        (October 1974): 376-407.

1366.   Pearce, K. S. "West Indian Boys in Community Home
        Schools." Community Schools Gazette 68
        (November 1974): 449-463.

1367.   Roberts-Holmes, Joy. "Culture Shock: Remedial Teach-
        ing and the Immigrant Child.: London Educational
        Review 2: 2 (Summer 1973): 72-79.

1368.   Sadler, G. T. "The Immigrant Child in the ESN School."
        Forward Trends 16 (July 1972): 52-55.

1369.   Scipio. L. "The Black Child in the British School
        System: A Personal View." Journal of Applied
        Educational Studies 2:1 (Summer 1973): 19-23.

1370.   Scott, Gavin. "D.E.S. Unit to Help Disadvantaged."
        Times Educational Supplement No. 3092
        (30 August 1974): 3.

1371.   Scott, Gavin. "Get Facts on Immigrants: Department
        of Education and Science Urged." Times Educa-
        tional Supplement No. 3131 (30 May 1975): 4.

1372.   Scott, Gavin. "New Inspector Will Lead I.L.E.A.
        Battle for Young Blacks." Times Educational
        Supplement No. 3118 (28 February 1975): 10.

1373.   Scott, Gavin. "Too Much Emphasis on the Needs of
        Immigrants." Times Educational Supplement
        No. 3125 (18 April 1975): 5.

1374.   "Special Classes Doom Immigrants to Failure." Times
        Educational Supplement No. 3158 (12 December
        1975): 7.

1375.   "Special Service for Reading." Education 145: 8
        (21 February 1975): 200.

1376.   Stadlen, Frances. "MPs Challenge Claim that Blacks
        are Doing Better." Times Educational Supplement
        No. 3206 (12 November 1976): 6.

1377.   Thompson, Dorothea. "Children's Unorganized Games."
        Remedial Education 10 (1975): 8-12.

1378.   Watson, Peter. "Stability of IQ of Immigrant and
        Non-Immigrant Slow-Learning Pupils." British
        Journal of Educational Psychology 43 (February
        1973): 80-82.

1379.   "West Indians Fail to Catch Up - Says Researcher."
        Times Educational Supplement No. 3187 (2 July
        1976): 7.

1380.   "Why the West Indians Feel Aggrieved." Education
        149:13 (1 April 1977): 230.

1381.   "Why West Indians Deserve Priority." Education
        143:18 (3 May 1974): 493.

1382.   Wight, James. "Testing West Indian Children." Times
        Educational Supplement No. 2854 (30 January
        1970): 2.

1383.   Willey, Richard. "Education: Supplementary Service
        for West Indian Pupils Set Up." New Community 2
        (Spring 1973): 210-212.

3. ENGLISH AS A SECOND LANGUAGE

A. Books

1384.   Andrews, John. Say What You Mean in English.
        Sunsbury-on Thames: Nelson, 1977. 114 p.

1385.   Bentley, John David. English Language Practice for
        West Indians. London: Hulton Educational, 1972.
        Unpaged.

1386.   Candlin, Christopher and June Derrick. Language.
        London: Community Relations Commission, 1972.
        67 p.

1387.   Candlin, Christopher and June Derrick. Language.
        Rev. 2d ed. London: Community Relations Commis-
        sion, 1973. 67 p.

1388.   Centre for Information on Language Teaching and
        Research. Language and Immigrants: Sources of
        Information and Teaching Materials. London:
        The Centre, 1972. 11 p.

1389.   Giuseppe, Undine. Nelson's New West Indian Readers.
        London: Nelson, 1971. 122 p.

1390.   Gray, Cecil and Joan Baker. Language for Living:
        A Caribbean English Course. Harlow: Longman,
        1971. 245 p.

1391.   Gray, Cecil. Language for Living: A Caribbean
        English Course. Rev. ed. Harlow: Longman,
        1976. 184 p.

1392.   Great Britain. Community Relations Commission.
        Evidence From the Community Relations Commission
        to the Committee of Enquiry into Reading and the
        Use of English. London: The Commission, 1974.
        10 p.

1393.   Great Britain. Community Relations Commission.
        Education Department. Voluntary Language
        Tutoring Schemes: A List of Organisers. London:
        The Commission, 1973. 11 leaves.

1394.   Great Britain. Department of Education and Science.
        A Language for Life: Report of the Committee of
        Enquiry Appointed by the Secretary of State
        for Education and Science Under the Chairmanship
        of Sir Alan Bullock; Department of Education and
        Science. London: H.M.S.O., 1975. 609 p.

1395. Great Britain. Schools Council. Immigrant Children
       in Infant Schools. London: Evans/Methuen
       Educational, 1970. 63 p.

1396. Great Britain. Schools Council. Teaching English
       to West Indian Children: The Research Stage of
       the Project. London: Evans, 1970. 72 p.

1397. Harrison, Brian. English As a Second and Foreign
       Language. London: Edward Arnold, 1973. 111 p.

1398. Jupp, Thomas Cyprian and Susan Hodlin. Industrial
       English: An Example of Theory and Practice in
       Functional Language Teaching. London: Heinemann
       Educational, 1975. 330 p.

1399. McEwen, Elizabeth Clare, C. V. Gipps and R. Sumner.
       Language Proficiency in the Multi-Racial Junior
       School: A Comparative Study. Windsor: NFER,
       1975. 113 p.

           Review by Nova Berrie. New Community 4
           (Winter/Spring 1975): 562-563.

1400. Mobbs, Michael C. Meeting Their Needs: An Account
       of the Language Tuition Schemes for Ethnic
       Minority Women. (Written) On Behalf of the
       Community Relations Commission's Education
       Department and Reference Division. London:
       Community Relations Commission, Reference and
       Technical Services Division, 1977. 64 p.

1401. Morgan, Marjories Lloyd and J. J. Percil. Vital
       English: A Pre-Intermediate Course. London:
       Macmillan, 1977. 152 p.

1402. National Union of Teachers. A Language for Life:
       The NUT's Commentary on the Bullock Report.
       London: NUT, 1976. 54 p.

1403. Readhead, Pamela. English Lessons at Work Pay Divi-
       dends. London: Runnymede Trust, 1972. 3 p.

1404. Scope: An Introductory English Course for Immigrant
       Children. London: Books for Schools, Ltd. for
       the Schools Council; Harlow: Distributed by
       Longman, 1970. 90 p.

1405. Scope: Pronunciation for Immigrant Children from
       India, Pakistan, Cyprus and Italy. London:
       Published for the School's Council by Books for
       Schools, Ltd., 1971. 164 p.

B. Periodical Articles

1406. Blake, H. E. "Written Composition in English Primary
         Schools." Elementary English 48 (October 1971):
         605-616.

1407. Bolt, S. "English in Further Education." Trends in
         Education 22 (April 1971): 34-39.

1408. Bradley, Sylvia. "English As an Acquired Language:
         To What End?" Spoken English 10 (January 1977):
         8-10.

1409. Brazier, Carolyn. "Teaching West Indian Children
         English." Special Education 59: 2 (June 1970):
         6-10.

1410. Brennan, M. B. "Centres of Confidence: Language
         Centres for England's New-Comers." Elementary
         School Journal 75 (December 1974): 168-171.

1411. Clark, E. P. "Mode Three GCE: 'O' Level English
         Language." Forum for the Discussion of New
         Trends in Education 18 (Spring 1971): 50-53.

1412. Clemens, Martyn. "Pathway to English." Trends in
         Education 19 (July 1970): 21-24.

1413. Clyne, Peter. "On the Fringes." Adult Education 44
         (July 1971): 94-99.

1414. Cotterell, Arthur. "Language for All the Community."
         Technical Journal 11: 2 (March 1973):14-15.

1415. Davis, D. "Everybody's Language." Times Educational
         Supplement No. 3258 (18 November 1977): 17.

1416. Denley, Gerald. "Teaching English to Indian Immi-
         grants." Higher Education Journal 17 (Spring
         1970): 17-20.

1417. Devlin, Tim. "Young Tariq Hits the Language Barrier
         Head On." Times Educational Supplement No. 2868
         (8 May 1970): 8.

1418. Dunn, Alison. "The Second Tongue." Education and
         Training 15 (April 1973): 131-132.

1419. Durojaiye, S. M. "Social Context of Immigrant Pupils
         Learning English." Educational Research 13
         (June 1971): 179-184.

1420. Edwards, Viv K. "Effect of Dialect on the Comprehen-
         sion of West Indian Children." Educational
         Research 18 (February 1976): 83-95.

1421.   "English Language Skills: Are Schools Failing?"
        Multiracial School 2: 2 (Spring 1973): 11-18.

1422.   Garvie, Edie. "Language Does Not 'Rub Off'." Times
        Educational Supplement No. 2907 (5 February
        1971): 4.

1423.   Garvie, Edie. "Teaching English As a Second Language
        at Pre-School Level." English in Education
        10: 1 (Spring 1976): 38-44.

1424.   Gipps, Caroline and Elizabeth McEwen. "Tests of
        English for Immigrant Children: Patterns of
        Performance." Trends in Education 33 (May
        1974): 31-35.

1425.   Griffiths, P. "Language Policy Across the Curriculum."
        Forum for the Discussion of New Trends in
        Education 12 (Spring 1970): 51-53.

1426.   Hankins, Brian. "Unstreamed English in a Senior High
        School." Forum for the Discussion of New Trends
        in Education 13 (Spring 1971): 58-59.

1427.   Heaton, J. B. and A. K. Pugh. "Real Test of Success
        is How Well They Read English." Times Higher
        Education Supplement No. 178 (14 March 1975):
        10.

1428.   "Help Yourself to English: BBC Radio 4 Series Designed
        to Improve Fluency in Spoken English." Educa-
        tion and Community Relations (July/August 1971):
        4-5.

1429.   Hinchliffe, Margaret. "Teaching English to Asian Men
        and Women." New Community 4 (Autumn 1975):
        342-344.

1430.   James, C. "Language Factors in the Education of
        Coloured Peoples in Britain." Modern Language
        Journal 54 (October 1970): 420-423.

1431.   James, Kenneth and Lloyd Mullen. "English As She is
        Heard: Aural Difficulties Experienced by Foreign
        Learners." English Language Teaching Journal 28
        (November 1973): 15-22.

1432.   Jordan, Robert R. and R. Mackay. "Overseas Students
        Have Difficulty with English." Times Higher
        Education Supplement No. 86 (8 June 1973): 8.

1433. Jordan, Robert R. and R. Mackay. "A Survey of the
       Spoken English Problems of Overseas Postgraduate
       Students at the Universities of Manchester and
       Newcastle Upon Tyne." Newcastle Institute.
       Education Journal 25 (November 1973): 39-46.

1434. Kirkcaldy, John. "Patois, Education and Jamaica."
       New Society (4 October 1973): 15-16.

1435. Levine, Josie. "An Outline Proposal for Testing
       Communicative Competence." English Language
       Teaching Journal 30 (January 1976): 128-135.

1436. McDonald, Joan E. "Commonwealth Immigrants in Adult
       Education." Trends in Education 30 (April
       1973): 33-38.

1437. Mace, Jane and Kate Harding. "Unreasonable Demands."
       Times Educational Supplement No. 3241 (15 July
       1977): 15.

1438. McEldowney, Patricia L. "Basic Working English for
       the Second Language Learner." Ideas No. 31
       (July 1975): 20-22.

1439. McEwen, Elizabeth and Caroline Gipps. "Tests of
       English for Immigrant Children." Multiracial
       School 2: 2 (Spring 1973): 22-24.

1440. McLean, Alan C. "The Uses of Follow-up: Television
       in the Classroom." English Language Teaching
       Journal 29 (July 1975): 303-309.

1441. Makins, Virginia. "English is Everybody's Job, Says
       Bullock." Times Educational Supplement No. 3117
       (21 February 1975): 3.

1442. Moorman, Paul. "Language for Life in the Old Country:
       EEC Pilot Project." Times Educational Supplement
       No. 3203 (22 October 1976): 10.

1443. Mundy, J. H. "Language Teaching and the Young Immi-
       grant." Trends in Education 20 (October 1970):
       21-26.

1444. Noble, R. W., et al. "EFL." Times Educational
       Supplement No. 3245 (12 August 1977): 21-28.

1445. Norbum, Roger. "Provision for the Coloured Immigrant."
       Adult Education 44 (January 1972): 298-302, 307.

1446. Norris, R. A. "Developing a Curriculum in English
       for West Indian Children." Urban Education 6
       (July 1971): 243-259.

1447. Parrott, F. "English As a Second Dialect." Trends
       in Education 3 (June 1975): 40-44.

1448. Pye, Michael. "Pidgins Come Home to Roost." Times
       Educational Supplement No. 3197 (10 September
       1976): 10.

1449. Radice, Francis. "Using Board Games." English
       Language Teaching 27 (June 1973): 271-276.

1450. Rudd, Elizabeth M. "Language for Immigrant Children."
       English Language Teaching 24 (May 1970):
       260-269.

1451. Rudd, Elizabeth M. "Language Tests for Immigrant
       Children." Multiracial School 1: 1 (Autumn
       1971): 26-29.

1452. Sinclair, J. M. "Integration of Language and Litera-
       ture in the English Curriculum." Educational
       Review 23 (June 1971): 220-234.

1453. Stanton, Michael and G. B. Shah: "Assessment of Non-
       English Speaking Immigrant Pupils." Remedial
       Education 9 (1974): 105-108.

1454. Stern, Vivien. "Immigrant Groups in the Community."
       Coombe Lodge Reports 7: 6 (1974): 383-388.

1455. Tough, Joan, et al. "Modern Language Teaching."
       Times Educational Supplement No. 2909 (19 Feb-
       ruary 1971): 33-39, 42-48.

1456. Townsend, Bert. "Holiday School for Immigrant
       Children." Community (October 1970): 15-16.

1457. Townsend, Bert and Elaine Brittan. "Immigrant Pupils-
       What Happens in School?" Multiracial School 2: 2
       (Spring 1973): 25-28.

1458. "V.S.O. Recruits Help Immigrants at Home." Times
       Educational Supplement No. 3091 (23 August
       1974): 4.

1459. Walker, George. "Sixth Form Tutors." Times Educa-
       tional Supplement No. 2892 (23 October 1970):
       26.

1460. Wallwork, Jean. "Language Teaching for Children from
       Immigrant Groups." Education for Teaching 90
       (Spring 1973): 24-29.

1461. Wight, James. "Dialect in School: Jamaican Creole."
       Educational Review 24 (November 1971): 47-58.

1462. Wilson, Amrit. "Asian Soap Opera." <u>Times Educa-
       tional Supplement</u> No. 3261 (9 December 1977):
       55.

1463. Yarmohammadi, Lotfollah. "Universal versus Language -
       Specific Tests." <u>English Language Teaching
       Journal</u> 29 (October 1974): 65-68.

4. MULTI-RACIAL EDUCATION

A. Books

1464. Arrowsmith, Pat. <u>The Colour of Six Schools</u>. London:
       Friends Community Relations Committee, Community
       and Race Relations Unit of the British Council
       of Churches, 1972. 132 p.

1465. Barnes, Jack, ed. <u>Curriculum Innovation in London's
       E.P.A.'s</u>. London: H.M.S.O., 1975. 289 p.

1466. Bolton, Felicity and Jennie Laishley. <u>Education for
       a Multi-Racial Britain</u>. London: Fabian Society,
       1972. 20 p.

1467. Day, Allison. <u>The Library in the Multi-Racial
       Secondary School: A Caribbean Book List</u>. London:
       The School Library Association, 1971. 6 p.

1468. <u>Education in Multi-Racial Schools: The Record of a
       Conference Organised by the Advisory Centre for
       Education</u>. London: Ginn, 1970. 50 p.

1469. Elkin, Judith. <u>Books for the Multi-Racial Classroom:
       A Select List of Children's Books Showing the
       Background of India, Pakistan and the West Indies</u>.
       Compiled in Collaboration with Birmingham Public
       Libraries. Birmingham: Library Association,
       1971. 67 p.

1470. Elkin, Judith. <u>Books for the Multi-Racial Classroom:
       A Select List of Children's Books Showing the
       Backgrounds of the Indian Sub-Continent and the
       West Indies</u>. 2d rev. ed. London, National
       Book League; Birmingham: Library Association,
       Youth Libraries Group, 1976. 112 p.

1471. Giles, Raymond. <u>The West Indian Experience in British
       Schools - Multi-Racial Education and Social
       Disadvantage in London</u>. London: Heimemann,
       1977. 170 p.

1472.   Great Britain. Community Relations Commission.
        Education for a Multi-Cultural Society: A
        Bibliography for Teachers. London: The Commis-
        sion, 1972. 35 p.

1473.   Great Britain. Community Relations Commission.
        Education for a Multi-Cultural Society: Audio-
        Visual Aids for Teachers. London: The Commis-
        sion, 1974. 26 p.

1474.   Great Britain. Community Relations Commission.
        Advisory Committee on Education. Education for
        a Multi-Cultural Society. London: The Commis-
        sion, 1970. 50 leaves.

1475.   Great Britain. Community Relations Commission.
        Advisory Committee on Education. Education for
        a Multi-Cultural Society. Rev. 2d ed. London:
        Community Relations Commisison, 1973. 67 p.

1476.   Hill, Janet. Books for Children; Homelands of Immi-
        grants in Britain: Africa, Cyprus, India and
        Pakistan, Ireland, Italy, Poland, Turkey, the
        West Indies. London: Institute of Race Relations;
        Distributed by Research Publications Services,
        1971. 85 p.

1477.   MacNeal, Julia and Margaret Rogers, eds. The Multi-
        Racial School: A Professional Perspective.
        Harmondsworth: Penguin, 1971. 154 p.

1478.   Morris, Sam. The Case and the Course: A Treatise
        on Black Studies. London: Committee on Black
        Studies, 1973. 37 p.

1479.   Scott, Rachel. A Wedding Man is Nicer Than Cats,
        Miss: A Teacher at Work With Immigrant Children.
        Newton Abbot: David and Charles, 1971. 192 p.

1480.   Scott, Rachel. A Wedding Man is Nicer Than Cats,
        Miss: A Teacher at Work With Immigrant Children.
        New York: St. Martin's Press, 1971. 192 p.

1481.   Taylor, Francine. Race, School and Community: A
        Study of Research and Literature on Education
        in Multi-Racial Britain. Slough: National
        Foundation for Educational Research, 1974.
        200 p.

        Review in New Community 3 (Summer 1974): 301.

1482. Townsend, Herbert Elwood Routledge and Elaine Mary
          Brittan. Multi-Racial Education, Need and Inno-
          vation: The Preliminary Report of the Schools
          Council's Education for a Multiracial Society
          Project. London: Evans; Methuen for the Schools
          Council, 1973. 104 p.

1483. Townsend, Herbert Ellwood Routledge and Elaine Mary
          Brittan. Organisation in a Multiracial School.
          Windsor: National Foundation for Educational
          Research, 1972. 172 p.

1484. Widlake, Paul. The Multiracial Class. London: Evans
          Bros., 1973. 40 p.

1485. World Religions: Aids for Teachers. London: Community
          Relations Commission, 1972. 138 p.

1486. World Religions: Aids for Teachers. Edited by Peter
          Woodward. 2d ed. London: Community Relations
          Commission, 1973. 144 p.

B. Periodical Articles

1487. Bagley, Christopher and Gajendra K. Verma. "Some
          Effects of Teaching Designed to Promote Under-
          standing of Racial Issues in Adolescence."
          Journal of Moral Education 1 (June 1972):
          231-238.

1488. Bennett, Robert. "Teaching Materials for Social
          Education." Multiracial School 1: 1 (Autumn
          1971): 21-25.

1489. Bennett, Robert. "Teaching Materials for Social
          Education." Multiracial School 1: 2 (Spring
          1972): 17-20.

1490. Bergman, Carol. "Colonial Colleges." Times Educa-
          tional Supplement No. 2894 (6 November 1970):
          53.

1491. Bhatnagar, Joti. "Teaching Race Tolerance." Race
          Today 2: 6 (June 1970): 171-173.

1492. "Black or White." Economist 255 (19 April 1975):
          14-15.

1493. Booth, John. "Black Skins, White Schools."
          Libertarian Education No. 23 (Winter 1977):
          3-4.

1494. Brittan, Elaine Mary. "Multi-Racial Education-2.
       Teacher Opinion on Aspects of School Life.
       Part 1: Changes in Curriculum and School
       Organisation." Educational Research 18
       (February 1976): 96-107.

1495. Brittan, Elaine Mary. "Multi-Racial Education-2.
       Teacher Opinion on Aspects of School Life.
       Part 2: Pupils and Teachers." Educational
       Research 18 (June 1976): 182-191.

1496. Brittan, Elaine Mary. "Organisation in Multi-Racial
       Schools." Journal of Applied Educational
       Studies 2: 1 (Summer 1973): 27-30.

1497. Burgin, Trevor. "Education in a Multi-Racial
       Huddersfield." Journal of Applied Educational
       Studies 2: 1 (Summer 1973): 31-34.

1498. Cameron, Sue. "Can Church Schools Fit into a Multi-
       Racial Society?" Times Educational Supplement
       No. 3010 (2 February 1973): 10.

1499. Cole, W. Owen. "Dreaming of a White Christmas."
       Times Educational Supplement No. 3262 (16 Dec-
       ember 1977): 24.

1500. Conti, Jon. "Bilingual and Bicultural Education -
       An Approach to Socio-Cultural Revolution." Race
       Today 3: 7 (July 1971): 233-234.

1501. Crick, Bernard and Sally Jenkinson. "Good Intentions
       and Muddled Thinking." Times Educational
       Supplement No. 2894 (6 November 1970): 20, 53.

1502. "Curriculum Change: New Approach to General Studies
       in a Multi-Racial School." Education and
       Community Relations (December 1971): 1-2.

1503. Davies, Graham. "Education for a Multi-Racial
       Britain." Contemporary Review 22 (November
       1972): 225-228.

1504. Davies, Margaret. "Different Approaches to Teaching
       About Race Relations in Schools and Colleges in
       Manchester and Stratford." Education and
       Community Relations (May 1971): 2-3.

1505. Day, Alison. "The Library in the Multi-Racial
       Secondary School: A Caribbean Book List." School
       Librarian 19 (September 1971): 197-203.

1506. Day, Alison. "Literature in the Multi-Racial
       Secondary School." Secondary Education 2
       (Autumn 1971): 9-12.

1507. Doe, Bob. "Race Understanding Questions Added
       Curriculum Review." Times Educational Supple-
       ment No. 3260 (2 December 1977): 3.

1508. Dove, Linda. "Learning About Race in School - Some
       Pupils' Views." New Era 56 (April 1975): 71-75.

1509. Dunning, Eric. "The Course on Race Relations for
       Sociology Undergraduates at Leicester University."
       Race 13: 2 (October 1971): 215-231.

1510. Edgington, David. "Education for a Multi-Racial
       Society - Schools' Council Project." Spectrum 7
       (May 1975): 7-8.

1511. "Education for a Multi-Racial Society Project."
       New Era 56 (April 1975): 81-82.

1512. "Ever So Coloured." Times Educational Supplement
       No. 3189 (16 July 1976): 15-16.

1513. Grimes, E. J. and Anthony Locke. "Adult Education
       and an Immigrant Community. 1. Life in a
       Resettlement Camp (by) E. J. Grimes. 2. Life in
       a New Community (by) Anthony Locke." Adult
       Education 46 (September 1973): 175-180.

1514. Guest, Juliet. "Playgroup in Walsall." Multiracial
       School 2: 3 (Summer 1973): 7-9.

1515. Hanks, Betty C. "The Multi-Racial School." Trends
       in Education 3 (September 1975): 10-14.

1516. Hodges, Lucy. "ILEA Moves to Improve Race Relations."
       Times Educational Supplement No. 3252 (7 October
       1977): 3.

1517. Hogbin, Jack W. G. "Moral Education for a Multi-
       Cultural Society." Learning for Living 10: 2
       (November 1970): 20-23.

1518. "How Teachers Can Help." Times Educational Supple-
       ment No. 3170 (5 March 1976): 6.

1519. "The Immigrant Revisited." Education 148: 1
       (2 July 1976): 6.

1520. Jackson, Mark. "No Racial Prejudice in Reverse."
       Times Educational Supplement No. 3165
       (30 January 1976): 4.

1521. Jeffcoate, Robert. "Curriculum Planning in Multi-
       Racial Education." Educational Research 18
       (June 1976): 192-200.

1522. Jeffcoate, Robert. "Schools and Prejudice." Trends
      in Education 3 (September 1975): 3-9.

1523. Jeffcoate, Robert. "Schools Council Project - Educa-
      tion for a Multi-Racial Society." Multiracial
      School 3: 1 (Autumn 1974): 7-12.

1524. Jelinek, Milena M. "Multi-Racial Education-3. Pupils'
      Attitudes to the Multi-Racial School." Educa-
      tional Research 19 (February 1977): 129-141.

1525. Khan, Nawab. "Multi-Racial Riches." Times Educa-
      tional Supplement No. 3233 (20 May 1977): 27.

1526. Kirkwood, Kenneth. "Ethnic, Cultural and Racial
      Pluralism: Awareness, Education and Policy."
      Oxford Review of Education 1 (1975): 107-116.

1527. Lewis, E. Glyn. "Immigrants: Their Languages and
      Development." Trends in Education 19 (July
      1970): 25-32.

1528. Midwinter, Eric. "The E.P.A. Community School."
      Urban Education 8 (April 1973): 7-19.

1529. "Mrs. Williams's Adviser Explains the DES Strategy."
      Education 149:14 (8 April 1977): 245.

1530. Morris, Sam. "Black Studies in Britain." New
      Community 2 (Summer 1974): 245-248.

1531. Multi-Racial Education: Symposium. Forum for the
      Discussion of New Trends in Education 20
      (Autumn 1977): 1-18.

1532. Mundy, J. H. "Teaching About the Third World."
      Trends in Education 3 (September 1975): 15-18.

1533. Munns, Roger. "A Full Time Course in Literacy and
      Numeracy for Unemployed Adults from Ethnic
      Minorities." Adult Education 49 (July 1976):
      75-81.

1534. "Nursery Staff Urged to Take a Multi-Racial Interest."
      Times Educational Supplement No. 3167 (13
      February 1976): 12.

1535. Parker, Bob, et al. "Will it Happen Here." Times
      Educational Supplement No. 3145 (12 September
      1975): 24-25.

1536. Parkinson, J. P. and Barry MacDonald. "Teaching
      Race Neutrally." Race 13: 3 (January 1972):
      299-313.

1537. Parsons, Dennis. "Education in a Multi-Racial
          Society." Secondary Education 5 (June 1975):
          39-41.

1538. "A Policy for Multi-Racial Schools: Commission Calls
          for More Resources." Education and Community
          Relations (June 1973): 1-2.

1539. Praeger, Peter. "Minority Languages." Times Educa-
          tional Supplement No. 3233 (20 May 1977): 27.

1540. "Race and the Role of the L.E.A.'s." Education
          149: 9 (4 March 1977): 159.

1541. "Reading Scheme for Multi-Racial Classes." Education
          and Community Relations (December 1972): 1-2.

1542. Rennie, John. "The Multi-Racial School." Secondary
          Education 2 (Autumn 1971): 3-4.

1543. Rhoden, Ernest L. "Multi-Racial School in England:
          Grove Junior School, Wolverhampton, England."
          Integrated Education 9 (November/December
          1971): 43-47.

1544. Richards, J. Kelvyn. "More Than Two Cultures." Times
          Educational Supplement No. 3261 (9 December
          1977): 25.

1545. Richardson, Stephen A. and A. Green. "When is Black
          Beautiful? Coloured and White Children's
          Reaction to Skin Colour." British Journal of
          Educational Psychology 41 (February 1971):
          62-69.

1546. Roberts, C. D. "Education in a Multi-Cultural
          Society." New Community 2 (Summer 1973):
          230-236.

1547. Rogers, Margaret. "Education in a Multi-Ethnic
          Britain: A Teacher's Eye View." New Community 2
          (Summer 1973): 221-229.

1548. Rudin, Jeff. "Black Studies Should Start at the
          Right End." Teacher 21: 4 (22 September 1972):
          12.

1549. "Runnymede Prods L.E.A.'s to Teach in Mother Tongue."
          Education 147:15 (9 April 1976): 348.

1550. Scott, S. E. "Curriculum Development in Ethnic
          Studies." Journal of Education 4: 4 (Summer
          1977): 21-24.

1551. Singh, P. "City Centre Schools and Community
      Relations." Trends in Education 33 (May
      1974): 27-30.

1552. "Social Education - New Teaching Materials for
      Secondary Schools." Education and Community
      Relations (April 1974): 1-3.

1553. "Talking of Race." Times Educational Supplement
      No. 3155 (21 November 1975): 22-23.

1554. Thomas, K. C. "Race in the Curriculum." New Era 56
      (September/October 1975): 10-13.

1555. Verma, Gajendra K. and Barry MacDonald. "Teaching
      Race in Schools: Some Effects on the Attitudinal
      and Sociometric Patterns of Adolescents."
      Race 13: 2 (October 1971): 187-202.

1556. Woodroffe, Bev. "Black Identity and Curriculum
      Change." New Era 56 (April 1975): 79-81.

1557. Woodward, Peter. "Teaching World Religions in a
      Multi-Racial Context." Secondary Education 2
      (Autumn 1971): 13-16.

1558. Worrall, Mary. "Ethnic Studies and Community Studies."
      Multiracial School 3: 1 (Autumn 1974): 17-19.

5. TEACHER TRAINING

A. Books

1559. Birmingham Educational Priority Area Project. A First
      Look at Asians: An Introduction to the Languages
      and Customs of Asian Immigrant Children for
      Teachers-in-Training, Probationary Teachers and
      Others Encountering Asian Children for the First
      Time. Birmingham: Birmingham Educational
      Priority Area Project, 1972. 4 p.

1560. Dakin, Julian. A Survey of English Courses for
      Immigrant Teachers. A Project Recommended by
      the Committee on Research and Development in
      Modern Languages Financed by the Department of
      Education and Science and Conducted by the Centre
      for Information on Language Teaching in 1969-70.
      London: Centre for Information on Language
      Teaching, 1971. 88 p.

1561. Great Britain. Community Relations Commission.
       In-Service Education of Teachers in Multi-Racial
       Areas: An Evaluation of Current Practice.
       London: The Commission, 1974. 58 p.

1562. Great Britain. Community Relations Commission.
       Practical Suggestions for Teachers of Immigrant
       Children. 3d ed. London: The Commission, 1970.
       32 p.

1563. Great Britain. Community Relations Commission.
       Teacher Education for a Multi-Cultural Society:
       The Report of a Joint Working Party of the
       Community Relations Commission and the Associa-
       tion of Teachers in Colleges and Departments
       of Education. London: The Commission, 1974.
       96 p.

1564. Hill, David. Teaching in Multi-Racial Schools: A
       Guidebook. London: Methuen, 1976. 136 p.

1565. Hobbs, Maurice. Teaching in a Multi-Racial Society.
       London: Association of Christian Teachers;
       Inter-School Christian Fellowship, 1976. 83 p.

                       B. Periodical Articles

1566. "Best Way to Help Immigrants." Times Educational
       Supplement No. 3100 (25 October 1974): 5.

1567. Brand, J. "Development of a Special Course for
       Immigrant Teachers." Educational Review 24
       (February 1974): 145-154.

1568. Davey, Alfred.G. "Racial Awareness in Children and
       Teacher Education." Education for Teaching
       No. 97 (Summer 1975): 25-33.

1569. Derrick, June. "The Language Needs of Immigrant
       Children." London Educational Review 2: 1
       (Spring 1973): 25-30.

1570. Dumon, W. A. "Educational Adaptation of Permanent
       Migrants." International Migration 12 (1974):
       270-292.

1571. "Failing to Meet the Needs of Blacks." Times Educa-
       tional Supplement No. 3075 (3 May 1974): 7.

1572. Griffiths, Ceri. "An Exercise in Non-Stereotyping."
       Education for Teaching No. 94 (Summer 1974):
       54-58.

1573.   Haines, John. "Teacher Training in Community Rela-
        tions." Multiracial School 2: 3 (Summer
        1973): 1-6.

1574.   Jackson, Mark. "The DES did not Seem to Know Much
        About Us." Times Educational Supplement
        No. 3137 (18 July 1975): 8-9.

1575.   Jones, Hywel. "Language Testing: A Strategy for
        Teaching." English Language Teaching Journal 30
        (October 1975): 56-61.

1576.   Millins, Ken. "The Preparation of Teachers to
        Educate Minority Groups." London Educational
        Review 2: 1 (Spring 1973): 5-11.

1577.   Shillian, David. "A Diploma in Education for a
        Multi-Cultural Society." New Community 4
        (Autumn 1975): 345-348.

1578.   "Staff Too Conservative." Times Educational Supple-
        ment No. 3187 (2 July 1976): 7.

1579.   "Training: Multi-Cultural Studies Urged for Teachers."
        Education 144: 1 (5 July 1974): 5.

1580.   Willey, Richard. "Teacher Education for a Multi-
        Cultural Society." Education for Teaching No. 97
        (Summer 1975): 34-39.

1581.   Willey, Richard. "Teacher Education for a Multi-
        Cultural Society." New Era 56 (April 1975):
        76-78.

1582.   Willey, Richard. "Teacher Training for a Multi-
        Cultural Society in the U.K." International
        Review of Education 21 (1975): 335-345. •

6. RACIAL DISCRIMINATION IN TEXTBOOKS

A. Books

1583.   Curry, Jennifer. Investigation Into the Colour
        Problem. Glasgow: Blackie, 1974. 43 p.

1584.   Foster, John L. Black and White: An Anthology.
        Exeter: Wheaton, 1976. 83 p.

1585.   Jay, Eric. Racial Discrimination. London: S.C.M.
        Press for the Christian Education Movement,
        1971. 32 p.

1586. Proctor, Chris. Racist Textbooks. London: National
          Union of Students, 1975. 41 p.

1587. Racist and Sexist Images in Children's Books. London:
          Writers and Readers Publishing Cooperative,
          1975. 49 p.

B. Periodical Articles

1588. "Bias in Textbooks: Survey by CRCs Suggest." Educa-
          tion and Community Relations (January 1972): 5.

1589. Cameron, Sue. "Prejudice on the Printed Page."
          Teacher 18:21 (19 November 1971): 3.

1590. Corbett, Anne. "Coloured Schoolbooks." New Society
          (28 October 1971): 834-835.

1591. Glendenning, F. J. "Attitudes to Colonialism and
          Race in British and French History Textbooks."
          History of Education 3: 2 (Summer 1974): 57-72.

1592. Glendenning, F. J. "Racial Stereotyping in History
          Textbooks." Race Today 3: 2 (February 1971):
          52-54.

1593. Glendenning, F. J. "School History Textbooks and
          Racial Attitudes, 1804-1911 (sic; i.e. 1804-
          1969)." Journal of Educational Administration
          and History 5: 2 (July 1973): 33-44.

1594. Jeffrey, Peter. "Books on the Black List." Special
          Education 61:1 (March 1972): 12.

1595. Parker, Jim. "Textbooks and Racial Prejudice: A
          Strategy for Change." Multiracial School 2: 1
          (Autumn 1972): 8-11.

1596. Price, Christopher. "Whiter Than White Textbooks."
          New Statesman (29 October 1971): 582.

1597. Townshend, John Rowe. "Racism and Sexism in Children's
          Books." New Community 5 (Summer 1976): 157-160.

XI.

HOUSING

A. BOOKS

1598. Bush, Martha, comp. Immigrant Housing. Compiled by
        Martha Bush for the Greater London Council
        Research Library. London: Greater London
        Council, 1976. 15 p.

1599. Buying a House; Building Societies: A Report from the
        Employment Working Party of the Co-ordinating
        Committee for the Welfare of the Evacuees from
        Uganda. London: Runnymede Trust, 1973. 3 p.

1600. Doherty, J. "Immigrants in London: A Study of the
        Relationship Between Spatial Structure and
        Social Structure." Doctoral dissertation,
        London School of Economics, University of London,
        1973.

1601. Duke, Christopher. Colour and Rehousing: A Study of
        Redevelopment in Leeds. London: Institute of
        Race Relations, 1970. 78 p.

1602. Fieller, N. R. J. "The Residential Segregation of
        Immigrants in Birmingham." M. Sc. thesis, Depart-
        ment of Mathematical Statistics, University of
        Birmingham, 1970.

1603. Great Britain. Commission for Racial Equality.
        Housing Need Among Ethnic Minorities: Comments
        on the Consultative Document on Housing Policy
        Presented to Parliament by the Secretary of
        State for the Environment and the Secretary of
        State for Wales. London: The Commission, 1977.
        9 p.

1604. Great Britain. Community Relations Commission.
       Reference Division. The Response to the Select
       Committee on Race Relations and Immigration.
       London: The Commission, 1974. 54 p.

1605. Great Britain. Department of Environment. Race
       Relations and Housing: Observation on the Report
       on Housing of the Select Committee on Race
       Relations and Immigration. Presented to Parlia-
       ment by the Secretary of State for the Depart-
       ment of Environment. London: H.M.S.O., 1975.
       23 p.

1606. Great Britain. Parliament. House of Commons. Select
       Committee on Race Relations and Immigration.
       Housing: Report of the Select Committee on Race
       Relations and Immigration, Session 1970/71.
       London: H.M.S.O., 1971. 3 Vols.

       Vol. 1. Report Vol. 2. Evidence
       Vol. 3. Evidence, Documents and Index.

1607. Hay, Hope. Friends and Neighbours in Islington: The
       Story of Friends Neighbourhood House. London:
       Race Relations Committee of the Social Respon-
       sibility Council of the Society of Friends,
       1972. 26 p.

1608. Hill, Clifford. Immigration and Integration: A Study
       of the Settlement of Coloured Minorities in
       Britain. Oxford: Pergamon, 1970. 214 p.

1609. Housing in Multi-Racial Areas. Prepared by a Working
       Party of Housing Directors. London: Community
       Relations Commission, 1976. 56 p.

1610. Installment Credit in Britain: A Report from the
       Employment Working Party of the Co-ordinating
       Committee for the Welfare of the Evacuees from
       Uganda. London: Runnymede Trust, 1973. 3 p.

1611. Johnston, Robert John. Urban Residential Patterns.
       London: Bell, 1971. 383 p.

1612. Lee, Trevor R. "Concentration and Dispersal: A
       Study of West Indian Residential Patterns in
       London, 1961-71." Doctoral dissertation,
       University of London, 1973.

1613. Lee, Trevor R. Race and Residence: The Concentration
       and Dispersal of Immigrants in London. Oxford:
       Clarendon Press, 1977. 193 p.

1614. Lomas, Glenys Barbara Gillian and Elizabeth M. Monck.
       The Coloured Population of Great Britain: A
       Comparative Study of Coloured Households in Four
       County Boroughs, Based on the 1971 Census of
       Population. London: Runnymede Trust, 1975.
       91 p.

              Review by Jenny Bourne. Race and Class 17: 4
              (Spring 1976): 448.

1615. London. Housing Research Group. Working Party on
       Race and Housing. Race and Local Authority
       Housing: Information on Ethnic Groups: A Report.
       London: Community Relations Commission, 1977.
       16 p.

1616. McKay, David H. Housing and Race in Industrial
       Society: Civil Rights and Urban Policy in Britain
       and the United States. London: Croom Helm, 1977.
       193 p.

1617. McKay, David H. Housing and Race in Industrial
       Society: The Civil Rights and Urban Policy in
       Britain and the United States. Totowa, N.J.:
       Rowman and Littlefield, 1977. 193 p.

1618. Pahl, R. E. London; What Next?: The Case for a
       Joint Inner London Rehabilitation Organisation.
       London: Runnymede Trust, 1973. 30 p.

1619. Parker, John and Keith Dugmore. Colour and the
       Allocation of GLC Housing: The Report of the GLC
       Lettings Survey, 1974-75. London: Greater
       London Council, 1976. 105 p.

1620. Perry, Jane. The Fair Housing Experiment: Community
       Relations Councils and the Housing of Minority
       Groups. With a foreword by Mark Bonham-Carter.
       London: Political and Economic Planning, 1973.
       53 p.

1621. Richmond, Anthony H. Migration and Race Relations in
       an English City: A Study in Bristol. London:
       Oxford University Press, 1973. 344 p.

              Review by Ruth Issacharoff. Race 15: 2
              (October 1973): 260-261.

1622. Runnymede Trust. Race and Council Housing in London:
       Census Returns Examined by the Runnymede Trust
       Research Staff. With a foreword by Elizabeth
       Parker. London: Runnymede Trust, 1975. 11 leaves.

1623. Smith, David John and Ann Whalley. Racial Minorities
       and Public Housing. London, P.E.P., 1975.
       119 p.

B. PERIODICAL ARTICLES

1624.   "Asians and Housing." Campaign to Repeal the Immigra-
         tion Act Bulletin 2 (1976): 2.

1625.   Barnett, A., C. G. Pickvance and R. H. Ward. "Some
         Factors Underlying Racial Discrimination in
         Housing." Race 12: 1 (July 1970): 75-85.

1626.   Bentley, Stuart. "Mortgages at Discount." Race Today
         3: 5 (May 1970): 169.

1627.   Blake, John. "The Planner and Immigration." Town
         and Country Planning 40 (November 1972): 513-515.

1628.   Bristow, Mike and Bert H. Adams. "Ugandan Asians and
         the Housing Market in Britain." New Community
         6 (Winter 1977/1978): 65-77.

1629.   Burney, Elizabeth. "Immigrant Housing in Britain."
         New Community 1 (Autumn 1971): 80-82.

1630.   "Changes in Allocation Procedures." Community Rela-
         tions in Social Services 3: 1 (May 1977): 11-12.

1631.   Clark, David. "Immigrant Responses to the British
         Housing Market: A Case Study in the West Midlands
         Conurbation." Working Papers on Ethnic Relations
         No. 7 (1977): 1-65.

1632.   Collar, D. A. "Exclusion by Estate Agents - An Analy-
         sis." Applied Economics 5: 4 (1974): 281-288.

1633.   Collard, David. "Price and Prejudice in the Housing
         Market." The Economic Journal 83:330 (June 1973):
         510-515.

1634.   Davies, Paul and K. Newton. "The Social Patterns of
         Immigrant Areas." Race 14: 1 (July 1972): 43-57.

1635.   Deakin, Nicholas and Brian Cohen. "Dispersal and
         Choice: Towards a Strategy for Ethnic Minorities
         in Britain." Environment and Planning 2 (1970):
         193-201.

1636.   Deakin, Nicholas. "Housing and Ethnic Minorities:
         An Overview." New Community 6 (Winter 1977/1978):
         4-7.

1637.   Dhanjal, Beryl. "Asian Housing in Southall: Some Im-
         pressions." New Community 6 (Winter 1977/1978):
         88-93.

1638. Fenton, Mike. "Asian Households in Owner-Occupation:
       A Study of the Pattern, Costs and Experiences of
       Households in Greater Manchester." Working Pa-
       pers on Ethnic Relations No. 2 (1977): 1-70.

1639. Fenton, Mike and David Collard. "Do Coloured Tenants
       Pay More? Some Evidence." Working Papers on
       Ethnic Relations No. 1 (1977): 1-9.

1640. Flett, Hazel and Margaret Peaford. "The Effect of
       Slum Clearance on Multi-Occupation." Working
       Papers on Ethnic Relations No. 4 (1977): 1-53.

1641. "Forcing the Council to Negotiate." Race Today 8:
       7/8 (July/August 1976): 159.

1642. Freeson, Reg. "Housing and Colour: The Problems and
       Some Answers." Spectator (19 May 1973): 630.

1643. "GLC Housing and Race." Community Relations in Social
       Services 2: 1 (May 1976): 8-9.

1644. Godfrey, W. R. "The Role of Local Authority Housing
       in the Integration of Coloured Immigrants."
       Housing 7 (March 1972): 22-23.

1645. "Government Policy on Housing and Race Relations."
       New Community 6 (Winter 1977/1978): 112-117.

1646. Gribbin, J. J. "The Implications of the 1976 Race
       Relations Act for Housing." New Community 6
       (Winter 1977/1978): 99-104.

1647. Haddon, R. "A Minority in a Welfare State: Location
       of West Indians in the London Housing Market."
       New Atlantis 2: 1 (1970): 80-123.

1648. Hall, Peter. "The Inner Cities Dilemma." New Society
       (3 February 1977): 223-225.

1649. Hammond, Robert. "Ethnic Records for Local Authority
       Housing." New Community 6 (Winter 1977/1978):
       105-111.

1650. Hill, Clifford. "Pentecostalist Growth - Result of
       Racialism." Race Today 3: 6 (June 1971): 187-
       190.

1651. "House Room." Economist 238 (6 February 1971): 41-42.

1652. "Housing Struggle: The Tiger is on the Loose." Race
       Today 8: 3 (March 1976): 52-53.

1653.   "Improvement in an Asian Area." Community Relations
        in Social Services 2: 1 (May 1976): 9.

1654.   Judge, Tony. "The Problems of Difficult Estates."
        New Community 6 (Winter 1977/1978): 45-48.

1655.   Karn, Valerie A. "The Financing of Owner-Occupation
        and Its Impact on Ethnic Minorities." New Com-
        munity 6 (Winter 1977/1978): 49-63.

1656.   Karn, Valerie A. "Housing: Uganda Asians - Houses or
        Jobs." New Community 2 (Winter 1972/1973): 90-
        95.

1657.   Knox, Valerie. "Housing Hopes in Camden." Community
        (July 1970): 8-12.

1658.   Lane, David. "Housing and Ethnic Minorities." New
        Community 6 (Winter 1977/1978): 483-485.

1659.   Langton, Pat. "Immigrants in Central London." Cam-
        paign to Repeal the Immigration Act Bulletin 2
        (1976): 7-8.

1660.   "Late Without Good Excuse: Housing and Race." Econo-
        mist 256 (6 September 1975): 24-25.

1661.   Leighton, Jeremy. "Needles in the Haystack." Com-
        munity (January 1970): 3-5.

1662.   Lindley, Richard. "Neighbours in No Man's Land."
        Listener 98 (8 September 1977): 290-291.

1663.   Lomas, Glenys Barbara Gillian. "Analysis of Census
        Data on Housing." New Community 6 (Winter 1977/
        1978): 8-15.

1664.   Lomas, Glenys Barbara Gillian. "The Black Tenant."
        New Society (1 April 1976): 19.

1665.   Mason, Tim. "Residential Succession, Community Fa-
        cilities and Urban Renewal in Cheetham Hill,
        Manchester." New Community 6 (Winter 1977/1978):
        78-87.

1666.   Mildon, Iva Wallis. "West Indian Home Owners in
        Croydon." New Community 6 (Winter 1977/1978):
        94-98.

1667.   Nandy, Dipak. "Public Housing and Chronic Discrimina-
        tion." New Community 4 (Winter/Spring 1975/
        1976): 541-542.

1668. Parker, John and Keith Dugmore. "Race and Allocation
       of Public Housing: A G.L.C. Survey." New Com-
       munity 6 (Winter 1977/1978): 27-40.

1669. Perry, Jane. "The Fair Housing Experiment." New
       Community 2 (Spring 1973): 206-209.

1670. Pickvance, C. G. "Life Cycle, Housing Tenure and
       Residential Mobility: A Path Analytic Approach."
       Urban Studies 11 (June 1974): 171-188.

1671. Plant, Martin A. "The Attitudes of Coloured Immi-
       grants in Two Areas of Birmingham to the Concept
       of Dispersal." Race 12: 3 (January 1971): 323-
       328.

1672. "Race and Housing: The Relevance of the Inner Area
       Studies (Birmingham, Lambeth and Liverpool)."
       New Community 6 (Winter 1977/1978): 119-122.

1673. Race Today Collective. "Fight for Better Housing:
       Forcing the Council to Negotiate." Race Today
       8: 7/8 (July/August 1976): 158-159.

1674. Race Today Collective. "The Right to Decent Housing."
       Race Today 8: 5 (May 1976): 104-105.

1675. Rex, John. "The Concept of Housing Class and the
       Sociology of Race Relations." Race 12: 3 (Janu-
       ary 1971): 293-301.

1676. Rex, John, et. al. "Housing, Employment and Race Re-
       lations in Birmingham." New Community 6 (Winter
       1977/1978): 123-126.

1677. Richmond, Anthony H. "Housing and Racial Attitudes
       in Bristol." Race 12: 1 (July 1970): 49-58.

1678. Rowley, Gwyn and Tipple Graham. "Coloured Immigrants
       Within the City: An Analysis of Housing and Tra-
       vel Preferences." Urban Studies 11 (February
       1974): 81-89.

1679. Smith, David J. "The Housing of Racial Minorities:
       Its Unusual Nature." New Community 6 (Winter
       1977/1978): 18-26.

1680. Taper, Toby. "The Allocation of Islington Housing
       to Ethnic Minorities." New Community 6 (Winter
       1977/1978): 40-44.

1681. Taylor, John Henry. "Community Action and Colour Con-
       flict." New Community 3 (Autumn 1974): 412-414.

1682.   Ward, Robin. "Urban Structure, the Housing Market
           and Race Relations: A Research Note." New Com-
           munity 6 (Winter 1977/1978): 127-129.

1683.   "We are Overcrowded: Plight of the Kotecha Family."
           Newsweek 80 (21 August 1972): 28-29.

1684.   "We Can Fight for Better Housing and Win." Race Today
           8: 7/8 (July/August 1976): 158.

1685.   "What House Mr. Biswas!" New Society (27 February
           1975): 506.

1686.   White, David. "Newham: An Example of Urban Decline."
           New Society (23 October 1975): 201-204.

1687.   Wilkinson, R. K. and S. Gulliver. "The Impact of
           Non-Whites on House Prices." Race 13: 1 (July
           1971): 21-36.

XII.

HEALTH

A. BOOKS

1688. Gish, Oscar. Doctor Migration and World Health: The Impact of the International Demand for Doctors on Health Services in Developing Countries. London: Bell, 1971. 151 p.

1689. Great Britain. Central Office of Information. Reference Division. Health Services in Britain. Rev. ed. London: British Information Service, 1974. 66 p.

1690. Great Britain. Community Relations Commission. Reference and Technical Services Division. Aspects of Mental Health in a Multi-Cultural Society: Notes for the Guidance of Doctors and Social Workers. London: The Commission Reference and Technical Services Division, 1976. 63 p.

1691. Great Britain. Community Relations Commission. Reference and Technical Services Division. Doctors From Overseas: A Case for Consultation. Prepared by the Commission's Reference and Technical Services Division with the assistance of the Social Services Section. London: The Commission, 1976. 32 p.

1692. Sen, Amya. Problems of Overseas Students and Nurses. London: N.F.E.R., 1970. 211 p.

1693. Skone, J. F. Public Health Aspects of Immigration. London: Community Relations Commission, 1970. 34 p.

1694. Van den Berghs and Jurgens, Ltd. Asians in Britain:
      A Study of Their Dietary Patterns in Relation to
      Their Cultural and Religious Backgrounds. Bur-
      gess Hill: The Author, 1976. 22 p.

1695. Varma, Ved P., ed. Stresses in Children. London:
      University of London Press, 1973. 165 p.

1696. Yudkin, Simon. The Health and Welfare of the Immi-
      grant Child. London: Community Relations Com-
      mission, 1970. 16 p.

B. PERIODICAL ARTICLES

1697. Bagley, Christopher and Steven Greer. "Black Sui-
      cide: A Study of 25 English Cases." Journal of
      Social Psychology 86 (April 1972): 175-179.

1698. Bagley, Christopher. "A Comparative Study of Mental
      Illness Among Immigrant Groups in Britain."
      Journal of Biosocial Science 3 (1971): 449-459.

1699. Bagley, Christopher. "Mental Illness in Immigrant
      Minorities in London." Journal of Biosocial
      Science 3 (1971): 461-471.

1700. Bagley, Christopher. "The Social Aetiology of
      Schizophrenia in Immigrant Groups." Interna-
      tional Journal of Social Psychiatry 17 (1971):
      292-304.

1701. Bosanquet, Nicholas. "Immigrants and the NHS."
      New Society (17 July 1975): 130-132.

1702. Burke, Aggrey W. "Attempted Suicide Among Asian Immi-
      grants in Birmingham." British Journal of Psy-
      chiatry 128 (May 1976): 528-533.

1703. Burke, Aggrey W. "Socio-Cultural Determinants of
      Attempted Suicide Among West Indians in Birming-
      ham: Ethnic Origin and Immigrant Status." British
      Journal of Psychiatry 129 (September 1976): 261-
      266.

1704. Burrowes, Horace. "Common Emotional Problems in Immi-
      grant Children." Therapeutic Education (Spring
      1972): 25-28.

1705. Duvoisin, Ann. "The Plight of Overseas Nurses."
      Focus 1: 2 (July 1973): 13-18, 59.

1706. Ford, J. A. "Asian Rickets and Osteomalacia." Nur-
      sing Times 70: 2 (10 January 1974): 49-50.

1707. Grainger, Ken. "Third World Workers in the N.H.S."
       Ethnic Minorities and Employment No. 3
       (December 1976): 11-12.

1708. Hunt, Sandra. "Disease and the Asian Diet." Health
       and Social Service Journal 86:4501 (1976): 1395.

1709. King, Jane. "Bereaved, Rejected, Deprived: The Emo-
       tional and Educational Experience of the West
       Indian Adolescent Immigrants in Britain."
       Labour Monthly 54 (October/November 1972):
       474-478, 515-519.

1710. Kitzinger, Sheila. "Speaking the Same Language,
       Working with W.I. (West Indian) Patients."
       Practitioner 213 (December 1974): 843.

1711. Kitzinger, Sheila. "West Indian Immigrant Children
       with Problems." Therapeutic Education (Spring
       1972): 5-19.

1712. Klein, Rudolf and Martin Buxton. "Health Inequities."
       New Society (7 November 1974): 357-358.

1713. Nicol. A. R. "Psychiatric Disorder in the Children
       of Caribbean Immigrants." Journal of Child
       Psychology and Psychiatry and Allied Disciplines
       12 (December 1971): 273-287.

1714. Nicol. A. R. "Psychiatric Disorder in West Indian
       School Children." Race Today 3: 1 (January
       1971): 1-15.

1715. Parry, W. H. "Health and Welfare of Immigrants.
       Proceedings of the Royal Society of Medicine
       63: 6 (1970): 633-636.

1716. Rutter, Michael et al. "Children of West Indian Immi-
       grants I. Rates of Behavioral Deviance and Psy-
       chiatric Disorder." Journal of Child Psychology
       and Psychiatry and Allied Disciplines 15
       (October 1974): 241-262.

1717. Stroud, C. "Nutrition and the Immigrant." British
       Journal of Hospital Medicine (May 1971):
       629-634.

1718. "Training Course for Staff Working with Asians."
       Nursing Times 73:12 (24 March 1977): 428-429.

1719. White, H. C. "Self-Poisoning in Adolescents." Brit-
       ish Journal of Psychiatry 123 (July 1973): 113.

1720. Woodhouse, Derrick F. "Tropical Eye Disease in Brit-
       ain." The Practitioner 214 (May 1975): 646-653.

XIII.

SOCIAL SERVICES

A. BOOKS

1721. Adamson, Giliray. The Caretakers. London: Bookstall
Publications, 1973. 276 p.

1722. Adeney, Martin. Community Action: Four Examples.
London: Runnymede Trust, 1971. 36 p.

1723. Association of Multi-Racial Playgroups. Action in
the Priority Areas. A Note on the Aims and
Workings of the Association of Multi-Racial Playgroups. Cambridge, England: Association of
Multi-Racial Playgroups, 1971. 10 p.

1724. Atkinson, Anthony Barnes. An Adequate Income for
One-Parent Families. London: National Council
for One Parent Families, 1977. 5 p.

1725. British Association of Social Workers. Guide to
Legal Aid (and) Questioned by the Police (and)
Immigration Act 1971. Birmingham: British Asso-
ciation of Social Workers, 1974. 11 p.

1726. Cheetham, Juliet. Social Work with Immigrants. London: Routledge and Kegan Paul, 1972. 230 p.

Review by Christopher Wood. New Community
2 (Autumn 1973): 435-436.

1727. The Commonwealth Foundation's Race Relations Bursary
Scheme: Report of a Conference of Bursars Held in
London Under the Auspices of the Community Rela-
tions Commission on 27 September 1972. London:
Commonwealth Foundation, 1973. 15 p.

1728. Croker, Susan K. Immigrants: The Problems They Pre-
       sent Public Libraries in Sweden (The Yugoslavs
       and Finns), the United Kingdom (The Indians and
       Pakistanis), the United States of America (The
       Spanish Speaking, i.e., the Mexican Americans,
       the Puerto Ricans and the Cubans). Aberystwyth:
       College of Librarianship, Wales, 1975. 54 p.

1729. Curtis, Sarah. Don't Rush Me: The Comic Strip, Sex
       Education and a Multi-Racial Society. London:
       Community Relations Commission, 1975. 52 p.

1730. Fisher, Thelma and Frank Fisher. All Our Children.
       Edited by Rachel Jenkins. London: Save the
       Children Fund, 1976. 24 p.

1731. Glennerster, Howard. Social Service Budgets and So-
       cial Policy: British and American Experience.
       London: Allen and Unwin, 1975. 272 p.

1732. Glennerster, Howard. Social Service Budgets and So-
       cial Policy: British and American Experience.
       New York: Barnes and Noble, 1976. 272 p.

1733. Great Britain. Community Relations Commission. A
       Home From Home: Some Policy Considerations on
       Black Children in Residential Care. London: The
       Commission, 1977. 39 p.

1734. Great Britain. Community Relations Commission. Pub-
       lic Library Service for a Multi-Cultural Society:
       A Report Produced by a Joint Working Party of the
       Library Advisory Council and the Community Rela-
       tions Commission. London: The Commission, 1976.
       27 p.

1735. Great Britain. Community Relations Commission. Sum-
       mer Programmes. London: The Commission, 1970.
       32 p.

1736. Great Britain. Community Relations Commission. Ref-
       erence and Community Services. Fostering Black
       Children: A Policy Document on the Needs of Eth-
       nic Minority Group Children. London: The Commis-
       sion, 1975. 36 p.

1737. Great Britain. Community Relations Commission. Ref-
       erence and Technical Services Division. Caring
       for Under-Fives in a Multi-Racial Society. Lon-
       don: The Commission, 1977. 60 p.

1738. Great Britain. Community Relations Commission. Ref-
       erence and Technical Division. Who Minds? A
       Study of Working Mothers and Childminding in
       Ethnic Minority Communities. London: CRC, 1975.
       77 p.

1739.   Great Britain. Home Office. Uganda Resettlement
            Board. Interim Report. London: H.M.S.O., 1973.
            22 p.

1740.   Greater London Services. London: Inner London Educa-
            tion Authority, 1967/68- . v. 1- . Annual.

1741.   Holman, Robert. Power for the Powerless: The Role of
            Community Action. London: Community and Race
            Relations Unit, British Council of Churches, 1972.
            19 p.

1742.   Holman, Robert, ed. Socially Deprived Families in
            Britain. London: Bedford Square Press of the
            National Council of Social Services, 1970. 235 p.

            ------- Supplement. London: Bedford Square
            Press; Distributed by Research Publication
            Services, 1973. 28 p.

1743.   Hood, Catriona, T. Oppe, I. Pless and E. Opte.
            Children of West Indian Immigrants - A Study of
            One-Year Olds in Paddington. London: The Insti-
            tute of Race Relations; Distributed by Research
            Publication Services, 1970. 108 p.

1744.   Implications of Youth Work in Asian Community: Report
            of a Conference Organised by National Association
            of Indian Youth. Written by Alec Oxford in co-
            operation with the Planning Group Resource Per-
            sons and Participants. Leicester: Youth Service
            Information Centre, 1973. 49 p.

1745.   Jackson, Brian and Joan Jones. One Thousand Children.
            Cambridge, England: Advisory Centre for Educa-
            tion, 1971. 14 p.

1746.   Jackson, Sonia. The Illegal Child-Minders: A Report
            on the Growth of Unregistered Child-Minding and
            the West Indian Community. Cambridge, England:
            Priority Area Children for the Cambridge Educa-
            tional Trust, 1972. 38 p.

1747.   Jones, Catherine. Immigration and Social Policy in
            Britain. London: Tavistock Publications, 1977.
            291 p.

            Review by Lee Bridges. Race and Class 19: 2
            (Autumn 1977): 211-212.

1748.   Kingswood District Council Services Information Hand-
            book. Carshalton: Forward Publicity, 1977. 40 p.

1749.   London Boroughs Association. LBA Handbook. London:
        The Association, 1970- . Vol. 1- .

1750.   The London Borough of Ealing Information Handbook.
        3rd ed. London: Burrow, 1977. 52 p.

1751.   Lozells Social Development Centre. Wednesday's Chil-
        dren: A Report on Under-Fives Provision in Hands-
        worth. London: Community Relations Commission.
        1975. 59 p.

1752.   Notting Hill Social Council. Leisure and Amenities
        Committee. Play Space in North Kensington:
        Report on Local Play Programmes, 1967/69. Lon-
        don: The Council, 1970. 68 p.

1753.   Public Library Statistics, 1973/74. Compiled by The
        Chartered Institute of Public Finance and
        Accountancy and the Society of County Treasurers.
        London: C.I.P.E.A.; Reading: The Institute,
        1975. 51 p.

1754.   Romijn, Jan. Tabu: Uganda Asians, the Old, the Weak,
        the Vulnerable: A Report on His Work with the
        Elderly and Handicapped Among the Uganda Asian
        Evacuees in London, Together with the LCSS's
        Recommendation and Suggestions for Further Action.
        London: London Council of Social Services, 1976.
        41 p.

1755.   Seen but Not Served: Black Youth and the Youth Ser-
        vice: Report of a Series of Six Seminars Held in
        1975/76 to Examine Statutory Provision for Young
        People from Racial Minorities. London: Community
        Relations Commission, 1977. 42 p.

1756.   Stott, John. Development Together: A Discussion of
        Some Issues Involved in Community Relations and
        Youth Work. London: Methodist Youth Department,
        1971. 24 p.

1757.   Triseliotis, John Paul, ed. Social Work with Coloured
        Immigrants and Their Families. London: Oxford
        University Press for the Institute of Race Rela-
        tions, 1972. 123 p.

        Review by Christopher Wood. New Community 2
        (Autumn 1973): 435-436.

1758.   Youth Service Information Centre. Youth Service Pro-
        visions for Young Immigrants: A National Survey
        of Local Authorities. Leicester: The Centre,
        1972. 67 p.

B. PERIODICAL ARTICLES

1759.   Barnes, Gill Gorrell. "Seen But Not Heard: Where is
        Home." Social Work Today 5:21 (23 January 1975):
        646-648.

1760.   Barnes, Gill Gorrell. "Seen But Not Heard: Where is
        Home." Social Work Today 5:20 (9 January 1975):
        606-609.

1761.   Bernard, William S. "How to Influence the Public for
        a Better Understanding of the Problems of Immi-
        grant Families and Social Welfare Measures Needed
        in Order to Facilitate a Better Integration of
        the Newcomers." International Migration 14
        (1976): 84-90.

1762.   "Black Children in Care." Community Relations in
        Social Services 2: 2 (July 1976): 1-2.

1763.   Boss, P. and J. Homeshaw. "Britain's Black Citizens."
        Social Work Today 6:12 (21 September 1975): 354-
        357.

1764.   Brown, R. "Library Service to Immigrant Groups."
        Greater London Council Intelligence Unit Quarter-
        ly Bulletin No. 21 (December 1972): 35-38.

1765.   Curtis, Sarah. "Free Pills for All." New Society
        (26 June 1975): 780.

1766.   Dixon, R. J. "How the Probation Service Copes with
        Immigrant Problems in Birmingham (England)."
        International Journal of Offender Therapy and
        Comparative Criminology 20: 1 (1976): 82-85.

1767.   Forester, Tom. "Out of the Library." New Society
        (21 August 1975): 425.

1768.   "Fostering Racial Confusion." Times Educational Sup-
        plement No. 3119 (7 March 1975): 5.

1769.   Gould, Donald. "The Dr. God Syndrome." New States-
        man (8 August 1975): 166.

1770.   Holman, Robert. "Social Workers and the Inadequates."
        New Society (5 September 1974): 608-610.

1771.   "Hostel for Asian Girls." Community Relations in
        Social Services 2: 1 (May 1976): 10-11.

1772.   "How to Bridge the Culture Gap." Times Educational
        Supplement No. 3171 (12 March 1976): 6.

1773. Jackson, Brian. "The Child Minders." New Society
       (29 November 1973): 521-524.

1774. Jackson, Sonia. "The Illegal Child-Minders." Where
       No. 63 (November 1971): 342-345.

1775. John, Gus. "Blaming the Victim." Times Educational
       Supplement No. 3239 (1 July 1977): 16-17.

1776. Judge, Ken. "The Social Services: Where the Money
       Goes." New Society (8 August 1974): 343-345.

1777. Knight, Lindsay. "Race: Where Were We?" Community
       Care No. 120 (21 July 1976): 14-16.

1778. Lees, Ray and Morag McGrath. "Community Work with
       Immigrants." British Journal of Social Work
       4: 2 (1974): 175-186.

1779. Lees, Ray and Morag McGrath. "Research and Community
       Work with Commonwealth Immigrants." New Commun-
       ity 3 (Winter/Spring 1974): 107-110.

1780. Lemon, Joyce P. "The Child's Need for Myths and
       Legends in the Mother Tongue." School Librarian
       20 (June 1972): 102-106.

1781. "Librarians Look at Children's Books." Education and
       Community Relations (November 1971): 1-3.

1782. Little, Alan. "Children in a Minority: A Need Unmet."
       Municipal Review 47:560 (September 1976): 180-
       182.

1783. McCulloch, J. W. and N. J. Smith. "Blacks and Social
       Work." New Society (25 April 1974): 191.

1784. "The Mixed Race Child." Community Relations in Social
       Services 3: 1 (May 1977): 3-4.

1785. Mukherjee, Bishwa Nath. "Reliability Estimates of
       Some Survey Data on Family Planning." Population
       Studies 29 (March 1975): 127-142.

1786. Naik, Don. "The Dilemma of Social Work in a Multi-
       Racial Society." Social Service Quarterly 45
       (January/March 1972): 84-88.

1787. Newell, David. "Immigrants: Advice Giving and Com-
       munity Relations Councils." New Community 4
       (Autumn 1975): 303-309.

1788. Page, Raissa C. "Have We Any Second-Rate Children?"
       Journal of the Association of British Adoption
       Agencies 1 (1973): 37-42.

1789. Pearl, David. "Social Security and the Immigrant."
        New Community 3 (Summer 1974): 272-279.

1790. "Race Relations Act and Fostering." Education 146:23
        (5 December 1975): 588.

1791. Scott, Gavin. "Gleam of Hope for Touchstone Kids."
        Times Educational Supplement No. 3113 (24 Janu-
        ary 1975): 8.

1792. "Shared or Special Needs?" Community Relations in
        Social Services 3: 1 (May 1976): 1-3.

1793. Tizard, Barbara. "Under Five and the Wrong Colour."
        Times Educational Supplement No. 3148 (3 October
        1975): 23.

1794. Wood, Christopher. "Among Saints and Swingers: De-
        fining the Social Work Task in Relation to West
        Indian Life-Styles." Social Work Today 5: 7
        (11 July 1974): 213-215.

1795. Wood, Christopher. "Community, Culture and Social
        Work." New Community 2 (Summer 1973): 278-282.

1796. Wood, Christopher. "Life Styles Among West Indians
        and Social Work Problems." New Community 3
        (Summer 1974): 249-254.

XIV.

RACE RELATIONS IN THE MASS MEDIA

A. BOOKS

1797. Evans, Peter. Publish and be Damned. London: Runnymede Trust, 1976. 37 p.

1798. Great Britain. Community Relations Commission. Future of Broadcasting: Community Relations Commission's Evidence to the Annan Committee. London: The Commission, 1975. 8 leaves.

1799. Hartmann, Paul G. and Charles Husband. Racism and the Mass Media: A Study of the Role of the Mass Media in the Formation of White Beliefs and Attitudes in Britain. London: Davis-Poynter, 1974. 279 p.

> Review by Peter Harland. New Community 3 (Summer 1974): 299-301.

1800. Husband, Charles. White Media and Black Britain. London: Arrow Books, 1975. 222 p.

1801. Jones, Clement, et al. Race and the Press. London: Runnymede Trust, 1970. 60 p.

1802. Race as News. Paris: UNESCO, 1974. 173 p.

B. PERIODICAL ARTICLES

1803. Bagley, Christopher. "Race Relations and the Press: An Empirical Analysis." Race 15: 1 (July 1973): 59-89.

1804. Chase, Louis A. "Ethnic Minorities and the Media.
       Shades of Black, White and Grey: A View of the
       West Indian Press." New Community 4 (Winter/
       Spring 1975/1976): 473-475.

1805. "Consensus Reporting." Journalism Today 2 (Spring
       1970): 101-118.

1806. "A Disorderly House." Economist 263 (14 May 1977):
       23-24.

1807. Faulkner, Graham. "Cricket, Race and the Media."
       New Community 2 (Autumn 1973): 392-394.

1808. "Grandeur Thrust Upon Them." Economist 259 (8 May
       1976): 32-34.

1809. Grigg, John. "Race Relations and the Mass Media."
       Community 2 (April 1971): 3-4.

1810. Half Moon Photography Workshop. "Lewisham: What are
       You Taking Pictures For?" Camerawork No. 8
       (1977): 1-15.

1811. Hanna, Max. "The Black Press." New Society (28 Au-
       gust 1975): 480-481.

1812. Harland, Peter. "The Media and Race Relations Today."
       New Community 4 (Winter/Spring 1975/1976): 453-
       460.

1813. Hartmann, Paul and Charles Husband. "The Mass Media
       and Racial Conflict." Race 12: 3 (January 1971):
       267-282.

1814. Husband, Charles. "Responsible Journalism for a Multi-
       racial Britain." New Community 4 (Winter/Spring
       1974/1975): 89-96.

1815. Marriott, Louis. "Race and the Press." New Community
       1 (Spring 1972): 197-200.

1816. New Society. "Race and the Press." New Society
       (13 January 1977): 64.

1817. Parker, John. "Ethnic Minorities and the Media.
       Blacks on the Box: Where Are They?" New Community
       4 (Winter/Spring 1975/1976): 465-466.

1818. "Press and Race." Christian Century 88 (29 December
       1971): 1515.

1819. "The Press and the Race." Race Today 8: 6 (June 1976):
       137-139.

1820. "Race and the Mass Media." Times Educational Supple-
         ment No. 3082 (21 June 1974): 11.

1821. "Race and the Press." Race and Class 18: 1 (Summer
         1976): 69-71.

1822. Race Today Collective. "Reviewing the Press." Race
         Today 8: 6 (June 1976): 137-140.

1823. Race Today Collective. "What the BBC Did Not Say."
         Race Today 8:10 (October 1976): 209-210.

1824. Rose, Eliot Joseph Benn. "Ethnic Minorities and the
         Media: An Employer's View." New Community 4
         (Winter/Spring 1975/1976): 461-462.

1825. Scott, George, et al. "Race Relations in Britain:
         Do We Get the Real News?" Listener 95 (17 June
         1976): 764-766.

1826. Wall, Max. "Ethnic Minorities and the Media - Caution
         or Credibility." New Community 4 (Winter/Spring
         1975/1976): 463-464.

XV.

POLICE AND THE COLORED MINORITIES

A. BOOKS

1827.   Banton, Michael Parker. <u>Police-Community Relations</u>.
        London: Collins, 1973. 176 p.

> "A guide for police officers receiving
> training in race relations."

1828.   Cain, Maureen E. <u>Society and the Policeman's Role</u>.
        London: Routledge and Kegan Paul, 1973. 315 p.

> Review by Tom Critchley. <u>New Community</u> 2
> (Spring 1973): 216-217.

1829.   Clarke, C. F. O. <u>The Police and Community Relations:
        Report of a Conference at Ditchley Park 29th of
        May to 1st of June</u>. Enstone: Ditchley Founda-
        tion, 1970. 44 p.

1830.   Great Britain. Home Office. <u>Police/Immigrant Rela-
        tions in England and Wales: Observations on the
        Report of the Select Committee on Race Relations
        and Immigration Presented to Parliament by the
        Secretary of State for the Home Department</u>.
        London: H.M.S.O., 1973. 14 p.

1831.   Great Britain. Parliament. House of Commons. Select
        Committee on Race Relations and Immigration.
        <u>Police/Immigrant Relations/Select Committee on
        Race Relations and Immigration, Session, 1971-
        72</u>. London: H.M.S.O., 1972. 3 vols.

> Vol. 1. Report. Vol. 2. Evidence.
> Vol. 3. Evidence, Document and Index.

1832. Humphry, Derek. Police Power and Black People. With
       a Commentary by Gus John. London: Panther Books,
       1972. 239 p.

           Review by John R. Lambert. Race 15: 1 (July
           1973): 131-133.

1833. Judge, Anthony. A Man Apart: The British Policeman
       and His Job. London: Arthur Barker, 1972. 230 p.

           Review by John R. Lambert. Race 15: 1
           (July 1973): 131-133.

1834. Lambert, John R. Crime, Police and Race Relations: A
       Study in Birmingham. With the Assistance of
       Robert F. Jenkinson, etc. London: Published for
       the Institute of Race Relations by Oxford Univer-
       sity Press, 1970. 308 p.

1835. Pulle, Stanislaus. Police Immigrant Relations in
       Ealing: Report of an Investigation Conducted on
       Behalf of the Ealing CRC. London: Published on
       Behalf of the Ealing Community Relations Council
       by Runnymede Trust, 1973. 88 p.

1836. Russell, Ken. Complaints Against the Police: A So-
       ciological View. Leicester: Milltak, 1976.
       124 p.

B. PERIODICAL ARTICLES

1837. Bantam, Michael. "The Definition of the Police Role."
       New Community 3 (Summer 1974): 164-171.

1838. Bogues, Tony. "Black Youth in Revolt." International
       Socialism No. 102 (October 1977): 12-15.

1839. Brown, John. "Police-Immigrant Relations." New Com-
       munity 4 (Winter/Spring 1974/1975): 69-78.

1840. "Call Your Police Off Our Backs: Black Parents and
       Students Warn the Home Secretary." Race Today
       8: 8/9 (July/August 1976): 155.

1841. Chase, Louis. "West Indians and the Police: Some
       Observations." New Community 3 (Summer 1974):
       205-210.

1842. Chopra, Subhash. "Immigrants and the Police." Race
       Today 2: 8 (August 1970): 283.

1843. Clarke, John, et al. "The Selection of Evidence and
       the Avoidance of Racialism: A Critique of the
       Parliamentary Select Committee on Race Relations
       and Immigration." New Community 3 (Summer 1974):
       172-192.

1844. Evans, Peter. "The Police As a Minority Group." New
       Community 4 (Winter/Spring 1974/1975): 65-68.

1845. Howe, Darcus. "Fighting Back: West Indian Youth and
       the Police in Notting Hill." Race Today 5:11
       (December 1973): 333-337.

1846. Judge, Anthony. "The Police and the Coloured Com-
       munities: A Police View." New Community 3
       (Summer 1974): 199-204.

1847. MacDonald, Ian Alexander. "The Creation of the Brit-
       ish Police." Race Today 5:11 (December 1973):
       331-333.

1848. Mark, Robert. "The Metropolitan Police: Their Role
       in the Community." Community (July 1970): 3-5.

1849. Marshall, Peter. "Policing: The Community Relations
       Aspect." New Community 3 (Summer 1974): 193-198.

1850. Nandy, Dipak. "Blacks and the Police." New Statesman
       (11 August 1972): 186.

1851. "Pigs in the Middle." Economist 264 (20 August 1977):
       18.

1852. "Police and Race. So What?" Economist 244 (16 Septem-
       ber 1972): 28.

1853. Race Today Collective. "Black Britishers and the
       Police." Race Today 8:12 (December/January 1976/
       1977): 243-246.

1854. Race Today Collective. "Black Self-Defence." Race
       Today 9: 2 (March/April 1977): 28-32.

1855. Race Today Collective. "Carnival Belongs To Us."
       Race Today 8: 9 (September 1976): 170-179.

1856. Race Today Collective. "How the Police Operate: Cases
       to Remember." Race Today 8: 7/8 (July/August
       1976): 151-152.

1857. Race Today Collective. "Lewisham Liaison Scheme in
       Ruins." Race Today 7:12 (December 1975): 272-
       274.

1858. Race Today Collective. "Remember, Remember, the 5th
       of November: The Bonfire Night Case." Race Today
       8: 9 (September 1976): 180-183.

1859. Race Today Collective. "Trials of the Cricklewood 12
       and the Stockwell 10." Race Today 7:11 (November
       1975): 243-245.

1860. Race Today Collective. "Up Against the Police."
       Race Today 8: 7/8 (July/August 1976): 147-149.

1861. Robinson, Clive. "Police/Immigrant Relations: The
       Community Relations Commission's Involvement."
       New Community 3 (Summer 1974): 239-241.

1862. Rolph, C. H. "Race and Police." Community (October
       1970): 4-6.

1863. "Time to Organise." Race Today 8: 7/8 (July/August
       1976): 153-154.

1864. Tobias, J. J. "Police-Immigrant Relations in England,
       1880-1910." New Community 3 (Summer 1974): 211-
       214.

1865. Troyna, Barry. "The Reggae War." New Society (10
       March 1977): 491-492.

1866. Underwood, Chris. "Police Five." Listener 95 (15
       April 1976): 462.

Appendix A.

LIST OF PERIODICALS, WITH ADDRESSES, THAT PRIMARILY DEAL WITH THE COLORED MINORITIES

CRC Journal. Community Relations Commission, 15-16 Bedford
    Street, London WC2E 8HX, 1972- Monthly.

    A journal of the Community Relations Commission.

CRC News. Community Relations Commission, 15-16 Bedford
    Street, London WC2E 8HX, 1970- Monthly.

Community: Quarterly Journal of the Community Relations Com-
    mission. Community Relations Commission, 15-16 Bedford
    Street, London WC2E 8HX, 1970-1971. v. 1-2.

    Superseded by New Community.

Community Relations in Social Services. Community Relations
    Commission, 15-16 Bedford Street, London WC2E 8 HX,
    1975- Bimonthly.

    Ceased in 1977.

Education and Community Relations. Community Relations Com-
    mission, 15-16 Bedford Street, London WC2E 8 HX, 1971-
    Bimonthly.

Education for a Multi-Cultural Society. Community Relations
    Commission, 15-16 Bedford Street, London WC2E 8 HX,
    1972-

English for Immigrants. Oxford University Press, Press Road,
    London NW10 81, 1967- Annual.

        Superseded by Multiracial School.

Equals. Race Relations Board. 5 Lower Belgrave Street, Lon-
    don SW1W, 1975- Bimonthly.

        Superseded by New Equals.

Ethnic Minorities and Employment: Quarterly Journal of the
    Employment Section of the Community Relations Commis-
    sion. Community Relations Commission, 15-16 Bedford
    Street, London WC2E 8HX, 1975- Quarterly.

Indian Messenger. Mithra Publishing Company, Ltd., 45a
    Market Street, Hyde, Cheshire SK14 2AB, 1975-
    Monthly.

        A journal which deals with the social adjustment
        problems of Indian youth.

Issues in Race and Education. National Association of
    Multi-Racial Education, 64 Lynmouth Road, London N16,
    1976- Monthly.

Multiracial School: Journal of the Association for the Educa-
    tion of Pupils from Overseas. Oxford University Press,
    Press Road, London NW10 81, 1971- 3 times a year.

        Supersedes English for Immigrants.

New Community. Journal of the Community Relations Commission.
    Community Relations Commission, 15-16 Bedford Street,
    London WC2E 8HX, 1971- Quarterly.

        Supersedes Community.

New Equals. Commission for Racial Equality, 15-16 Bedford
    Street, London WC2E 8HX, November/December 1977-
    6 issues a year.

        Supersedes Equals.

New Society: The Social Science Weekly. International Pub-
    lications Corporation Magazines, Ltd., King's Reach
    Tower, Stamford Street, London SE1 9LS.

Race and Class: The Journal of the Institute of Race Relations
    and Transnational Institute. 247 Pentonville Road,
    London N1, 1974- Vol. 16, No. 2 Quarterly.

        Supersedes Race.

Race: The Journal of the Institute of Race Relations. Issued
        under the auspices of the Institute of Race Relations
        by the Oxford University Press, Press Road, London
        NW10 81. Semi-annual, 1959-1974.

        Superseded by Race and Class.

Race Relations. Race Relations Board, 5 Lower Belgrave
        Street, London SW1 WONR, 1967-1977. Quarterly.

        Ceased in 1977 when Race Relations Board was
        abolished.

Race Relations Abstracts. Institute of Race Relations;
        Distributed by Research Publications Services, Ltd.,
        11 Nelson Road, Greenwich, London SE10, 1968-

        Ceased in 1974. Superseded by Sage Race Relations
        Abstracts.

Race Relations Bulletin: Industrial Supplement. Runnymede
        Trust Industrial Unit, 62 Chandos Place, London WC2N
        4HG, 1970- Monthly.

Race Today. 184 King's Cross Road, London WC1, 1969-
        Monthly.

        It started as the newsletter of the Institute
        of Race Relations. Now it is an independent
        journal covering issues of race relations and
        ethnic minorities.

Runnymede Trust Bulletin. Runnymede Trust, 62 Chandos
        Place, London WC2N 4HG, 1969- Monthly.

Runnymede Trust Report. Runnymede Trust, 62 Chandos Place,
        London WC2N 4HG, 1969- Annual.

Sage Race Relations Abstracts. Sage Publications Ltd., 44
        Hatton Garden, London EC1N 8ER, 1975- 3 times a year.

        Supersedes Race Relations Abstracts. Published
        on behalf of the Institute of Race Relations.

Samaj. Samaj, 98 Gifford Street, London N1.

        A journal of the Indian Community in London.
        Published at irregular intervals.

West Indian World. Lenmond Publishing, Ltd., 859 Harrow
        Road, London NW10, 1971- Weekly.

Appendix B.

LIST OF ORGANIZATIONS CONCERNED WITH THE BRITISH COLORED MINORITIES' PROBLEMS

The British Council of Churches, 10 Eaton Gate, London
    SW1W.

Campaign Against Racial Discrimination, 23 St. George's
    House, Gunthorpe Street, London E1.

Commission for Racial Equality, 15-16 Bedford Street, London
    WC2E.

Commonwealth and Overseas Families Association, 85a Ball's
    Pond Road, London N1.

Community Relations Commission, 15 Bedford Street, London
    WC2E.

Counter Information Services, 9 Poland Street, London W1.

Institute of Race Relations, 247-249 Pentonville Road, Lon-
    don N1.

London Council of Social Services, 68 Charlton Street, Lon-
    don NW1 1JR.

Minority Rights Group, 36 Craven Street, London WC2N5 NG.

National Association of Indian Youth, 32 High Street, South-
    all, Middlesex.

National Association of Multi-Racial Education, 64 Lynmouth
    Road, London N16.

National Council for Civil Liberties, 186 King's Cross Road, London WC1X.

National Foundation for Educational Research in England and Wales, The Mere, Upton Park, Slough, England.

Political and Economic Planning, 12 Upper Belgrave Street, London SW1X.

Runnymede Trust, 62 Chandos Place, London WC2N.

Towards Racial Justice, 184 King's Cross Road, London WC1.

Youth Development Trust (Manchester), 22 Cromwell Buildings, 11 Blackfriars Street, Manchester, M35BJ.

AUTHOR INDEX

Numbers refer to item number, not to page number.

Abbott, Simon, 39, 378
Abraham, A. S., 1330
Adam, Corinna, 596, 597, 719, 720, 846
Adams, Bert N., 1074, 1628
Adams, F. J., 1209
Adamson, Giliray, 1721
Adeney, Martin, 598. 1722
Akram, Mohammed, 119, 543, 1066, 1148
Alcock, A. E., 40
Allen, Sheila, 425, 699, 796, 797, 848, 1159
Anderson, C. Arnold, 1210
Andrews, John, 1384
Anglo-French Conference on Race Relations in France and Great Britain, 1968, 1
Angus, Anne, 1331
Ankrah-Dove, Linda, 286
Anwar, Muhammad, 147, 287-289, 1160
Armitage, J., 428
Armor, David J., 1211
Armstrong, Michael, 829
Arrowsmith, Pat, 1464
Ashby, B., 1212
Asher, Wayne, 290
Association for the Education of Pupils from Overseas, 1199
Association of British Adoption and Fostering Agencies, 706

Association of Christian Teachers, 1565
Association of Multi-Racial Playgroups, 1723
Association of Teachers of English to Pupils from Overseas, 1313
Athisayam, Gillian, 721
Atkins, Liz, 133
Atkinson, Anthony Barnes, 1724
Avent, Catherine, 850
Azim, Tariq, 432
Aziz, Khalid, 1067

Bagley, Christopher, 2, 41, 293, 379, 722, 723, 791, 1000-1002, 1134, 1161, 1207, 1332, 1487, 1697-1700, 1803
Bainbridge, Dennis, 1302
Baker, Joan, 1390
Baker, Peter, 700
Ball, R., 42
Ballard, Roger, 851, 852, 1068
Bandali, Sultan G., 1003
Bandopadhyay, Nirmalaya, 853
Banner, Stephen, 701
Banton, Michael Parker, 3, 4, 5, 43, 44, 1069, 1827, 1837
Barclay, William, 223
Barnes, Gill Gorrell, 1216, 1759, 1760

Barnes, Jack, 1465
Barnett, A., 1625
Barot, Rohit, 1070
Batta, I. D., 1004
Baxton, Martin, 1712
Baxtor, Paula Trevor William, 702
Bayles, Michael D., 294
Beaumont, Tim, 1071
Beeson, T., 149, 433, 434, 854
Beetham, David, 798
Beith, Alan, 295
Bell, Geoff, 799
Bellamy, J., 435
Beloff, Max, 45
Bennett, Robert, 1488, 1489
Bennion, Francis, 724
Bentley, John David, 1385
Bentley, Stuart, 297, 436, 726, 797, 855, 965, 1217, 1626
Berger, Michael, 1135, 1312
Bergman, Carol, 1333, 1490
Berkeley, Humphry, 224
Bermant, Chaim, 966
Bernard, William S., 1761
Berry, James, 968
Beswick, W. A., 727
Bhatnager, Joti, 1186, 1491
Bhatt, S., 1171
Bhatti, F. M., 1005
Bidwell, Sidney, 380
Bindman, Geoffrey, 544, 545, 586, 587, 601, 602, 856
Bingham, Stella, 728
Birmingham Educational Priority Area Project, 1559
Bishop, Terry, 857
Black People in Britain. The Way Forward (Conference), London, 1975, 967
Blair, Carol, 1219
Blake, H. E., 1406
Blake, John, 1627
Blakeley, Madeleine, 1048
Bloom, Leonard, 6
Bogan, Robert, 381
Bogues, Tony, 1838
Bolt, Christine, 225, 302
Bolt, S., 1407
Bolton, Felicity, 1466
Bonham-Carter, Mark, 46, 120, 303, 603, 604, 730
Bonhomme, Samuel, 226

Booth, John, 1162, 1493
Bornat, Joanna, 796, 797
Bosanquet, Nicholas, 800, 861, 1701
Boss, P., 1763
Bottomley, Arthur, 121
Boulter, Hugh, 1314
Bourhis, R. Y., 1091
Bourne, Jenny, 320, 321
Bourne, Richard, 150, 304
Bowker, Gordon, 7
Boyle, Edward Charles Gurney, Baron Boyle, 1187
Bracken, H. M., 47
Bradley, Sylvia, 1408
Brah, A. M. Fuller, 1073
Brand, J., 1567
Brannen, P., 801
Brazier, Carolyn, 1409
Brendon, David, 969
Brennan, M. B., 1410
Bridger, Peter, 1049
Bridges, Lee, 305, 306
Bristow, Mike, 307, 1628
Bristow, S., 308, 1074
British Association of Social Workers, 1725
British Broadcasting Corporation, 253
British Council of Churches, 9, 1055, 1062, 1741
Brittan, Elaine Mary, 731, 756, 1457, 1482, 1483, 1494-1496
Brock, George, 438
Bronnert, David, 382
Brooks, Dennis, 439, 732, 802, 862, 863
Brough, D. I., 733
Brown, G. A., 734
Brown, John, 803, 1839
Brown, R., 1764
Browne, Gilbert, 864
Buchanan, John, 25
Burgin, Trevor, 1497
Burke, Aggrey W., 440, 1702, 1703
Burke, Anthony, 865
Burney, Elizabeth, 546, 1629
Burnham, Colin, 8
Burrowes, Horace, 1704
Bush, Martha, 1598
Butcher, H., 1212
Butterworth, Eric, 735, 1050
Buxton, Martin, 1712

Byrne, David, 1315
Byrne, E. M., 1225

CIS, 383, 804
Cain, Maureen E., 1828
Callinicos, Alex, 442
Cambridge, A. X., 866
Cameron, Gordon Campbell, 970
Cameron, James, 311
Cameron, Sue, 1498, 1589
Campbell-Platt, Kiran, 9,
    122, 805
Candlin, Christopher, 1386,
    1387
Carby, Keith, 806
Carrier, John, 7
Cashmore, Ernest, 1075
Castles, Stephen, 971
Catholic Commission for Racial
    Justice, 384
Catholic Truth Society, 709
Centre for Information on
    Language Teaching and
    Research, 1388, 1560
Channon, Omkar Nath, 685
Chansarkar, B. A., 1076
Chase, Louis A., 1006, 1804,
    1841
Cheetham, Juliet, 1726
Chopra, Subhash, 1842
Christopher, Lancelot, 1334
Churchill, R. C., 1077
Claiborne, Louis F., 547,
    606-608
Clark, David, 443, 1631
Clark, E. P., 1411
Clarke, Alva, 444
Clarke, C. F. O., 1829
Clarke, John, 1013, 1843
Clarke, Susan E., 972
Clemens, Martyn, 1412
Clyne, Peter, 1413
Coard, Bernard, 1149, 1316,
    1333
Coard, Phyllis, 1149
Cohen, Abner, 10
Cohen, Brian, 385, 1635
Cohen, Elizabeth G., 736
Cohen, Gerda, 1078
Cohen, Robin, 494
Cole, Porter, 807
Cole, William Owen, 1051, 1499
Collar, D. A., 1632
Collard, David, 48, 1633, 1639
Colling, Clive, 1226

Collins, Joyce, 1079
Collins, Paul, 868
Collymore, Yvonne, 869
Committee on Black Studies,
    1478
Community Relations Commis-
    sion see Great Britain.
    Community Relations Commis-
    sion
Community Work Group, 1052
Confederation of British
    Industry, 808
Conference on Cultural Con-
    flict and the Asian Family,
    1150
Connell, Richard, 941
Connelly, Tom, 870, 871
Constable, John, 612, 613
Conti, Jon, 1500
Cooper, Mark N., 49
Corbett, Anne, 1590
Cosgrave, Patrick, 156, 157,
    158, 313
Cotterell, Arthur, 1414
Cottle, T. J., 1007, 1080,
    1228, 1336
Counter Information Services
    see CIS
Coupland, D. E., 872
Cousins, Frank, 873, 874
Cox, Margaret, 1337
Crabbe, Pauline, 314
Crewe, Ivor, 227
Crick, Bernard, 1501
Crishna, Seetha, 1053
Croker, Susan K., 1728
Cross, Crispin P., 1008
Cross, Malcolm, 1009
Cunningham, Sir Charles, 315-
    317
Curry, Jennifer, 1583
Curtis, Sarah, 739, 1729,
    1765

Dahya, Badr, 1081, 1082
Dakin, Julian, 1560
Dalton, M., 1083
Daly, O., 875
Davenport, Maureen, 1102
Davey, Alfred G., 1229, 1568
Davies, Evelyn, 822
Davies, Graham, 1503
Davies, Margaret, 1504
Davies, Paul, 973, 1634
Davis, Anthony, 1339

Davis, D., 1415
Day, Alison, 1467, 1505, 1506
Deakin, Nicholas, 11, 159, 160,
  319-321, 385, 1635, 1636
Deaton, David, 876
Deming, A., 446
Denley, Gerald, 1416
Dennett, Margaret, 1163-1165
Derrick, June, 1386, 1387,
  1569
Devlin, Tim, 1417
Dewitt, John, 974
Dhanjal, Beryl, 1084, 1637
Dhavan, Rajeev, 967
Dhesi, A., 322
Dhondy, Farrukh, 1230
Dhondy, Mala, 877
Dickey, Anthony, 614-616
Dickie-Clarke, Hamish, 50
Dickinson, Leslie, 1326
Dimbleby, Jonathan, 740
Dixon, R. J., 1766
Dockrell, Bryan, 447
Doe, Bob, 448, 1085, 1507
Doeringer, P. B., 861
Doherty, J., 1600
Dolan, Paul J., 401
Donnelly, Lewis, 825
Donnison, David, 989
Douglas, J. W. B., 1086
Dove, Linda, 741, 1231, 1508
Drake, S., 51
Driver, Geoffrey, 1188, 1232
Dugmore, Keith, 991, 1619,
  1668
Duke, Christopher, 1601
Dummett, Ann, 386, 550, 1166
Dummett, M., 323
Dumon, W. A., 1570
Dunn, Alison, 1418
Dunning, Eric, 1509
Durojaiye, M. O. A., 742
Durojaiye, S. M., 1419
Duvoisin, Ann, 1705
Dykes, Hugh, 164

Ealing Community Relations
  Council, 1835
Edgar, David, 449
Edgington, David William,
  387, 1510
Edwards, J. H., 450
Edwards, Viv K., 1191, 1420
Egbuna, Obi Benue Joseph,
  451, 975, 976

Ehrlich, Paul R., 12
Elkin, Judith, 1469, 1470
Elkin, S. L., 452
Elliot, Jan, 119
Emecheta, Buchi, 388, 389,
  453, 454
Emerson, Patricia, 773
English, David, 457
European Commission on Human
  Rights, 165
Evans, Jane Marix, 551, 617
Evans, Peter, 458, 977, 1797,
  1844
Evans, Roger Warren, 544
Eversley, David Edward
  Charles, 124, 989
Ewen, Elizabeth Clare see
  McEwen, Elizabeth Clare
Eysenck, Hans Jurgen, 390.
  1192

Farid, S. M., 77
Faulkner, Graham, 1807
Feinmann, Jane, 1341
Feldman, Shirley, 12
Fenton, James, 168, 461, 878
Fenton, Mike, 1638, 1639
Fethney, Valerie, 1342,
  1343
Field, A. M., 107
Field, Frank, 13, 1189
Fieller, N. R. J., 1602
Figueroa, Peter M. E., 879
Filkin, C. J., 57
Findlay, Roslyn, 880
Finnegan, Brian, 1167
Fisher, Frank, 1730
Fisher, Thelma, 1730
Fletcher, Barbara, 1315
Flett, Hazel, 1640
Flew, Antony, 463, 464
Foner, Nancy, 881, 882, 1088,
  1089
Foot, Paul, 391
Ford, J. A., 1706
Forester, Tom, 883, 1767
Foster, John L., 1584
Fowler, Bridget, 884, 885
Fox, A. D., 170
Francis, H., 1344
Frasure, Robert C., 326
Freeman, Gary Pete, 126
Freeson, Reg, 1642

Gardiner, Susan, 1194
Garner, J. F., 618
Garvie, Edie, 1422, 1423
Gates, H. L., 172
Ghuman, Paul Avtar Singh, 1151
Gibbs, Norma, 1235
Giles, H., 1091
Giles, Raymond H., 1471
Gillie, Oliver, 978
Gilpin, Sylvia, 825
Gilroy, Beryl, 393, 1236
Gipps, Caroline V., 1399,
  1424, 1439
Gish, Oscar, 1688
Giuseppi, Undaine, 1389
Glean, Marion, 465
Glendenning, F. J., 1591-1593
Glennerster, Howard, 1731,
  1732
Godfrey, W. R., 1644
Goldthorpe, John H., 886
Goody, Esther, 1121
Gorz, Andre, 887
Gould, Donald, 1769
Gould, Stuart H., 888
Graham, Tipple, 1678
Grainger, Ken, 1707
Grant, L., 620
Gray, Cecil, 1390, 1391
Gray, John, 1345
Great Britain. Central Office
  of Information, 14, 15, 127,
  1193, 1689
Great Britain. Central Statis-
  tical Office, 78, 79
Great Britain. Commission for
  Racial Equality, 228, 1603
Great Britain. Commonwealth
  Immigration Advisory Coun-
  cil, 80
Great Britain. Community Rela-
  tions Commission, 16-22,
  229-235, 552-554, 703, 704,
  809-811, 979, 980, 1054,
  1194, 1317, 1318, 1392,
  1393, 1400, 1472-1475, 1485,
  1486, 1561-1563, 1604, 1690,
  1691, 1727, 1733-1738, 1755,
  1798
Great Britain. Department of
  Education and Science, 81,
  82, 1195, 1196, 1319-1321,
  1394

Great Britain. Department of
  Employment, 83, 84, 85, 812,
  889
Great Britain. Department of
  Health and Social Security,
  86, 87
Great Britain. Department of
  the Environment, 88, 89,
  90, 1605
Great Britain. Government Ac-
  tuary, 91
Great Britain. Home Depart-
  ment, 92-95
Great Britain. Home Office,
  236-238, 555-572, 1322,
  1830
Great Britain. Home Office.
  Uganda Resettlement Board,
  239, 1739
Great Britain. Laws, Sta-
  tutes, etc., 573-575
Great Britain. Ministry of
  Housing and Local Govern-
  ment, 96, 108
Great Britain. Office of Man-
  power Economics, 813
Great Britain. Office of Popu-
  lation Censuses and Sur-
  veys, 97-105, 814
Great Britain. Parliament,
  128
Great Britain. Parliament.
  House of Commons. Select
  Committee on Race Relations
  and Immigration, 106, 240-
  247, 327, 576-578, 815,
  1323, 1605, 1606, 1830,
  1831
Great Britain. Parliament.
  House of Commons. Select
  Committee on the Anti-Dis-
  crimination (No. 2) Bill,
  579
Great Britain. Parliament.
  House of Commons. Standing
  Committee B on Immigration
  Bill, 580
Great Britain. Parliament.
  House of Lords, 581, 582
Great Britain. Prime Minis-
  ter, 129
Great Britain. Race Relations
  Board, 248

Great Britain. Schools Council, 1197, 1324, 1395, 1396, 1404, 1405, 1482
Greater London Council, 107, 116, 404, 991, 1598, 1619
Greaves, Mary, 328
Green, A., 1545
Greer, Steven, 1697
Gretton, John, 466, 1238, 1239
Gribbin, J. J., 1646
Griffith, John, 621, 622
Griffiths, Ceri, 1572
Griffiths, P., 1425
Grigg, John, 1809
Grimes, E. J., 1513
Grove, John, 52
Grubb, Martyn, 1240
Guest, Juliet, 1514
Gullick, Mary, 1241
Gulliver, S., 1687
Gundara, Jagdish, 1346
Gunther, K., 891
Gupta, A., 175
Gupta, Y. P., 1242

Haddon, R., 1647
Haikin, Patricia, 13
Haines, John, 1573
Half Moon Photography Workshop, 1810
Hall, Peter, 1648
Hall, Stuart, 1168, 1169
Hallam, Roger, 1092
Halls, W. D., 1243
Halsey, A. H., 1325, 1347
Hamilton-Paterson, James, 329
Hammond, Robert, 1649
Hamnet, Chris, 981
Hankins, Brian, 1426
Hanks, Betty C., 1515
Hanna, Max, 467, 1811
Harden, Jane, 1203
Hardie, Alan, 893
Harding, Kate, 1437
Hardy, Allan F., 894
Harland, Peter, 744, 1812
Harrington, I., 624, 1010
Harris, Sydney, 468
Harrison, Brian, 1397
Harrison, Paul, 745, 1011, 1093
Harrison, Robert M., 817
Hartley, Tim, 583
Hartmann, Paul, 746, 1799, 1813

Harwood, Jonathan, 4
Hatch, Stephen, 53
Hatchet, Alastair, 442
Hay, Hope, 1607
Haynes, Judith Mary, 1198, 1244
Headley, Jane, 747
Heaton, J. B., 1427
Hedayatullah, M., 1094
Heinemann, Benjamin W., 394
Hepple, Bob, 818
Herbert, Martin, 1103
Hibbert, C., 469
Higgins, Rosalyn, 625
Hill, Barry, 1095, 1348
Hill, Clifford, 1012, 1055, 1608, 1650
Hill, David, 748, 982, 1096, 1097, 1564
Hill, Janet, 1476
Hill, Michael J., 249, 330
Hinchliffe, Margaret, 1429
Hines, Vince, 983
Hiro, Dilip, 395, 396, 470, 471
Hitchens, Christopher, 179, 878
Hobbs, Maurice, 1247, 1565
Hodges, Lucy, 1516
Hodgkinson, C. A., 1248
Hodlin, Susan, 1398
Hogbin, Jack W. G., 1517
Hogg, Quintin, 626
Holden, Bronwen M., 851, 852
Holland, M., 895
Hollings, Michael, 749
Holman, Robert, 1741, 1742, 1770
Holmes, Colin, 472
Holroyde, Geoffrey, 1249
Holroyde, Peggy, 1056
Homeshaw, J., 1763
Hood, Catriona, 1743
Hooper, Rachel, 397
Hope, Francis, 750, 1098
Hopkins, Adam, 1250
Horowitz, Dan, 331
Houghton, Vic, 514, 1349
Howe, Darcus, 1845
Howell, D., 1190
Howells, William W., 55
Hubbard, Alan, 752
Hudson, Bob, 1350
Humphry, Derek, 398, 584, 1832

Hunt, Sandra, 1708
Husband, Charles, 746, 1799, 1800, 1813, 1814
Husen, Torsten, 1351
Huttenback, Robert Arthur, 250
Huxley, E., 182

Incomes Data Services, 819
Inner London Education Authority see London. Inner London Education Authority
Institute of Economic Affairs, 123
Institute of Personnel Management, 806, 843
Institute of Practitioners in Advertising, 705
Institute of Race Relations, 125, 378, 1834
Iqbal, Mohammed, 1056, 1100, 1253
Irvine, Keith, 252
Issacharoff, Ruth M., 249

Jackson, Barbara, 706
Jackson, Brian, 1745, 1773
Jackson, Mark, 1254, 1520, 1574
Jackson, Mary, 1238
Jackson, Ray, 1255
Jackson, Sonia, 1746, 1774
Jacobs, David M., 1170
Jahoda, G., 1171
Jahoda, Marie, 56
James, Alan Geoffrey, 1057
James, C., 1430
James, Kenneth, 1354, 1431
Janner, Greville Ewan, 820
Jay, Eric, 1585
Jeffcoate, Robert, 754, 755, 1521-1523
Jefferson, Tony, 1013
Jeffrey, Patricia, 1058, 1101
Jeffrey, Peter, 1594
Jelinek, Milena M., 756, 1524
Jenkins, Rachel, 1730
Jenkins, Simon, 707
Jenkinson, Robert F., 1834
Jenkinson, Sally, 1501
Jensen, Arthur Robert, 476, 1256
John, Augustine, 985

John, Gus, 398, 1775
Johnson, R. W., 332
Johnson, S. F., 1257, 1258
Johnston, Robert John, 1611
Johnstone, T., 333
Jones, Catherine, 130, 1747
Jones, Clement, 1801
Jones, Huw R., 1102
Jones, Hywel, 1575
Jones, Joan, 1745
Jones, Kathleen, 131, 184, 821
Jones, Mervyn, 477, 631
Jones, P. N., 1014
Jordan, Robert R., 1432, 1433
Jordanhill College of Education, 1326
Jowell, R., 898
Judge, Anthony, 1833, 1846
Judge, Ken, 1776
Judge, Tony, 1654
Jupp, Thomas Cyprian, 822, 899, 1398

Kallarackal, A. M., 1103
Kanitkar, H. A., 1015
Kannan, C. T., 1152
Kapo, Remi, 900
Kareh, Diana, 708
Karmi, H. S., 1104
Karn, Valerie A., 1655, 1656
Katznelson, Ira, 132, 334
Kawwa, T., 774
Kelly, Cheryl, 34
Kelly, Michael, 1167
Kendall, Michael N., 901
Kentish, Barbara, 709
Kerr, Alice, 903
Ketchum, Sara Ann, 478
Khan, Asif, 904
Khan, Naseem, 986
Khan, Nawab, 1525
Khan, Verity Saifullah, 1105, 1106
Kidman, Brenda, 253
Kiernan, E. Victor Gordon, 254
King, Jane, 1709
King, R., 403
Kinnibrugh, Donald, 1050
Kirby, Alexander, 185, 633
Kirkcaldy, John, 479, 1434
Kirkham, Pat, 905

Kirkwood, Kenneth, 1526
Kirp, David, 1259
Kitzinger, Sheila, 1710, 1711
Klein, Rudolf, 1712
Knappman, Edward W., 480
Knight, Lindsay, 1777
Knox, Valerie, 906, 1657
Koestler, Arthur, 481
Kohler, David Frank, 58, 109-
   113, 186-191, 634, 635, 823
Kosack, Godula, 971
Kramer, J., 1107
Krausz, Ernest, 23, 24, 757,
   1016
Kuepper, William George, 255,
   1108
Kumar, Krishna, 223
Kuper, Leo, 417, 710, 987

Labor Party (Great Britain)
   see Labour Party (Great Bri-
   tain)
Labour Party (Great Britain),
   133, 134, 399
Lackey, G. Lynne, 255, 1108
Laird, A. F., 335
Laishley, Jennie, 482, 758,
   1466
Laishley, Jenny, 759
Lambert, John R., 57, 1834
Lambeth Libraries, 25
Lancelot, Christopher, 1355
Lane, David, 1658
Langton, Pat, 1659
Lapping, Sir A., 1017
Lapping, Anne, 192
Lawrence, Daniel, 711
Lawrence, Susanne, 484, 760
Layton-Henry, Zig, 336, 337
Leach, Bridget, 907, 1109
Leach, Edmund, 485
Lee, G. L., 824
Lee, Trevor R., 1018, 1612,
   1613
Lees, Ray, 1778, 1779
Legum, Colin, 193, 637
Leicester Teachers, 1199
Leigh, Sarah, 543
Leighton, Jeremy, 1661
Lemon, Joyce P., 1780
Lengermann, Patricia Madoo,
   1110
Lester, Anthony, 586, 587,
   638, 639, 988

Lestor, J., 486
Lethbridge, J., 1355
Levine, Josie, 1435
Levine, Ned, 761
Lewis, E. Glyn, 1527
Liberal Party (Great Britain).
   Panel on Immigration, Race
   and Community Relations,
   135, 136
Library Advisory Council,
   1734
Lindley, Richard, 1662
Lines, S., 908
Little, Alan, 58, 762, 1111,
   1260, 1782
Little, Kenneth, 256
Littlewood, Barbara, 884
Liu, W. H., 640
Locke, Anthony, 1513
Lodge, Bert, 1261
Lomas, Glenys Barbara Gil-
   lian, 114, 122, 194, 827,
   909, 1614, 1663, 1664
Lomas, Graham Maurice, 825
London, Louise, 487
London Boroughs Association,
   1749
London. Centre for Environ-
   mental Studies, 989
London Council of Social Ser-
   vices, 825, 1754
London Housing Research
   Group, 1615
London. Inner London Educa-
   tion Authority, 1200, 1740
Lorimer, Douglas Alendarder,
   257
Louden, D., 1073, 1172
Lozells Social Development
   Centre, 1751
Lucas, Eileen, 1112, 1113
Lydamore, Margaret, 1063
Lyon, Alex, 196
Lyon, Michael H., 59, 763,
   1114
Lyttle, John, 641

Mabey, Christine, 1201
McCulloch, J. W., 1004, 1019,
   1783
MacDonald, Barry, 1536, 1555
MacDonald, Ian Alexander, 588,
   589, 1847
McDonald, Joan E., 1436

MacDonald, Marcia, 1115
McDowell, D., 1262
Mace, Jane, 1437
McEldowney, Patricia L., 1438
McEwen, Elizabeth Clare,
    1399, 1424, 1439
McFie, J., 1263
McGlashan, Colin, 1020, 1021,
    1173, 1264
McGrath, Morag, 911, 1778,
    1779
Machie, Lindsay, 505
MacInnes, Colin, 1022, 1116
McIntosh, Neil, 400
Mack, Joanna, 1356
McKay, David H., 1616, 1617
Mackay, R., 1432, 1433
McKenzie, Robert, 197
Mackie, Lindsay, 505
McLean, Alan C., 1440
McNeal, Julia, 385, 1477
MacShane, Denis, 489
Madge, Nic, 590
Madge, Nicola, 996
Madigan, Ruth, 884
Makins, Virginia, 338, 1441
Mamdani, Mahmood, 137
Marjoribanks, Kevin, 1118
Mark, Robert, 1848
Marks, Laurence, 198
Marriott, Louis, 1815
Marsh, Alan, 490, 491, 764,
    1174
Marshall, Peter, 1849
Marshall, Roy, 492
Martin-Jenkins, Christopher,
    765
Marvell, J., 766
Mason, Philip, 26, 27, 493,
    990
Mason, Tim, 1665
May, Roy, 494
Mazov, V., 258
Mazrui, Ali A., 1175
Meacher, Michael, 495
Medlicott, Paul, 1119, 1265,
    1266, 1357
Melgert, Willy, 418
Meth, Monty, 826
Middleweek, Helene, 825
Midwinter, Eric, 1528
Mildon, Iva Wallis, 1666
Miles, R., 913, 1073
Miller, Henry, 496
Miller, Ruth, 401

Millins, Ken, 1576
Milner, David, 60, 497, 992,
    1176, 1177
Minority Rights Group, 392,
    547
Mobbs, Michael C., 1400
Monck, Elizabeth M., 827,
    1614
Moore, G., 993
Moore, Robert Samuel, 61,
    138, 402, 498, 914
Moorman, Paul, 1442
Morgan, Marjorie Lloyd, 1401
Morrell, William Parker, 259
Morrey, C. R., 116
Morris, Sam, 1120, 1478,
    1530
Morrish, Ivor, 1059
Morrison, A., 1212
Morrison, Lionel, 712, 767,
    915, 916
Morton, Janis, 1134
Moseley, Caroline, 1358,
    1359
Mowat, John, 1360
Muir, Christine, 1121
Mukherjee, Bishwa Nath, 1785
Mullard, Christ, 260
Mullen, Lloyd, 1431
Mundy, J. H., 1361, 1443,
    1532
Mungham, Geoff, 828
Munns, Roger, 1533
Munro, Colin, 643
Murari, Timeri, 1178

Nagenda, John, 768
Naik, Don, 1786
Nandy, Dipak, 117, 644, 839,
    1667, 1850
Narayan, Rudy, 339
National Association for
    Multi-racial Education,
    1191
National Association of In-
    dian Youth, 1744
National Council for Civil
    Liberties, 590, 594
National Council for One-
    Parent Families, 1724
National Council of Social
    Services, 1743
National Foundation for Educa-
    tional Research, 1271, 1327,
    1328, 1399, 1483

National Union of Teachers,
   1402
Nayar, Tripta, 761
New Society, 1816
Newall, Venetia, 1123
Newell, David, 918, 1787
Newton, Kenneth, 261, 973,
   1634
Nicholson, Geoffrey, 786
Nicol, A. R., 1713, 1714
Nicolson, Colin, 139
Nikolinakos, Marios, 499
Noble, R. W., 1444
Norbum, Roger, 1445
Norris, R. A. 1446
North, David, 919
Norton, Philip, 647
Notting Hill Social Council,
   1752
Nugent, Neill, 403, 501

Obler, Jeffrey L., 972
Obrien, Justin, 262
Omar, Barbara, 648, 1363
O'Muircheartaigh, Colin, 922
Onyeama, Dillibe, 263
Oppe, T., 1743
Opte, E., 1743
Ottevanger, Tim, 1273
Oxford, Alec, 1744

Page, Raissa C., 1788
Pahl, R. E., 1618
Palmer, Godfrey, 503
Palmer, Howard, 140
Panning, W. H., 452
Parekh, Bhikhu, 994, 1150
Parekh, Pramila, 1150
Parker, Bob, 1535
Parker, Jim, 1595
Parker, John, 1619, 1668,
   1817
Parkinson, J. P., 1536
Parliamentary Group on the
   Feasibility and Usefulness
   of a Register of Dependents,
   128
Parrott, F., 1447
Parry, Jann, 1024-1026
Parry, W. H., 1715
Parsons, Dennis, 1537
Patel, Praful R. C., 504
Paterson, Peter, 829

Patterson, Sheila, 770, 1124
Payne, Joan, 1202
Peach, G. C. K., 200, 1028
Peaford, Margaret, 1640
Peaker, Gilbert Fawcett, 1327
Pearce, K. S., 1364-1366
Pearl, David, 655-665, 1789
Pearn, M. A., 666
Pearson, David G., 344, 1125
Pearson, Geoff, 828
Peirce, G., 620
Percil, J. J., 1401
Pereira, Cecil, 1074
Perry, Jane, 1620, 1669
Perry, Norman, 1029
Pettigrew, J., 1126
Phillips, K. Diana, 141
Phillips, Melanie, 345
Phillips, Michael, 346
Phillips, Mike, 505
Phillips, Ron, 347
Philpott, Stuart B. 142
Phizacklea, A., 913
Pickvance, C. G., 1625, 1670
Pierce, Christine, 478
Pirani, M., 1179
Plant, Martin A., 1671
Plender, Richard, 201, 591,
   667-669
Pless, I., 1743
Political and Economic Plan-
   ning, 409, 838
Pollak, Margaret, 995
Pollard, Paul, 1127
Potter, Tim, 348
Poulter, S., 1128
Power, Jonathan, 349, 924
Praeger, Peter, 1539
Prescotte, Patricia Clarke,
   898
Prest, Mike, 1030
Preston, Barbara, 1031
Preston, Maurice, 506
Price, Christopher, 1596
Prickett, John, 1129
Pritt, D. N., 670
Proctor, Chris, 1586
Proffit, N., 446
Prosser, Hilary, 1158
Pryce, Kenneth, 771
Pugh, A. K., 1427
Pulle, Stanislaus, 830, 1835
Pye, Michael, 1448

Raban, Jonathan, 1032, 1033
Race Today Collective, 508-
    512, 928, 929, 1673, 1674,
    1822, 1823, 1853-1860
Radice, Francis, 1449
Raphael, Adam, 193
Raspberry, William 1130, 1180,
    1181
Raynor, John, 1203
Raynor, Lois, 713
Readhead, Pamela, 1403
Redman, Michael J. 595
Rees, Tom, 833, 922
Reid, Vince, 772
Rennie, John, 1542
Reubens, Edwin P., 1034
Rex, John, 28, 264, 354, 1675,
    1676
Reynolds, Paul, 513
Reynolds, V., 65
Rhoden, Ernest L., 1543
Richard, J. K., 1544
Richards, Martin, 1153
Richardson, C., 355
Richardson, Ken, 514, 1153
Richardson, Stephen A., 773,
    1545
Richmond, Anthony H., 66,
    834, 1621, 1677
Ridgeway, C., 961
Rimmer, Malcolm, 835
Ritchey, P. Neal, 1035
Road, Alan, 1279
Roberts, C. D., 1546
Roberts, Celia, 932
Roberts-Holmes, Joy, 1367
Robertson, T. S., 774
Robinson, Clive, 1861
Rogaly, Joe, 836
Rogers, Margaret, 1280, 1477,
    1547
Rolph, C. H., 67, 1862
Romijn, Jan, 1754
Rose, Arnold Marshall, 29
Rose, Caroline B., 29
Rose, Eliot Joseph Benn, 1824
Rose, Hannan, 356, 677-681
Rose, John, 515
Rose, Paul, 682
Rose, Richard, 68
Rose, Steven, 516
Roser, J. S., 404
Rossiter, Ann, 517, 933
Roswith, Gerloff, 714

Roth, Andrew, 265
Rowan, Iain, 1132
Rowland, V. I., 934
Rowley, Gwyn, 1678
Roy, Amit, 357, 1133
Rudd, Elizabeth M., 1450,
    1451
Rudin, Jeff, 1548
Runciman, W. G., 1036
Runnymede Trust, 9, 118, 119,
    251, 266, 267, 405, 550,
    585, 592, 593, 831, 837,
    842, 1622
Russell, Alan Gladney, 268
Russell, Ken, 1836
Russell, Ralph, 1136
Rutter, Michael, 996, 1134,
    1135, 1312, 1716

Sadler, G. T., 1368
Samuels, Alec, 683
Sanders, Peter, 684
Sansbury, Kenneth, 406
Sansom, Basil, 702
Santa Cruz, Hernan, 30, 31
Sargeant, A. J., 776
Scase, Richard, 69
Schaefer, Richard T., 358,
    407, 408, 518, 777
Schoen, Douglas E., 269, 270,
    332
Schofield, D., 685
Schools Council see Great
    Britain. Schools Council
Scipio, L., 1369
Scobie, Edward, 271, 519
Scott, Duncan, 359
Scott, Elizabeth, 839
Scott, Gavin, 360, 936, 1239,
    1282, 1370-1373, 1791
Scott, George, 1825
Scott, Rachel, 1479, 1480
Scott, S. E., 1550
Seabrook, Jeremy, 778
Seaman, J. M., 1083
Searle, Chris, 1037, 1154,
    1155
Select Committee on Race Re-
    lations and Immigration
    see Great Britain. Parlia-
    ment. House of Commons.
    Select Committee on Race
    Relations and Immigration

Seminar on Measures to be
   Taken on the National Level,
   32
Sen, Amya, 1692
Sengupta, Susan, 937
Sevinc, Muzeyyen, 789
Shah, G. B., 1453
Shamsher, Joginder S., 939,
   1136
Sharma, Ursula, 1060
Shepherd, Robin, 1063
Sherman, Barrie, 594
Shillian, David, 1577
Shiner, Roger A., 780
Shyllon, Folarin Olawale,
   272, 273, 686
Sibley, Tom, 940
Siddiqui, Hamid Rabbani, 1204
Silk, Andrew, 520
Sills, Patrick, 361
Silver, Robert, 521
Simmonds, Kenneth, 941
Simms, Ruth P. 223
Simpson, R. E. D., 1137, 1138
Simpson, William, 942
Simsova, S., 1182
Sinclair, Sir George, 121
Sinclair, J. M., 1452
Singh, Karamjit, 439, 862
Singh, P., 1551
Sivanandan, Ambalavaner, 33,
   34, 274, 522-524, 1038
Skone, J. F., 1693
Slatter, Stuart, 809
Smith, A. D., 131, 184
Smith, David John, 400, 409,
   410, 838, 943, 944, 1623,
   1679
Smith, Derek, 411
Smith, Jef, 362
Smith, N. J., 1004, 1783
Smith, Peter B., 781
Smith, Richard, 1139
Social Science Research Coun-
   cil, 35
Solanki, Ramniklal, 945
Sookhdeo, Patrick, 1061
Sparks, Colin, 525, 526
Sparks, D. F., 946
Spears, David, 1153
Spittles, Brian, 527, 1140
Stacey, Tom, 275
Stadlen, Frances, 363, 1039,
   1285-1287, 1376

Stafford-Clark, David, 412
Stanton, Michael, 782, 1453
Stapleton, John, 364
Stephen, Andrew, 947, 948
Stephen, David, 143, 365,
   689, 839
Stephens, Leslie, 36
Stern, Vivian, 1194, 1289-
   1292, 1454
Stevenson, D., 949
Stewart, Margaret, 840, 950
Stewart, Philippa, 997
Stock, A. K., 1190
Stoker, Diana, 1205
Stott, John, 1756
Stroud, C., 1717
Studler, Donley T., 366, 783
Sumner, R., 1399
Swinerton, E. Nelson, 255,
   1108
Sye, Robert J., 208
Syer, Michael, 1294

Tajfel, Henri, 1183
Tambs-Lyche, Harald, 1141
Taper, Toby, 1680
Taylor, Francine, 1481
Taylor, John Henry, 715, 952,
   1142, 1206, 1295, 1681
Taylor, Laurie, 528, 529
Taylor, Robert, 953
Taylor, Stan, 337, 367
Thakur, Manab, 806, 841, 954
Thomas, Brinley, 144
Thomas, Clem, 786
Thomas, K. C., 1554
Thomas, Roger Edmund, 716
Thomas, S., 1171
Thompson, Dorothea, 1377
Thompson, J. A., 1263
Thompson, John, 787
Thompson, Marcus, 1184
Thompson, Susan S., 1156
Thomson, Grant, 37
Tilbe, Douglas, 1062
Tinker, Hugh, 145, 276, 277,
   369
Tizard, Barbara, 531, 1793
Tobias, J. J., 1864
Tomilson, Sally, 1298
Tough, Joan, 1455
Townsend, Bert, 1456, 1457

Townsend, Herbert Elwood Rout-
  ledge, 1299, 1328, 1482,
  1483
Townshend, John Rowe, 1597
Toynbee, Josephine, 762
Triseliotis, John Paul, 1757
Troyna, Barry, 1865
Trudgian, Raymond, 1063
Trussler, Denis, 1041
Tucker, Peter, 278, 691
Tunteng, P-Kiven, 532
Turner, Charles, 789

Underwood, Chris, 373, 1866
Union of Muslim Organisations
  of United Kingdom and Ire-
  land, 1204
United Nations. Commission on
  Human Rights, 625
United Nations Educational,
  Scientific and Cultural Or-
  ganization, 417
United Nations. General Assem-
  bly, 413, 414
United Nations. Institute for
  Training and Research, 378
United Nations. Secretary
  General, 415, 416
United Nations. Subcommission
  on Prevention of Discrimi-
  nation and Protection of
  Minorities, 30

Van den Berghe, Pierre L.,
  888
Van den Berghs and Jurgens,
  Ltd., 1694
Van Haute, Hans, 418
Varma, Ved P., 1695
Vennings, Philip, 1300
Verma, Gajendra K., 791, 792,
  1207, 1487, 1555
Vestey, Michel, 533
Vetta, Atam, 1301
Vincent, John James, 419
Vohra, Dharam Kumar, 1056

Wade, Donald William, 717
Wainwright, David, 843
Wakefield, Bernard, 1302
Walker, David, 1303

Walker, Douglas James, 595
Walker, George, 1459
Walker, Peter, 534
Wall, Max, 1826
Wallace, Tina, 138
Wallis, P., 949
Wallis, Susan, 214, 1145
Wallwork, Jean, 1460
Walvin, James, 70, 279, 280
Wandsworth Council for Com-
  munity Relations, 844, 998
Ward, George, 845
Ward, Michael, 584
Ward, Robin H., 215, 374,
  375, 1625, 1682
Waters, Hazel, 33, 71
Watkins, Alan, 694, 695
Watson, George, 535, 1185
Watson, James Lee, 1157
Watson, Peter, 38, 536, 537,
  794, 958, 1378
Waugh, Auberon, 538
Wedge, Peter, 1158
Weightman, Gavin, 1042
Weintraub, Allen L., 281
Weir, Stuart, 1043
Weissert, William, 919
Wells, John Christopher, 1064
Werner, Eric, 1044
West, Katharine, 1045
West, Richard, 217, 959
Whalley, Ann, 1623
Whitaker, Ben, 392
White, David, 1046, 1146,
  1686
White, H. C., 1719
White, Sarah, 420
Whitehouse, R., 1147
Whitfield, Sylvia, 146, 697
Wicker, B., 219, 540
Widlake, Paul, 1484
Wight, James, 1382, 1461
Wilby, Peter, 960
Wild, Raymond, 961
Wilke, Ingeborg, 1308
Wilkinson, R. K., 1687
Willes, Mary, 1329
Willey, Richard, 1383, 1580-
  1582
Williams, Roger, 954
Williamson, Bill, 1315
Willke, I., 1309
Wilson, A. T. M. 809
Wilson, Amrit, 795, 1462

Wilson, David, 962
Wilson, Sir Geoffrey, 1047
Wilson, Michael J., 781
Winchester, S. W. C., 200, 221
Wingo, Lowdon, 970
Winter, J. M., 541
Wolverhampton Council for Com-
    munity Relations, 701
Wood, Christopher, 1794-1796
Wood, D., 335
Wood, John, 282
Wood, Susanne, 222
Woodhouse, Derrick F., 1720
Woodroffe, Bev, 1556
Woods, Robert Ivor, 999
Woodward, Peter, 1557
Workers' Fight, 832
Workman, G., 377
World Council of Churches,
    421

Worrall, Mary, 1558
Worrell, Keith, 1310
Wrench, K. J., 824
Wright, Derek, 542

Yarmohammadi, Lotfollah, 1463
Yorkshire Committee for Com-
    munity Relations, 717
Youth Service Information Cen-
    tre, 1758
Yudkin, Simon, 1696
Yule, Bridget, 1134, 1312
Yule, William, 1135, 1312

Zellick, Graham, 698
Zubaida, Sami, 422

TITLE INDEX

This index includes all titles of books, published
reports, and theses which are cited in the text.
In some cases titles have been shortened.
Titles of journal articles are not included.

Accidents are Colour Blind,
  824
Act Now, 397
Action in the Priority Areas,
  1723
Adequate Income for One-Parent
  Families, 1724
Adoption and the Coloured
  Child, 708
Adoption of Non-White Chil-
  dren, 713
After Four Years, 546
Aliens, 555, 556
All Our Children, 1730
Annual Abstract of Greater
  London Statistics, 72
Annual Abstract of Statis-
  tics, 78
Arts Britain Ignores,
  986
As They See It, 712
Asians in Britain, 1061,
  1694
Aspects of Mental Health,
  1690
Assimilation of Jamaicans,
  716
Attitudes of Ethnic Minori-
  ties, 982
Attitudes of Young Immigrants,
  977

Attitudes to the Coloured
  People in Glasgow, 700
Audio-Visual Aids, 16

Background and Employment of
  Asian Immigrants, 822
Background of Immigrant Chil-
  dren, 1059
Banyan Tree, 145
Battle of Grunwick, 799
Because They are Black, 398
Between Two Cultures, 1157
Black and White, 279, 1584
Black Britain, 260
Black Britannia, 271
Black British, White Bri-
  tish, 395, 396
Black Britons, 13, 25
Black Churches, 1055
Black Men, White Cities, 132
Black Migrants, White Na-
  tives, 711
Black People in Britain, 272
Black People in Britain: The
  Way Forward, 967
Black Presence, 280
Black Slaves in Britain, 273
Black Teacher, 393
Bluefoot Traveller, 968
Books for Children, 1476

Books for the Multi-Racial
  Classroom, 1469, 1470
Born to Fail, 1158
Britain: Ann Official Hand-
  book, 73
Britain, the Black Man and the
  Future, 983
British and French Policies,
  126
British Attitudes to the Ne-
  gro, 257
British Nationality Law, 557
British Overseas Expansion,
  259
British Right, 403
Brothers to All Men, 826
Brown Britons, 262
Buying a House, 1599

CRC Evidence, 810
Caretakers, 1721
Caring for Under-Fives, 1737
Case and the Course, 1478
Census 1971, 97-99, 114, 122,
  814
Chaos or Cummunity, 709
Children and Race, 992
Children of West Indian Immi-
  grants, 1743
Christians and Colour in Bri-
  tain, 387
Cities, Regions and Public
  Policy, 970
Citizens Without Status, 988
Citizenship and Nationality,
  550
Citizenship, Immigration and
  Integration, 134
Citizenship of the United
  Kingdom and Colonies, 229,
  278
Colloque Franco-Britannique,
  1
Colour and Rehousing, 1601
Colour and the Allocation of
  GLC Housing, 1619
Colour, Citizenship and Bri-
  tish Society, 385
Colour, Culture and Cons-
  ciousness, 994
Colour in Britain, 74
Colour of Six Schools, 1464
Colour Prejudice in Britain,
  834

Colour, Race and Empire, 268
Coloured Population of Great
  Britain, 104, 1614
Combating Racism, 406
Commonwealth Citizens, 558
Commonwealth Foundation's
  Race Relations Bursary
  Scheme, 1727
Commonwealth Immigrants Acts
  1962 and 1968, 548, 559-
  561
Commonwealth Immigration, 821
Community Action, 1722
Community Action and Race Re-
  lations, 249
Community Relations, 1063
Complaints Against the Po-
  lice, 1836
Concentration and Dispersal,
  1612
Continuing Needs of Immi-
  grants, 1319
Control of Commonwealth Im-
  migration, 121, 576-578
Control of Immigration Sta-
  tistics, 92
Country of Birth and Colour,
  105
Crime, Police and Race Rela-
  tions, 1834
Cross'd With Adversity, 1324
Cultural Conflict and the
  Asian Family, 1150
Cultural Contents of Think-
  ing, 1151
Current Issues in Community
  Work, 1052
Current Tempo of Fertility,
  77
Curriculum Innovation in Lon-
  don's E.P.A.'s, 1465
Cycles of Disadvantage, 996

Department of Employment Ga-
  zette, 83
Destroy This Temple, 975, 986
Development of Ethnic Con-
  cepts, 1156
Development Together, 1756
Digest of Views, 549
Doctor Migration and World
  Health, 1688
Doctors from Overseas, 1691
Don't Rush Me, 1729
Dutch Plural Society, 2

E.P.A. Problems and Policies,
 1325
E.P.A. Surveys and Statistics,
 1202
East Comes West, 1056
Economic Impact of Common-
 wealth Immigration, 131
Economic Issues in Immigra-
 tion, 123
Education, 1323
Education and the Urban Cri-
 sis, 1189
Education, Employment and
 Integration, 715
Education for a Multi-Cul-
 tural Society, 1472-1475
Education for a Multi-Racial
 Britain, 1466
Education for Adult Immi-
 grants, 1190
Education in Britain, 1193
Education in Multi-Racial
 Schools, 1468
Education of Immigrants,
 1320
Education Service for the
 Whole Community, 1200
Education Statistics, 75
Education Survey, 81
Educational Assessment of
 Immigrant Pupils, 1198
Educational Disadvantage,
 1321
Educational Needs of Chil-
 dren, 1318
Elimination of All Forms of
 Racial Discrimination, 415,
 416
Employer's Guide to Equal Pay,
 829
Employer's Guide to the Law,
 820
Employment, 815
Employment and Socio-Economic
 Conditions, 827
Employment of Black People,
 823
Employment of Non-English
 Speaking Workers, 809
Employment Policies in the
 Hosiery Industry, 830
End Colonial and Racial
 Crimes, 258
English as a Second and
 Foreign Language, 1397

English Language, 1385
English Lessons at Work
 Pay Dividends, 1403
Enoch Powell, 265
Enoch Powell and the Powel-
 lites, 269, 270
Enoch Powell and the West
 Indian Immigrants, 226
Entering the World of Work,
 801
Equal Pay, 813
Ethnic Minorities in Bri-
 tain, 23, 24, 109-113
Ethnic Minorities in Society,
 9
Ethnic Relations, 35
Ethnicity, Cultural Compe-
 tence and School Achieve-
 ment, 1188
Evidence from the Community
 Relations Commission, 1392
Extent and Content of Racial
 Prejudice, 407, 408
Extent of Racial Discrimina-
 tion, 400

Facts and Figures 1972, 76
Facts of Racial Disadvantage,
 409
Facts Paper on the United
 Kingdom, 125
Fair Housing Experiment,
 1620
Family Experiences of Inter-
 Racial Adoption, 706
Far Upon the Mountain, 1148
Film Catalogue, 17
Final Report of Uganda Re-
 settlement Board, 239
Firm But Unfair, 119
First Fifteen Months,
 266
First Look at Asians, 1559
Foreigners in Our Community,
 418
Forsaken Lover, 1154
 1155
Fort Grunwick, 845
Fostering Black Children,
 1736
Fourth World, 392
Friends and Neighbours in
 Islington, 1607
From Citizen to Refugee, 137
Future of Broadcasting, 1798

Getting to Know Ourselves,
  1149
Girls of Asian Origin in Bri-
  tain, 1053
Greater London Services, 1740
Grunwick, 816, 836
Guide to Legal Aid, 1725

Half-Way Generation, 1206
Handful of Tears, 253
Health and Welfare, 1696
Health Services in Britain,
  1689
Here to Live, 707
Hindu Family in Britain, 1049
Home from Home, 1733
Housing, 1606
Housing and Construction Sta-
  tistics, 88
Housing and Race in Indus-
  trial Society, 1616, 1617
Housing in Multi-Racial Areas,
  1609
Housing Need Among Ethnic Mi-
  norities, 1603
Housing Statistics, 89
Housing Survey Reports, 108
How Black?, 701
How the West Indian Child is
  Made Educationally Subnor-
  mal, 1316
How to Calculate Immigration
  Statistics, 117
Human Rights and Race in the
  U.K., 36

Idea of Race, 3
Illegal Child-Minders, 1746
Illegal Immigration and the
  Law, 585
Immigrant Children in Infant
  Schools, 1205, 1395
Immigrant Housing, 1598
Immigrant Pupils in England,
  1328
Immigrant School Learner, 1326
Immigrant Workers and the
  Class, 971
Immigrants, 997, 1728
Immigrants and Crime, 993
Immigrants at School, 1186
Immigrants in Europe, 11
Immigrants in London, 1600

Immigration, 136
Immigration Act 1971, 573,
  1725
Immigration and Enoch Powell,
  275
Immigration and Integration,
  1608
Immigration and Race Rela-
  tions, 135, 143, 251
Immigration and Racialism,
  133
Immigration and Settlement,
  118
Immigration and Social Policy
  in Britain, 1747
Immigration and the Rise of
  Multi-Culturalism, 140
Immigration Appeals, 141
Immigration Bill, 562-564,
  581, 582
Immigration Bill and the In-
  dustrial Relations Bill,
  594
Immigration Bill 1971, 544,
  580
Immigration from the Common-
  wealth, 129
Immigration into Britain, 127
Immigration Law, 551
Immigration Statistics, 93
Implications of Youth Work
  in Asian Community, 1744
Indian Workers Associations
  in Britain, 974
Industrial English, 1398
Industry as Seen by Immigrant
  Workers, 841
Inequality of Man, 390
Inner City, 825
In-Service Education of
  Teachers, 1561
Inside Out, 804
Installment Credit in Bri-
  tain, 1610
Interim Report of Uganda
  Resettlement Board, 1739
International Asian Guide and
  Directory, 984
Inter-Racial Marriages in
  London, 1152
Investigation into the Colour
  Problem, 1538

Jamaican Pronunciation in
  London, 1064

John Bull's Nigger, 263

Kingswood District Council
  Services Information Handbook, 1748

Language, 1386, 1387
Language and Immigrants, 1388
Language for Life, 1394, 1402
Language for Living, 1390,
  1391
Language Proficiency, 1399
LBA Handbook, 1749
Library in the Multi-Racial
  Secondary School, 1467
List of Community Relations
  Councils, 230
Local Housing Statistics, 90,
  96
London, 989, 1618
London Borough of Ealing In-
  formation Handbook, 1750
London Facts and Figures, 115
Lords of Human Kind, 254

Making Audio-Visual Materials,
  1199
Man Apart, 1833
Meeting Their Needs, 1400
Migrants and Refugees, 1058
Migration and Distribution,
  991
Migration and Economic Growth,
  144
Migration and Race, 120
Migration and Race Relations,
  1621
Minority Problems, 29
Monthly Digest of Statistics,
  79
Multiple Deprivation and the
  Inner City, 981
Multiracial Class, 1484
Multi-Racial Community, 979
Multi-Racial Education, 1482
Multi-Racial School, 1477
Museums in Education, 1195
Muslim Burials, 1054

Nahda's Family, 1048
Negroes in Britain, 256

Nelson's New West Indian
  Readers, 1389
New Earnings Survey, 84
New Immigration Law, 588
New Minorities, Old Con-
  flicts, 699
New Race Law and Employment,
  819
1971 Census, 116
1971 Census Data on London's
  Overseas Born Population,
  107
No Bloody Suntans, 844
No Problems Here, 806
No To the Fascists, 411
Not Proven, 969

Odyssey of Enoch Powell, 224
On the State of the Public
  Health, 86
One Thousand Children, 1745
One Year On, 235
Organisation in a Multira-
  cial School, 1483
Organisation of Race Rela-
  tions Administration, 236,
  241

Pakistan Act 1974, 574
Partnership in Black and
  White, 714
Passports and Politics, 584
Patterns of Dominance, 26
People in Paper Chains, 146
Pity of it All, 710
Play Space in North Kensing-
  ton, 1752
Plowden Children Four Years
  Later, 1327
Point of Arrival, 966
Police and Community Rela-
  tions, 1829
Police-Community Relations,
  1827
Police-Immigrant Relations,
  1831
Police/Immigrant Relations
  in Ealing, 1835
Police Immigrant Relations
  in England and Wales, 1830
Police Power and Black Peo-
  ple, 1832
Policy or Drift?, 833

Politics of Race, 227
Politics of the Powerless,
   394
Population Projections 1970,
   91, 100
Population Trends, 101
Portrait of English Racism,
   386
Potential and Progress in a
   Second Culture, 1196
Poverty of Education, 1315
Powell and the 1970 Election,
   282
Power for the Powerless, 1741
Practical Suggestions for
   Teachers, 1562
Prejudice in the Community,
   412
Prevention of Racial Discrimi-
   nation in Britain, 378
Problems of Coloured School
   Leavers, 1322
Problems of Overseas Students
   and Nurses, 1692
Programme to Combat Racism,
   421
Promotion of Racial Harmony,
   705
Prospero's Magic, 990
Psychology and Race, 38
Public Health Aspects of Im-
   migration, 1693
Public Library Service for a
   Multi-Cultural Society,
   1734
Publish and be Damned, 1797

Question of Numbers, 124
Questioned by the Police, 1725
Questions and Answers on Race
   Relations and Immigration,
   592

Race, 8, 382
Race and Council Housing in
   London, 1622
Race and Education Across
   Cultures, 1207
Race and Employment, 843
Race and Employment in Bri-
   tain, 800
Race and Ethnic Relations, 7
Race and Industrial Conflict,
   835

Race and Jobs, 831, 839
Race and Labour in London
   Transport, 802
Race and Law, 586
Race and Law in Britain and
   the United States, 547
Race and Law in Great Bri-
   tain, 587
Race and Local Authority
   Housing, 1615
Race and Local Politics in
   England, 281
Race and Racialism, 422
Race and Residence, 1613
Race and Resistance, 274
Race and Social Difference,
   702
Race and the Dangers of
   'Benign Neglect', 405
Race and the Press, 1801
Race as News, 1802
Race Awareness, 401
Race Bomb, 12
Race, Class and Power, 987
Race, Colonialism and the
   City, 264
Race Concept, 4
Race Conflict and the Inter-
   national Order, 276
Race, Culture and Intelli-
   gence, 1153
Race in the Inner City, 985
Race, Intelligence and Edu-
   cation, 1192
Race, Jobs and the Law in
   Britain, 818
Race Race, 419
Race Relations, 27, 37, 589
Race Relations Act 1976, 575
Race Relations and Education,
   1187
Race Relations and Housing,
   1605
Race Relations and the Cur-
   riculum, 1197
Race Relations and the Law
   in Britain, 591
Race Relations Audit, 837
Race Relations in Britain,
   14, 15, 18-22
Race Relations in Employ-
   ment, 808
Race Relations in Sociologi-
   cal Theory, 28
Race Relations Law, 552

Race Relations Research, 238
Race, School and Community, 1481
Race, Science and Society, 417
Racial Conflict Discrimination and Power, 223
Racial Disadvantage in Britrain, 410
Racial Disadvantage in Employment, 838
Racial Discrimination, 30, 31, 237, 565, 590, 593, 595, 1585
Racial Equality, 703
Racial Minorities, 5
Racial Minorities and Public Housing, 1623
Racial Prejudice, 381
Racialism, 399
Racialism and the Working Class, 832
Racism, 383
Raciam and Black Resistance, 402
Racism and Empire, 250
Racism and the Mass Media, 1799
Racist and Sexist Images in Children's Books, 1587
Racist Textbooks, 1586
Rampal and His Family, 1060
Readings in Urban Education, 1203
Red, White and Black, 380
Refuge or Home, 234
Register of Dependents, 128
Register of Research on Commonwealth Immigrants, 33, 34
Registrar General's Annual Estimate of the Population, 102
Registrar General's Statistical Review, 103
Religious Education for Muslim Children, 1204
Report of Commonwealth Immigration Advisory Council, 80
Report of Community Relations Commission, 231
Report of Race Relations Board, 248
Report of the Committee on the Elimination of Racial Discrimination, 413

Report of the Work Group on West Indian Pupils, 1313
Residential Segregation of Immigrants in Birmingham, 1602
Response to the Select Committee, 1604
Review of the Race Relations Act, 553
Rise of the Coloured Races, 252
Road Made to Walk on Carnival Day, 420

Say What you Mean in English, 1384
Scope, 1404, 1405
Second Chance, 1194
Second City Politics, 261
Second Class Citizen, 388
Seen But Not Served, 1755
Seminar on Measures to be Taken...Aimed at Combating and Eliminating Racial Discrimination, 32
Separate and Unequal, 277
Sikh Children in Britain, 1057
Sikh Family in Britain, 1051
Slamming the Door, 138
Slave Girl, 389
Social and Ethnic Mix in Schools, 1201
Social and Political Patterns of Immigrant Areas, 973
Social Background of Immigrant Children, 1050
Social Psychology of Race Relations, 6
Social Security Statistics, 87
Social Service Budgets and Social Policy, 1731, 1732
Social Structure and Prejudice in Five English Boroughts, 379
Social Work with Coloured Immigrants, 1757
Social Work with Immigrants, 1726
Socially Deprived Families in Britain, 1742
Society and the Policeman's Role, 1828
Some of My Best Friends, 704

Special Report of Select Com-
  mittee, 242, 579
Statement of Change in Immi-
  gration Rules, 566-569
Statement of Immigration
  Rules, 570-572
Statistics of Education, 82
Statistics of Foreigners
  Entering and Leaving, 94
Statistics of Immigrant School
  Pupils, 106
Statistics of Persons Acquir-
  ing Citizenship, 95
Statistics on Incomes, Prices,
  Employment and Production,
  85
Stitch in Time, 840
Stochastic Analysis of Immi-
  grant Distribution, 999
Strangers to England, 139
Strategy and Style in Local
  Community Relations, 267
Strategy Statement, 228
Stresses in Children, 1695
Structure of Leadership, 965
Study of Violence on London
  Transport, 404
Subject of Inquiry, 243-246
Summary of Immigration Act,
  545
Summary of the PEP Report,
  232
Summer Programmes, 1735
Supplement on the Immigration
  Bill 1971, 554
Survey of Books About the Edu-
  cation of Immigrants, 1329
Survey of English Courses for
  Immigrant Teachers, 1560

Tabu, 1754
Take 7, 812
Teacher Education for a Multi-
  Cultural Society, 1563
Teaching English to West In-
  dian Children, 1396
Teaching in a Multi-Racial
  Society, 1565
Teaching in Multi-Racial
  Schools, 1564
Time for Growing, 1317
Today's Three Year Olds in
  London, 995
Towards a Multi-Racial Soci-
  ety, 233

Trade Union Movement and Discrimination, 842
Transport and Turbans, 798

Uganda Asian and Employment,
  807
Uganda Asians in Wandsworth,
  998
Ugandan Asian Crisis, 1062
Ugandan Asians in Great Bri-
  tain, 255
Under One Law, 583
Unemployment and Homeless-
  ness, 811
Unions and Immigrant Workers,
  796
Union Policy and Workplace
  Practice, 817
United Nations Declaration...
  Elimination of all Forms of
  Racial Discrimination, 414
Unmelting Pot, 803
Urban Deprivation, 980
Urban Ethnic Conflict, 972
Urban Ethnicity, 10
Urban Residential Patterns,
  1611

Victorian Attitudes to Race,
  225
Vital English, 1401
Voluntary Language Tutoring
  Schemes, 1393

Wedding Man is Nicer Than
  Cats, Miss, 1479, 1480
Wednesday's Children, 1751
West Indian Community, 247
West Indian Experience in
  British Schools, 1471
West Indian Language, 1191
West Indian Migration, 142
West Indians in Great Bri-
  tain, 1065
Where Creed and Colour Mat-
  ter, 384
Where Do You Keep Your String
  Beds?, 543
White Media and Black Bri-
  tain, 1800
Who Do You Think You Are,
  978

Who Minds?, 1738
Work of A.T.E.P.O., 1314
Work, Race and Immigration,
  797
Workers Against Racism, 391
Workers in Britain, 805
Working Class Youth Culture,
  828

World Religions, 1485, 1486

Yearbook of Social Policy,
  283
Yorkshire Survey, 717
Youth Service Provisions for
  Young Immigrants, 1758

SUBJECT INDEX

The numbers after each name refer to
item numbers in the bibliography.

Acculturation, 757, 1182, 1419
Adaptation, 761, 1570
Adoption, inter-racial, 706,
  708, 713, 728, 753, 768,
  1788
Affirmative action,
  see Positive discrimination
Amnesty, 154
Anti-Discrimination Law, 579,
  599, 641
Anti-immigrant organizations
  see Right wing organizations
Anti-Racism conference, 431
Aptitude tests, 872
Asian press, 945
Asians, 43, 66, 148, 344, 504,
  699, 761, 762, 787, 1061,
  1115, 1140
  assaults on, 429, 508
  crime, 1019
  culture conflict, 1150
  diet, 1694, 1708
  education, 1214, 1233, 1558,
    1559
  employment, 822, 830, 877,
    884, 898, 904, 911, 933,
    954
  family life, 1053, 1093,
    1142, 1146, 1150, 1160,
    1353
  housing, 1624, 1638, 1653,
    1671
  identity problem, 1178

Asians (cont.)
  juvenile delinquency, 1004,
    1771
  police attitudes, 1837
  social life and customs,
    1053, 1067, 1160
  social problems, 1095,
    1168, 1771
  trade unions, 953
  voting behavior, 287, 322,
    357
  women, 517, 795, 816, 928,
    933, 1005, 1053, 1067,
    1771
  working conditions, 928,
    944
  See also Bangladeshis, Ben-
    galis, Indians, Kenyan
    Asians, Pakistanis, Pun-
    jabis, Sikhs, Ugandan
    Asians
Assimilation, 704, 716, 722
Association for the Education
  of Pupils from Overseas,
  1314
Association of Multi-Racial
  Playgroups, 1723
Association of Teachers in
  Colleges and Departments of
  Education, 1563, 1580
Audio-Visual aids, 16, 1199,
  1473

BBC, 1428, 1823
Bangladeshis, 145
  voting behavior, 297
Batley
  Asians, 911
  economic conditions, 911
Bedford
  colored population, 803
  social conditions, 803
Bengali Housing Action Group,
  1641, 1652, 1673, 1674
Bengalis, 1017, 1072
  assaults on, 430
  housing, 1641, 1652, 1674
  See also Indians
Bennion, Francis, 725
Bibliography, 9, 16-22, 25,
  33, 71
Bilingual and bi-cultural edu-
  cation, 1442, 1500, 1539
Bill of Rights, 622
Birmingham
  Asians, 1559
  colored population, 999,
    1014
  education, 1250, 1559
  employment, 1676
  housing, 973, 1602, 1671,
    1672, 1675, 1676
  Indians, 1702
  Pakistanis, 146
  politics, 261, 539
  race relations, 985, 1676,
    1834
  race riots, 456
  West Indians, 1313, 1703
Birth control see Family
  planning
Black churches, 1055, 1139
  Birmingham, 714
  London, 714
Black militancy, 510, 512,
  521, 526, 530
Black power, 398, 451, 479,
  527, 975, 976
Black press, 1811
Black studies, 1305, 1478,
  1530, 1548, 1556
Black teachers, 1304
  experiences, 393, 1236
  See also Immigrant teachers
Blackburn
  race relations, 778
Blacks in television, 1817
Bonham-Carter, Mark, 554

Bradford
  Asians, 787, 1004
  Bengalis, 1072
  busing, 1238
  education, 1209
  employment, 797, 827
  housing, 1614, 1626
  police, 1854
  racial discrimination, 355,
    437
  socio-economic status, 827
Brent
  race relations, 712
  Ugandan Asians, 217
Bristol
  housing, 1621, 1677
  Pakistanis, 1058, 1101
  racial attitudes, 1677
British Broadcasting Corporation see BBC
British churches
  attitudes, 406
British Council of Churches,
  406, 433
British left. 1030
British Nationality Law, 550,
  557, 640, 691, 988
Brixton
  race problem, 454
  welfare services, 1756
  West Indians, 1119, 1228
Bullock, Alan, 1402, 1441
Busing, 1211, 1220, 1222-1224,
  1238, 1240, 1267, 1286,
  1288, 1307

CARD see Campaign Against
  Racial Discrimination
CBI see Confederation of Bri-
  tish Industry
Camden
  housing, 1657
Campaign Against Racial Dis-
  crimination, 323, 394, 465
Career training, 1221
Census 1966, 200
Census 1971, 98, 99
  colored population, 107,
    114, 122, 187, 194, 436
  economic conditions, 814
  Indians, 147, 200
  Pakistanis, 147, 200
  West Indians, 200

Child care services, 1723,
    1737, 1738, 1746, 1751,
    1762, 1772-1774, 1782, 1793
    See also Day care centers
Children
    academic achievement, 1212
    aspirations, 1231
    behavior problem, 1086, 1161
    communication problem, 1358-
        1360, 1435
    culture conflict, 1158, 1160
    educational problems, 1208,
        1227, 1338, 1352
    family life, 1059, 1134
    heritage, 1166, 1183
    identity problem, 1164, 1165,
        1171, 1176, 1177, 1184
    language, 1112, 1113
    potential, 1196
    social background, 1050,
        1059, 1079
    social problems, 1180, 1185
    teachers' attitudes, 1229
    See also Child care ser-
        vices, Color awareness
        amongst children, Day care
        centers, English children,
        West Indian children
Christiantiy and race, 382,
    384, 387, 397, 406, 419,
    421, 709, 714, 1061, 1063,
    1139, 1498
Church Missionary Society, 397
Cities
    racial discrimination, 452
    social structure, 379
Citizenship, 134, 229, 278,
    385, 395, 396, 697
    history, 988
    law, 550, 638, 640, 691,
        692, 988
    statistics, 95
City planning, 1627
Coggan, Frederick Donald, Abp
    of York, 610
Colonialism, 254, 258, 264,
    268, 276, 306, 369, 494
Color awareness amongst chil-
    dren, 741, 759, 773, 1174,
    1545, 1554, 1568
Colored intellectuals, 994,
    1038
Colored population, 13, 114,
    120, 122, 222

Colored population (cont.)
    country of birth, 99, 105
    decline, 209
    London, 107
    statistics, 13, 74, 76, 104,
        109-113, 124, 125, 191,
        199
Commission for Racial Equal-
    ity, 228, 325, 338, 345,
    602, 1239, 1273
Commonwealth
    history, 259
    India, 277
Commonwealth countries, 163
Commonwealth Immigrants Act,
    1962, 548, 559, 560, 561
Commonwealth Immigrants Act,
    1968, 548, 559-561
Community action, 1741
    case studies, 1722
Community relations commit-
    tees, 249
Community Relations Coun-
    cils, 330, 361, 1787
    list, 230
    role, 918, 946
Community relations organi-
    zations, 735
Community work 1779
Confederation of British In-
    dustry, 873
    racial policy, 950
Conservatism
    racial prejudice, 293, 331
Conservative Party, 290
Co-ordinating Committee for
    the Welfare of the Evacuees
    from Uganda, 1599, 1610
Council housing, 1622, 1649
    See also Public housing
Courtaulds, 804
Courts, 698
    immigrants, 686
Cousins, Frank, 376, 873
Cousin's Commission see
    Great Britain. Community
    Relations Commission
Coventary, 221
Coventary Community College,
    1249
Crime, 404, 686, 993, 1013,
    1019-1023, 1834
Croyden
    housing, 1666

Curriculum, 1446, 1452, 1465,
   1507, 1521, 1550, 1554, 1556

Day care centers, 1723, 1730
   See also Child care services
Department of Education and
   Science, 1259, 1287, 1338
   1361, 1370, 1371, 1457,
   1529, 1574
Dependents, 183, 342, 350, 644
   analysis, 128
   immigration control, 629
   register, 128
   rights, 655, 669
Deportation, 434, 564, 632,
   633, 698
Desegregation see Integration
Devon
   Ugandan Asians, 537
Discrimination in education,
   774, 1234, 1237, 1246, 1247,
   1259, 1262, 1309
Discrimination in employment,
   11, 400, 546, 603, 800, 831,
   832, 835-839, 841, 843-845,
   847, 848, 854, 858, 860,
   861, 872, 879, 884, 885,
   888, 898, 909, 910, 930,
   931, 934, 944
   employers, 808, 843
   grievances, 891
   law, 943
Diseases, 1706, 1708
Dundee
   Pakistanis, 1102
Drug abuse, 1719

ESN children see Educationally
   subnormal children
Ealing
   busing, 1224, 1240, 1286,
      1307
   colored population, 1083
   social services, 1750
East African Asians, 165, 171,
   619
   See also Kenyan Asians, Ugan-
      dan Asians
Economic conditions, 409, 410
Economic status
   race, 1002

Education, 1186-1597
   adult, 1190, 1413, 1429,
      1436, 1437, 1445, 1513,
      1533
   bibliography, 1298, 1308
   elementary, 1327
   higher, 1194, 1290, 1300,
      1351
   race, 1285
   religious, 1129, 1204,
      1485, 1486, 1557
   research, 1299, 1481
   statistics, 75, 81, 82, 1202
   surveys, 1202, 1320
   See also Children - educa-
      tional problems, Discrim-
      ination in education, Edu-
      cational needs, Education-
      al performance, Education-
      ally subnormal children,
      Equal educational oppor-
      tunity, Integration -
      education, Multi-racial
      education, Socially dis-
      advantaged children -
      education, Special educa-
      tion, Women - Education
Education priority areas,
   1465, 1528
Education vouchers, 960
Educational aspirations
   Asians, 1242, 1311
Educational needs, 1283, 1289,
   1292, 1310, 1318, 1319,
   1321, 1350, 1370, 1373,
   1569, 1571
Educational performance, 1244,
   1260, 1337
   Asians, 1213, 1295
   Indians, 1206, 1276
   Pakistanis, 1206
   West Indians, 1232, 1312,
      1382
Educationally disadvantaged
   see Children - educational
   problems
Educationally subnormal chil-
   dren, 1235, 1316, 1333,
   1340, 1342, 1343, 1348,
   1349, 1362, 1363, 1368,
   1380
Election 1970, 282, 320, 321

Election 1972
  Pakistani participation, 288
Election 1974
  Asian participation, 287
  National Front, 367
Election 1976, 284
Election surveys, 170
Employers
  recruitment practices, 888,
    915, 945
  See also Discrimination in
    employment
Employment, 796-964
  graduates, 851, 852, 954
  immigration laws, 831, 839
  integration, 833
  politics, 798
  promotion, 899, 926
  protection, 820
  report, 815
  statistics, 83-85
  working condition, 834, 835
  See also Discrimination in
    employment, Economic con-
    ditions, Equal employment
    opportunities, Equal Pay
    Act, Fair employment prac-
    tices
Employment agencies, 946
English as a second language,
  1384-1463
  teaching, 1388, 1402, 1403,
    1409, 1416, 1421, 1423,
    1443, 1449, 1460
  See also Industrial English
English Calico, Ltd., 906
English children
  attitude towards color, 701,
    721
  behavior problem, 1001
  education, 1219
  intelligence, 1000
Equal educational opportunity,
  1203, 1210, 1273, 1277,
  1284, 1351
Equal employment opportunity,
  806, 818-820, 829, 840, 875,
  899, 926, 941
  employers, 840
Equal Pay Act 1970, 813, 829
Equal Rights Commission, 285
Ethnic identity, 1073, 1171

Ethnic services, 333
Ethnicity, 10, 200, 1045,
  1114
  concept, 1156
  education, 1217
  intelligence, 1118, 1188
  politics, 1217
  race, 763
European Convention on Human
  Rights, 588
European Economic Community,
  1442

Fair Employment Agency, 963
Fair employment practices,
  963
  laws, 870
Fair housing, 1620, 1632,
  1669
Family planning, 1035, 1138,
  1765, 1769, 1785
  instruction, 1729
Fascism, 525, 526
Fertility, 1099, 1137
  See also Family planning
Films, 17
Ford Motor Company, 929
Foster care, 667, 771, 1121,
  1721, 1736, 1768, 1784,
  1790
Frost, David, 208

Glasgow
  colored population, 700
  Pakistanis, 1326
Great Britain. Community Re-
  lations Commission, 340
  376, 1227, 1290, 1292,
  1341, 1538, 1571, 1861
Greater London Council, 1643
Grievances
  educational, 1282
Grove Junior School, Wolver-
  hampton, 1543
Grunwick Photo Processing
  Laboratories, 890, 925,
  928, 959
Grunwick strike, 799, 816
  836, 845, 925, 928, 959
Gujaratis, 877, 1114, 1141
  See also Indians

Hain, Peter, 720, 725
Handsworth
  day care centers, 1751
  race relations, 985
Health, 1688-1720
  mental, 1690, 1695, 1704,
    1709, 1711
  public, 1693
  racial discrimination, 1707,
    1712
  statistics, 86
Hinduism, 1056
Homelessness, 811, 936, 969
Hospital workers, 857
House of Commons, 647
House of Lords, 614
House of Lords, Appellate
  Committee, 141
Housing, 1598-1687
  allocation, 1630, 1668
  census data, 1663
  concentration, 1614
  discrimination, 11, 400,
    546, 1604, 1617, 1623,
    1625, 1632, 1639, 1641,
    1642, 1650, 1651, 1660,
    1667, 1674
  government policy, 1603,
    1616, 1617, 1645
  law, 1646
  price, 1633, 1687
  report, 1604-1606
  segregation, 1602, 1605,
    1656
  social patterns, 1634
  statistics, 80, 88-90, 96,
    108
  See also Council housing;
    Fair housing, Public hous-
    ing
Housing mobility
  Asian's attitudes, 1671
Huddersfield
  education, 1497
  Pakistanis, 359
  race relations, 359, 712
Human rights, 36, 40, 69, 588,
  625

IQ, 450, 485, 1301, 1378
  genetic controversy, 463,
    531
  race, 514
  tests, 1198, 1337, 1378,
    1382

Illegal immigration, 154, 183,
  188, 585, 610
  law, 612, 632
  public opinion, 189
Immigrant doctors, 1688, 1691
Immigrant nurses, 901, 917,
  1692, 1705
Immigrant population
  see Colored population
Immigrant teachers, 1574, 1575
  employment, 897
  training, 1560, 1567
Immigration, 119-222
  Asian, 148
  attitude, 197
  economic aspects, 144, 184,
    821
  history, 139, 314
  social aspects, 140
  statistics, 76, 80, 92-94,
    117, 118, 156, 169, 186,
    198
Immigration Act 1971, 138, 141,
  545, 573, 585, 588, 617, 619,
  625, 627, 632, 644, 668, 670,
  677, 678, 680, 683, 696,
  1725
  See also Immigration Bill
    1971
Immigration Appeal Tribunal,
  141
Immigration appeals, 141, 613
Immigration Bill 1971, 298,
  544, 562-564, 580, 581, 594,
  605, 628, 650, 694
  amendment, 582
  criticism, 583, 652
  patrial clause, 650, 654
  report, 598
  supplement, 554
  See also Immigration Act
    1971
Immigration control, 119, 146,
  167, 192, 205, 206, 209,
  555, 556, 558, 585, 600
  administration, 138
  commonwealth citizens, 121,
    129, 160, 437, 559-563,
    566-572, 576-578, 609,
    610, 620
Immigration law and non-
  Christian oaths, 685
Immigration laws, 204, 543,
  551, 596, 611, 637-639, 642,
  688, 693
  history, 640

Immigration policy, 126, 127,
  132-134, 155, 157-159, 170,
  182, 196, 203, 212, 215, 216,
  295, 689
  Asians, 119, 185, 214
  Commonwealth countries, 121,
    129, 149, 150, 152, 153,
    163, 548, 629, 681
  economic aspects, 123, 131
  Liberal Party, 135, 136
  questions and answers, 592
  Whites, 163
Immigration rules, 647, 668
Imperial Typewriters, 877
Incitement to racial hatred,
  615
  law, 645
Income
  distribution, 810
  statistics, 85
India
  commonwealth, 277
Indian Workers Association,
  515, 974
Indians, 145, 147, 200, 432,
  965, 1025, 1070, 1076, 1078,
  1103, 1133
  diet, 1644
  education, 715, 1206, 1335,
    1404, 1405
  elites, 1032
  employment, 715, 797, 836,
    845, 939
  family life, 1049, 1051, 1114
  juvenile delinquency, 1004
  mental health, 1702
  social conditions, 443, 470
  social life and customs,
    1050, 1053
  social status, 1015
  suicide rate, 1702
  unemployment, 952
  women, 1162
  working conditions, 845
  youth, 1744
  See also Asians, Bengalis,
    Marathas, Punjabis, Sikhs
Industrial conflict, 855
Industrial English, 809, 865,
  893, 894, 932, 1398, 1403
Industrial relations, 862
Industrial Relations Act, 594
  dismissals, 870

Industry and race relations,
  684, 830, 833, 837, 838,
  840-843, 854, 863, 871, 900,
  902, 910, 940, 942, 947,
  948, 958, 959, 962
  surveys, 812
Inequality, 390
  economic, 868, 886, 896
  educational, 1225, 1251,
    1256
  social, 886
  See also Discrimination in
    education, Discrimination
    in employment, Racial
    discrimination
Inner London Education Authority, 1331, 1372, 1516
  See also London Education
    Authority
Institute of Race Relations,
  260, 310, 370, 493, 522
  history, 274
Integration
  educational, 1195, 1243,
    1249, 1252, 1267-1269,
    1272, 1274, 1275
  employment, 833, 906, 923
  housing, 1608, 1609, 1635,
    1644, 1661
  racial, 134, 233, 398, 519,
    760, 833
  schools, 1201, 1215, 1220,
    1222-1224, 1281, 1288,
    1293, 1297, 1307
  social, 722, 724, 1761
Intelligence and race, 450,
  482, 485, 496, 516, 1153,
  1192, 1301
  genetic influence, 476, 481,
    978
Inter-ethnic friendship, 704,
  730, 731, 736, 742, 756
  youth, 792
Inter-group relations, 297,
  707, 733, 777, 782, 783,
  787, 789
Islam, 1056
Islington
  housing, 1607, 1630, 1680
  social integration, 1607

Jamaicans, 311, 716, 1064,
  1088, 1127

Jamaicans (cont.)
  education, 1089, 1361
  folklore, 1123
  language, 1434, 1461
  women, 881, 882
  See also Negroes, West In-
    dians
Jensen, Arthur, 463
Joint Inner London Rehabilita-
  tion Organization, 1618
Joseph, Sir Keith, 301
Juvenile delinquency, 969,
  1004, 1044, 1169

Katznelson, Ira, 335
Kent
  Ugandan Asians, 253
Kenyan Asians, 171, 177
Kingswood
  social services. 1748
Labor Party see Labour Party
Labor strikes, 849, 855, 866,
  877, 902, 905, 925, 928,
  933
  See also under specific name,
    e.g. Grunwick Strike
Labour Party
  immigration laws, 639
  minorities, 631
Ladywood
  election 1977, 337
  politics of race, 336
Lambeth
  housing, 1672
  welfare services, 1756
Lancashire, 906
Language barrier, 1111, 1430
  Asians, 1005, 1418
Lane, David, 338
Language proficiency, 1399,
  1400, 1427, 1430, 1451,
  1453, 1457, 1463
  tests, 1424, 1439
Language training of workers,
  809, 865, 893, 894, 932
Leadership, 965, 1130
Leeds
  housing, 1601
  Sikhs, 1143
  West Indians, 907, 1858
Leeds Career Association, 1221
Legal aid, 1725
Legal decisions, 651, 658-664

Legal status, 606
Leicester
  busing, 1238
  education, 1339
  employment, 827
  housing, 1614
  race problem, 460
  socio-economic status, 827
  Ugandan Asians, 1098
Leicestershire
  race riots, 469
Lemington Spa
  Sikhs, 707
Lewisham, 348
  employment, 823
  police, 1851, 1857
  race problem, 442, 1810
  race riots, 456
Library services, 1728, 1734,
  1753, 1764, 1767, 1780,
  1781
Liverpool, 740
  housing, 1672
  race riots, 426, 494
  West Indians, 834
London
  Asians, 1115
  Bengalis, 430, 1017, 1641,
    1652
  colored population, 107,
    116, 172, 509, 529, 719,
    1018
  economic conditions, 991
  education, 1199, 1250
  employment, 823, 825, 844
  Gujaratis, 1142
  housing, 825, 1598, 1600,
    1615, 1618, 1619, 1622,
    1641, 1643, 1647, 1652,
    1659, 1673, 1674, 1684-
    1686
  Indians, 1076
  Jamaicans, 881, 882, 1064,
    1088, 1089, 1127
  police, 1853
  race problem, 989, 1017
  race riots, 446
  social conditions, 989
  social life, 966
  social services, 1740
  social status, 991
  statistics, 72, 115
  Trinidadians, 1127
  welfare services, 1749, 1756

London (cont.)
  West Indians, 823, 995,
    1017, 1127, 1285, 1316
London Education Authority,
  1328, 1540, 1549
  See also Inner London Educa-
    tion Authority
London transport
  crime, 404
  immigrants, 798, 876
  West Indians, 802, 876
Loughborough
  employment, 847, 866, 918,
    927
  race relations, 918, 927

Macmillan, Harold, 160
Management attitudes, 822
Managerial positions, 941
Manchester
  colored population, 347,
    798
  employment, 827
  housing, 1614, 1620, 1625,
    1640, 1665, 1669, 1670
  race relations, 1504
  socio-economic status, 827
Marathas, 1076
  See also Indians
Marriage, interracial, 730,
  740, 1152
  law, 656
  legal problems, 657
  London, 1152
  statistics, 723
Marriage, Moslem, 665
Media see Race relations in
  the mass media
Media, hiring practices, 945,
  1817, 1824
Members of Parliament
  racial attitudes, 326
Mental illness, 1697-1700,
  1702, 1703, 1713, 1714,
  1716, 1719
Midlands
  employment, 859
  Gujaratis, 1141
  racial discrimination, 817,
    835
Milton Keynes, 1661
Minorities
  problem, 42

Minorities (cont.)
  protection of, 40
  rights, 67
Mirpur see Yorkshire
Montserrat, 142
Moody, Harold A., 1120
Moral education, 1517
Moslem organizations, 1122
Moslems, 1092, 1094, 1100
  divorce, 1128
  education, 1085, 1100,
    1122, 1131, 1204, 1253
  marriage, 1128
  social customs, 1122
Multi-cultural society, 140,
  1474, 1475, 1479, 1480
Multi-racial education, 1464-
  1558
  bibliography, 1467, 1469,
    1470, 1472, 1473, 1476,
    1505
  funding, 1519
  pupils' attitudes, 1524
  teachers' opinions, 1494,
    1495, 1547
Multi-racial schools, 1464,
  1468, 1477, 1502, 1503,
  1515, 1524, 1538, 1542,
  1543
  organization, 1483, 1496
  teaching, 1561-1565
Multi-racial society, 233,
  758, 979, 1510, 1511,
  1517, 1537
Muslims see Moslems

National Association for
  Multi-racial Education,
  1523
National Foundation for Educational Research, 1363
National Front, 348, 367,
  411, 428, 442, 449, 456,
  459, 460, 462, 467, 468,
  501, 521, 526, 539, 1254,
  1810
National Health Service,
  917, 1701, 1707
National Party, 462
Negroes, 256, 263, 271-273,
  279, 280
  See also West Indians,
    Jamaicans

New Castle upon Tyne, 1206
  Asians, 1295
Non-patrials, 630
Notting Hill
  race riots, 427
  welfare services, 1752
  West Indians, 1845
Notting Hill Carnival 1976,
  483, 488, 1855
Notting Hill Carnival 1977,
  420, 500
Nottingham
  education, 1334, 1445
  housing, 1620, 1669
  racial discrimination, 334,
  711
  West Indians, 334, 1334,
  1355
Nottingham Committee for Commonwealth Immigrants, 335
Nutrition, 1694, 1708, 1718

Organizations
  Asian, 984
  West Indian, 1125
Osteomalacia, 1706
Overseas students, 1261

Paki-Bashing, 429, 487, 502
Pakistan Act 1973, 146
Pakistan Act 1974, 574
Pakistanis, 145-147, 200, 221,
  432, 487, 543, 965, 1025,
  1066, 1078, 1081, 1082, 1102,
  1106, 1145
  citizenship, 697
  diet, 1694
  education, 715, 1206, 1326,
  1404, 1405
  employment, 715, 796, 797,
  828, 846
  family life, 1048, 1058,
  1101, 1104
  juvenile delinquency, 1004
  legal status, 636
  marriage customs, 665, 1128
  social conditions, 1148
  social life and customs,1054
  unemployment, 952
  voting behavior, 288, 289,
  297, 359
  voting rights, 574

Pakistanis (cont.)
  women, 1105
  See also Asians, Moslems
Patrials, 650, 654, 682
Performing arts, 986
Pinkerton, Jamie Horace, 1080
Pluralism, 41, 49, 68, 374,
  750, 757, 763, 764, 1009,
  1159, 1175, 1526
Police and race, 1827-1866
Police attitudes towards
  blacks, 1832, 1839, 1841,
  1850, 1853, 1854, 1856,
  1860, 1863
Police brutality, 1840,
  1841, 1856
Political and economic plan-
  ning, 232
Political ideology and race,
  293, 358, 532
Political rights
  minorities, 319
Politicians and racial attitudes, 326
Politics and race, 26, 130,
  132, 227, 228, 251, 261,
  269, 270, 275, 281, 290,
  299, 301, 305, 309, 319,
  332, 356, 360, 626, 634
Politics of race, 587, 606
Population see Colored population
Population census 1971 see
  Census 1971
Population projections
  statistics, 91, 100
Positive discrimination, 856
  education, 1345
Powell, Enoch, 202, 224, 265,
  269, 270, 275, 290, 296,
  312, 332, 341, 350, 653,
  1805
  election 1970, 282, 320,
  321
  immigration, 198
  Immigration Bill 1971, 650
  public opinion, 366
  Ugandan Asians, 371
  West Indians, 226
Prejudice, 56, 1522
  against commonwealth immigrants, 412
  color, 474, 480, 834
  immigrant children, 497

Prejudice (cont.)
  racial, 38, 276, 379, 381,
    407, 408, 468, 475, 491,
    497, 1522
  surveys, 379, 407, 408
Pre-school education, 1534
Press coverage of racial is-
  sues see Race relations in
  the mass media
Pressure groups, 309
Probation service
  Birmingham, 1766
Public housing, 1615, 1619,
  1623, 1640
  allocation, 1668
  discrimination, 1667
  See also Council housing,
    Housing
Publishing, 62
Punjabi magazines, 1136
Punjabis, 877, 1151, 1184,
  1276
  See also Indians

Race awareness, 401
Race problem, 458, 461, 507,
  987
Race relations, 1, 2, 5, 15,
  27, 37, 46, 240, 380, 903
  administration, 236, 241,
    327, 343
  black viewpoint, 712
  case studies, 710
  history, 3, 225, 268, 302,
    303
  law and legislation, 591,
    616, 643
  political aspects, 52
  public opinion, 363, 366
  questions and answers, 251,
    592
  reports, 242-248
  research, 33-35, 39, 44, 48,
    53, 57, 59, 60, 65, 238,
    306, 354
  role of law, 608
  social aspects, 6, 7, 14,
    28, 50
  sociology, 61
  surveys, 52, 58, 397, 518,
    711, 712, 781
  teaching, 792, 1197, 1487,
    1504, 1508, 1509, 1536,
    1553, 1555

Race Relations Act 1965, 547,
  614, 615, 676, 831
Race Relations Act 1968, 546,
  547, 614, 641, 676, 831,
  837, 844
  amendment, 553
  application, 684
  foster care, 667
  interpretation, 621
Race Relations Act 1971, 646,
  651, 653, 839
Race Relations Act 1976, 565,
  575, 589, 595, 602, 623,
  671-673, 819, 820, 1261
  employment, 856
  guide, 687, 806
  housing, 1646
  positive discrimination,
    856
Race Relations Bill 1976,
  674, 676, 1273
  See also Race Relations
    Act 1976
Race Relations Board, 372,
  675, 938
Race relations in the mass
  media, 1797-1826
Race relations laws, 552,
  586, 587, 607, 649
  employment, 635
  review, 549
  See also Anti-Discrimina-
    tion Law
Race relations organizations,
  231, 266, 267, 323, 372
Race riots, 426, 427, 446,
  469, 494
Racial attitudes, 727, 739,
  755, 1040
  children, 747, 754, 794,
    992
  White, 14, 385, 700, 746,
    748
  youth, 791
Racial discrimination, 23,
  24, 29-31, 33, 34, 54, 63,
  143, 237, 258, 260, 423,
  441, 492, 520, 523, 524,
  542, 565, 699, 990
  case studies, 392, 394, 400,
    417
  elimination, 413-416, 473
  fight against, 318, 385,
    395, 396, 406, 417, 418,
    421, 431, 435, 489, 519

Racial discrimination (cont.)
  law and legislation, 590,
    593, 595, 601, 604
  prevention, 40, 378
  reports, 232
  schools, 448
  sociology, 51
  social services, 495
  surveys, 409, 410
Racial discrimination in
  sports, 455, 597, 720, 727,
  729, 737, 738, 744, 751,
  752, 765, 775, 785, 786,
  788, 790, 793
Racial discrimination in textbooks, 1583-1597
Racial equality, 64, 69, 703
Racial harmony, 12, 705
Racial prejudice see Prejudice, racial
Racial Preservation Society,
  501
Racial tolerance, 739, 764,
  1490, 1491
  children, 721
  teaching, 1491, 1501
Racial violence, 404, 429,
  430, 472, 487, 502, 503,
  508, 511, 529
Racism, 41, 49, 133, 348, 350
  Christianity, 406
  colonial, 250
  economic aspects, 499
  history, 256, 264
  institutional, 402, 425
  psychological aspects, 490
  urban areas, 264
Radio in education, 1428
Reading problems, 1344, 1347
Redbridge Community Relations
  Council, 1277
Refugee camps, 329, 352
  See also Ugandan Asians-
    settlements
Refugees, 137, 168, 234, 235
  See also Ugandan Asians
Remedial reading, 1375, 1377,
  1541
Reparation, 294
Repatriation, 440, 445, 498
  Asian viewpoint, 432
Repatriation Bill, 648
Rickets, 1706
Right wing organizations, 356,
  403, 428, 437, 467, 501

Rochdale
  Election 1972, 288
  Election 1973, 289
Roman Catholic Church and
  race, 709
  See also Christianity and
    race
Roman Catholic schools
  immigrant children, 384
Royal Commission on the Dis-
  tribution of Income and
  Wealth, 810
Runnymede Trust, 1549

Schizophrenia, 1700
School dropouts, 1218, 1228,
  1270, 1322
  employment, 879, 884, 921
  politics, 286
  unemployment, 921, 952
School enrollment, 106, 1230,
  1250, 1294
Schools Council, 1482, 1523
Select Committee on Race Relations and Immigration,
  121, 236, 343, 1235
  education, 1278, 1304,
    1306, 1321, 1323, 1370
  housing, 1604-1606, 1626
  police/immigrant relations,
    1830, 1831, 1843
Sheffield
  housing, 1620, 1669
Shockley, William Bradford,
  496
Sidney stringer school, 1249,
  1544
Sikhism, 1056
Sikhs, 707, 1071, 1084, 1133
  diet, 1644
  family life, 1051, 1057,
    1068, 1093, 1126
  marriage patterns, 1068
  social life and customs,
    1093, 1126, 1143
  social problems, 1184
  women, 1084
Slough
  Asians, 761
  election 1971, 308
Smithfield
  race problem, 533
Social class, 971, 990

Social clubs
  racial discrimination, 1010,
    1011, 1037, 1047
Social conditions, 409, 410,
  803, 827, 1614
Social differences, 702
Social education, 1488, 1489,
  1552
Social environment, 1000
Social justice, 1009
Social mobility, 1016
Social policy, 283, 304, 360,
  916
  urban, 305, 980
Social security, 1789
  statistics, 87
Social services, 1721-1796
  social policy, 1731, 1732,
    1747
Social status, 827, 987, 1012
  race, 1002
Social stratification, 1045
Social structure, 379, 971,
  1600
Social work, 1726, 1757, 1761,
  1763, 1770, 1783, 1786,
  1794-1796
Social workers, 1777
Socialism, 486, 535
Socialist Workers Party, 348
Socialists, 535
Socialization, 766
Socially disadvantaged chil-
  dren, 996, 1745
  education, 1189, 1209,
    1324, 1341
Sociology of work, 801
Southall, 1093, 1133, 1558
  housing, 1637
  race relations, 749
  racial violence, 511, 1777
Southall Youth Movement, 515
Special education, 1248, 1357,
  1374, 1383
Sports, 769, 770, 772, 776
  See also Racial discrimina-
    tion in sports
Statistical sources, 72-118
Stereotypes
  against Asians, 937
  racial, 388, 447, 450, 463,
    514
Stratford
  race relations, 1504
Suicide, 1697, 1702, 1703

Swaminarayan sect, 1070

TUC see Trade Union Congress
Teacher attitudes, 1296
Teacher training, 1559-1582
Television in education,
  1041, 1437, 1440, 1462
Third World, 1532
Tinker, Hugh, 370
Trade Union Congress, 873,
  931, 1254
  black workers, 913, 951
  racial policy, 950
Trade Unions, 864
  Asians, 836, 953
  black workers, 796, 912,
    940, 955
  race relations, 594, 817,
    826, 842, 845, 864, 866,
    877, 902
  racial attitudes, 853, 956,
    957
  women, 816, 905
Training services agencies,
  869
Transport workers, 863, 876,
  908
  Jamaican, 716
  West Indian, 876
  See also London transport
Trinidadians, 1127, 1167
  values, 1110
Turbans, use of
  employment, 798
  law, 646
Tyneside
  Indians, 952
  Pakistanis, 952

Uganda
  racism, 300
Ugandan Asians, 149, 150, 152,
  153, 161, 171, 173-175, 178,
  180, 181, 195, 207, 210-212,
  216, 217, 220, 262, 291,
  292, 300, 372, 375, 537,
  584, 1003, 1062, 1074, 1090,
  1098, 1107, 1144
  attitudes towards, 190, 197,
    219
  dependents, 176, 669
  employment, 807
  expulsion, 201

Ugandan Asians (cont.)
  housing, 1599, 1610, 1628,
    1656, 1683
  resettlement, 137, 234, 235,
    239, 253, 255, 307, 315-
    317, 329, 353, 365, 368,
    1108
  social conditions, 998, 1043
  welfare services, 1739, 1754
  women, 176
Ugandan Asians Resettlement
  Board, 315-317, 365, 368
Unemployment, 811, 858, 880,
  889, 920
  racism, 439
Unions see Trade Unions
Unionization, 890
United Nations Commission on
  Human Rights, 625
United Nations Year for Action
  to Combat Racism and Racial
  Discrimination, 418
Urban aid, 1039
Urban areas
  public policy, 970
  racial discrimination, 574,
    980, 981, 985
Urban ghettoes, 1017, 1028,
  1034, 1611, 1648
  concentration, 1018, 1612,
    1613
Urban renewal, 1665

V.S.O. see Voluntary Service
  Overseas
Vocational education, 964,
  1255
Voluntary Service Overseas,
  1458

Wandsworth
  race relations, 712
  Ugandan Asians, 998
Warwickshire
  race relations, 985
Welfare services, 1724, 1727,
  1733
West Indian associations, 1125
West Indian children, 995,
  1135, 1270, 1743
  academic achievement, 1188,
    1191, 1232, 1287, 1312

West Indian children (cont.)
  behavior problems, 1001,
    1161
  cultural background, 1147
  educational problems, 1241,
    1257, 1258, 1280, 1310,
    1313, 1316, 1333-1335,
    1338, 1340, 1342, 1355,
    1356, 1363-1367, 1375,
    1376, 1379, 1446, 1448,
    1571
  family life, 1134, 1135
  identity problems, 1149,
    1154, 1155, 1709
  intelligence, 1000, 1263
  language, 1191
  mental health, 1709, 1711
  mental illness, 1713, 1714,
    1716
West Indians, 43, 66, 200,
  218, 263, 334, 344, 398,
  505, 506, 519, 520, 699,
  995, 1007, 1017, 1024,
  1065, 1075, 1116, 1119,
  1125, 1127, 1285, 1380,
  1381
  acculturation, 1172
  crime, 1013
  employment, 433, 797, 802,
    823, 834, 876, 879, 904,
    907, 925, 1340
  family life, 1134
  health, 1710, 1711, 1713,
    1714, 1716, 1719
  heritage, 1120
  history, 271-273, 362
  homelessness, 811, 936, 969
  housing, 1647
  justice, 624
  juvenile delinquency, 969
  poets, 968
  police attitudes, 483,
    1837, 1841, 1852, 1863,
    1865
  Powell, E., 226
  pronunciation, 1091
  religion, 1139
  social conditions, 143, 247,
    272, 273, 453, 534, 967,
    983, 1042, 1316
  social problems, 1168
  social services, 1759, 1760,
    1791, 1794, 1796
  sports, 772, 776

West Indians (cont.)
  suicide rate, 1697, 1703
  unemployment, 811, 920, 936,
    949, 1340
  values, 1110
  voting behavior, 339
  welfare services, 1756
  women, 867
  See also Jamaicans, Negroes,
    Trinidadians
West Midlands
  housing, 1631
  West Indians, 1232
White Defence League, 501
Willesden
  race relations, 281
William Tyndale School, 1520
Wolverhampton
  employment, 798, 827
  minorities, 798
  socio-economic status, 827
Women
  Asian, 795, 816, 905, 933,
    1005, 1053, 1067, 1400,
    1462, 1771
  career opportunities, 850
  discrimination against, 388,
    517
  education, 1400, 1454, 1462
  employment, 881, 882, 905,
    933
  Jamaican, 881
  language training, 1041
  Pakistani, 1105
  Sikh, 1084
  social problems, 1095, 1771
  West Indian, 867, 1454
  working conditions, 867
Workers, 391, 805, 914, 924
  Asian, 549
  exploitation, 804, 830, 832
  housing, 1678
  industrial accidents, 824
  job satisfaction, 961
  job training, 875
  language training, 809, 865,
    893, 894, 932
  management, 822

skills, 919
  social conditions, 972
  work ethic, 919
  working conditions, 877,
    883, 958
  See also under specific
    terms, e.g. Transport
    workers
Working Group Against Racism,
  424
World Conference to Combat
  Racism and Racial Discrimination, 431
World Council of Churches,
  419, 421

Yorkshire
  Indians, 1078, 1479, 1480,
    1778
  Pakistanis, 1078, 1778
  race relations, 717
Young, George, 498
Youth, 515, 748
  aspirations, 1179
  attitudes, 977, 982, 1096,
    1555
  culture conflict, 1148-1185
  education, 715, 1206
  employment, 715, 801, 828,
    892, 904, 977, 1218
  integration, 715
  job training, 869, 916
  juvenile delinquency, 1169
  personality traits, 1097
  police, 1838, 1845
  social adjustment, 1169
  social problems, 1173,
    1179, 1181, 1744
  social services, 1755,
    1758, 1775, 1791
  surveys, 977
  unemployment, 512, 880,
    892, 904, 920, 921, 936,
    952, 1340
  vocational training, 964
Youth clubs
  Asians, 1008
  West Indian, 1008

ABOUT THE COMPILER

Raj Madan is librarian and head of acquisitions at Drake Memorial Library, State University College, Brockport, N.Y. His article "The Status of Librarians in Four-Year Colleges and Universities" was published in *College and Research Libraries.*